Lecture Notes in Computer Science **16356**

Founding Editors

Gerhard Goos
Juris Hartmanis

AF665004

Editorial Board Members

Elisa Bertino, *Purdue University, West Lafayette, IN, USA*
Wen Gao, *Peking University, Beijing, China*
Bernhard Steffen, *TU Dortmund University, Dortmund, Germany*
Moti Yung, *Columbia University, New York, NY, USA*

The series Lecture Notes in Computer Science (LNCS), including its subseries Lecture Notes in Artificial Intelligence (LNAI) and Lecture Notes in Bioinformatics (LNBI), has established itself as a medium for the publication of new developments in computer science and information technology research, teaching, and education.

LNCS enjoys close cooperation with the computer science R & D community, the series counts many renowned academics among its volume editors and paper authors, and collaborates with prestigious societies. Its mission is to serve this international community by providing an invaluable service, mainly focused on the publication of conference and workshop proceedings and postproceedings. LNCS commenced publication in 1973.

Yuting Chen · Hiroyuki Okamura · Shaoying Liu
Editors

Software Fault Prevention, Verification, and Validation

Second International Symposium, SFPVV 2025
Shanghai, China, November 8–9, 2025
Proceedings

Springer

Editors
Yuting Chen
Shanghai Jiao Tong University
Shanghai, China

Hiroyuki Okamura
Hiroshima University
Hiroshima, Japan

Shaoying Liu
East China Normal University
Shanghai, China

ISSN 0302-9743 ISSN 1611-3349 (electronic)
Lecture Notes in Computer Science
ISBN 978-981-95-6031-8 ISBN 978-981-95-6032-5 (eBook)
https://doi.org/10.1007/978-981-95-6032-5

© The Editor(s) (if applicable) and The Author(s), under exclusive license
to Springer Nature Singapore Pte Ltd. 2026

This work is subject to copyright. All rights are solely and exclusively licensed by the Publisher, whether the whole or part of the material is concerned, specifically the rights of translation, reprinting, reuse of illustrations, recitation, broadcasting, reproduction on microfilms or in any other physical way, and transmission or information storage and retrieval, electronic adaptation, computer software, or by similar or dissimilar methodology now known or hereafter developed.
The use of general descriptive names, registered names, trademarks, service marks, etc. in this publication does not imply, even in the absence of a specific statement, that such names are exempt from the relevant protective laws and regulations and therefore free for general use.
The publisher, the authors and the editors are safe to assume that the advice and information in this book are believed to be true and accurate at the date of publication. Neither the publisher nor the authors or the editors give a warranty, expressed or implied, with respect to the material contained herein or for any errors or omissions that may have been made. The publisher remains neutral with regard to jurisdictional claims in published maps and institutional affiliations.

This Springer imprint is published by the registered company Springer Nature Singapore Pte Ltd.
The registered company address is: 152 Beach Road, #21-01/04 Gateway East, Singapore 189721, Singapore

If disposing of this product, please recycle the paper.

Preface

Software fault prevention, verification, and validation are essential and important approaches to ensuring software productivity, reliability, and quality. Fault prevention focuses on how to prevent the introduction and occurrence of faults in software systems. Verification is a means to rigorously check whether software systems satisfy their specification or properties. Validation refers to technologies and activities for confirming whether the behavior and performance of software systems satisfy the user's requirements. Various techniques and supporting tools have been developed to fulfill the tasks of software fault prevention, verification, and validation, but many difficulties and open problems remain unaddressed.

The 2nd International Symposium on Software Fault Prevention, Verification, and Validation (SFPVV 2025), which took place on November 8-9, 2025, in Shanghai, aimed to bring together researchers and practitioners dedicated to advancing software quality assurance. The symposium encouraged the exchange of ideas and discussion on how formal methods, testing-based techniques, AI-driven approaches, and their combinations can be explored, established, and refined to achieve the goals of software fault prevention, verification, and validation.

There were 31 submissions, each undergoing a two-step review process. Initially, the program committee (PC) chair screened all submissions to verify that they aligned with the symposium's scope and met the formatting and page limit requirements. Submissions failing to meet these criteria were excluded from further review. In the second step, each remaining submission was reviewed by three program committee members or additional reviewers. Ultimately, 11 submissions were accepted for both presentation at the symposium and inclusion in the proceedings.

The SFPVV 2025 program featured two keynote talks given by Jian Zhang from the Institute of Software, Chinese Academy of Sciences (ISCAS) Hironori Washizaki from Waseda University, and 11 paper presentations on techniques and approaches for software fault prevention, verification, and validation, including formal methods, testing and analysis, formal semantics, defect detection, specification, and implementation. The SFPVV 2025 program also included a track of 9 presentations only for exchanging ideas between participants. A presentation paper was not required to report mature research results but was expected to include new ideas or progress in ongoing research projects. This year, the symposium welcomed around 30 attendees from over 6 countries worldwide.

The successful organization of SFPVV 2025 was due to the invaluable contributions of numerous individuals and institutions. We extend heartfelt thanks to all authors for submitting and presenting their papers at SFPVV 2025. We are deeply grateful to the program committee members for their dedication and efforts in reviewing and selecting papers. Our sincere appreciation also goes to the conference organizing committee for their hard work in handling the many complex tasks required. Our thanks also go to the EasyChair team for their user-friendly platform that helped us efficiently manage the files needed for this volume, and to Springer-Nature for their support in publishing the SFPVV 2025 proceedings.

November 8, 2025

Yuting Chen
Hiroyuki Okamura
Shaoying Liu

Organization

General Chair

Shaoying Liu	East China Normal University, China

Program Committee Chairs

Yuting Chen	Shanghai Jiao Tong University, China
Hiroyuki Okamura	Hiroshima University, Japan

Steering Committee

Tadashi Dohi	Hiroshima University, Japan
Shaoying Liu	East China Normal University, China
Geguang Pu	East China Normal University, China
Tatsuhiro Tsuchiya	University of Osaka, Japan

Program Committee

Yamine Ait Ameur	IRIT/INPT-ENSEEIHT, France
Yuting Chen	Shanghai Jiao Tong University, China
Yoonsik Cheon	University of Texas at El Paso, USA
Yujun Dai	Hiroshima University, Japan
Jin Song Dong	National University of Singapore, Singapore
Mara Downing	University of California Santa Barbara, USA
Dingbang Fang	Fujian Normal University, China
Sun Jun	Singapore Management University, Singapore
Jingyue Li	Norwegian University of Science and Technology, Norway
Jiandong Li	Peking University, China
Yang Li	Hiroshima University, Japan
Chen-Kai Lin	Academia Sinica, Taiwan
Ai Liu	Nanjing University of Aeronautics and Astronautics, China
Haiyi Liu	Jiangsu Second Normal University, China

Shaoying Liu	East China Normal University, China
Fumiko Nagoya	Nihon University, Japan
Shin Nakajima	National Institute of Informatics, Japan
Kazuhiro Ogata	JAIST, Japan
Hiroyuki Okamura	Hiroshima University, Japan
Jun Pang	University of Luxembourg, Luxembourg
Lei Rao	Southwest Petroleum University, China
Yuji Sato	Hosei University, Japan
Wuwei Shen	Western Michigan University, USA
Xinfeng Shu	Xi'an University of Posts and Telecommunications, China
Tatsuhiro Tsuchiya	Osaka University, Japan
Pingyan Wang	Guangdong University of Petrochemical Technology, China
Xi Wang	Shanghai University, China
Zhen You	Jiangxi Normal University, China
Tao Zhang	Macau University of Science and Technology, China
Jianjun Zhao	Kyushu University, Japan

Software Analysis

Jian Zhang

Institute of Software, Chinese Academy of Sciences (ISCAS), China

Abstract. Software analysis is an important class of techniques for preventing faults in software. In particular, various static program analysis methods are quite effective for identifying bugs before the software is deployed. This talk will give an overview of our works on the analysis of C/C++ programs and Android apps. Then I will discuss various issues such as benchmarking, false warning elimination, cross-language analysis, and the use of AI techniques in software analysis.

Jian Zhang is a research professor with the Institute of Software, Chinese Academy of Sciences (ISCAS), and an adjunct professor with the University of Chinese Academy of Sciences (UCAS). His research interests include software testing, program analysis, automated reasoning and constraint solving. He has served on the program committees of well-known international conferences such as ICSE, ISSTA, ISSRE, VSTTE, FM, ICFEM, IJCAR, CADE, SAT and QSIC/QRS. Currently, he serves on the editorial boards of several journals including Frontiers of Computer Science, Journal of Computer Science and Technology, and Chinese Journal of Computers. He has published several books, including Automatic Generation of Combinatorial Test Data (with Zhiqiang Zhang and Feifei Ma), Logic in Computer Science (with Hantao Zhang).

Impact of IEEE Computer Society in Advancing Technologies, including AI SE based on Modeling with Patterns and MLOps

Hironori Washizaki

Waseda University, Tokyo, Japan

Abstract. This talk first provides an overview of IEEE Computer Society's strategic areas, including engaging our members, engaging the industry, and leading new areas such as AI and Society. Then, the talk explains the latest version of the Technology Predictions 2025, which foresees 22 breakthrough technologies (incl. LLM/AI Agents) to shape the future of our world for decades to come, and the Guide to the Software Engineering Body of Knowledge (SWEBOK Guide) V4.0, which reflects the current state of generally accepted knowledge, including a new topic, AI and Software Engineering (SE). Then, as a part of AI and SE, the talk presents AI software engineering, with a particular focus on a multi-view modeling framework and engineering patterns for Machine Learning and LLM systems (including design patterns and assurance argument patterns), with ML pipeline integration, to address multi-dimensional aspects and the probabilistic nature of ML/LLM, and its experimentative development approach involving ML training, performance monitoring, repair pipelines, and security risk management.

Hironori Washizaki is the 2025 IEEE Computer Society (CS) president. He is a professor and the associate dean of the Research Promotion Division at Waseda University. He is a visiting professor at the National Institute of Informatics and an advisor at the University of Human Environments. He also works in the industry as an outside director and advisor at eXmotion and SI&C. He has led professional and educational activities at the IEEE CS, including the evolution of the Guide to the Software Engineering Body of Knowledge (SWEBOK) and the CS Juniors program. He has led many academia-industry joint research and large-funded projects in systems and software requirements, design, reuse, quality assurance, and AI software engineering. He leads a professional IoT/AI/DX education project called "Smart SE." Since 2015, he has been the convenor of ISO/IEC/JTC1/SC7/WG20 to standardize bodies of knowledge and certifications in systems and software engineering.

Contents

Can Generative AI Enhance the Effectiveness of N-Version Programming? 1
Junjun Zheng, Hiroyuki Okamura, and Tadashi Dohi

QRAT: A Reachability Analysis Tool for Quantum Programs 17
Canh Minh Do and Kazuhiro Ogata

An Empirical Study on Software Defect Prediction Based on Neural Network DeepDebugger Technique 34
Yuxiang Shang, Shaoying Liu, and Jin Song Dong

Fuzzing the Solidity Compiler Solc with Fuzz4All 48
Haruto Igaki and Tatsuhiro Tsuchiya

Diagnosing and Repairing Field Access Hallucinations in LLM-Based Test Generation 59
Xiujing Guo and Tatsuhiro Tsuchiya

Data-Driven and Scenario-Based Risk Analysis Considering Uncertainty in Machine Learning Systems 78
Toshiya Okubo, Hironori Washizaki, Naoyasu Ubayashi, Nobukazu Yoshioka, Hironori Takeuchi, and Truong Vinh Truong Duy

Similarity Evaluation Between Queries and Chunks in RAG Systems 98
Shun Noguchi, Kozo Okano, Shipei Ogata, and Shin Nakajima

A Support Tool for Verification of Simulation Relations Between State Machines with Maude 112
Takanori Ishibashi, Masaki Nakamura, and Kazuhiro Ogata

Design and Implementation of a Software Tool to Support Agile-SOFL 130
Ran Chen and Shaoying Liu

Model Checking the Two-Phase Commit Protocol for Distributed Database Systems 141
Yisong Yu, Naipeng Dong, Jun Pang, and Jin Song Dong

Formal Verification of Measurement-Based Quantum Computation in Maude 160
Ryuichi Nagoshi and Tsubasa Takagi

Author Index 179

Can Generative AI Enhance the Effectiveness of N-Version Programming?

Junjun Zheng(✉), Hiroyuki Okamura, and Tadashi Dohi

Graduate School of Advanced Science and Engineering, Hiroshima University, 1-4-1 Kagamiyama, Higashihiroshima 739-8527, Japan
{jzheng,okamu,dohi}@hiroshima-u.ac.jp

Abstract. N-version programming (NVP) is a classical fault-tolerance technique that enhances software reliability by executing multiple independently developed program variants in parallel. Despite its effectiveness, NVP has seen limited adoption in practice due to its high development cost. With the emergence of large language models (LLMs), generative AI offers a new opportunity to automate the creation of diverse program variants. But can generative AI truly enhance the effectiveness of NVP? In this paper, we attempt to answer this question through an empirical evaluation of LLM-generated code, focusing on two key factors: correctness and diversity. We explore the impact of model quality by comparing high-performing (e.g., GPT-4o) and lower-performing LLMs, and evaluate two diversity-promoting strategies; i.e., temperature tuning and conversation history reuse. Our results show that generative AI can improve NVP effectiveness when using high-quality models, enabling more reliable outcomes through majority voting. However, the benefits are limited with lower-accuracy models. Furthermore, while diversity can be increased by adjusting temperature and leveraging conversation history, such measures do not always translate into improved reliability. These findings highlight both the promise and the limitations of incorporating generative AI into fault-tolerant software development workflows.

Keywords: N-version programming · Generative AI · Software reliability · Large language models · Fault tolerance · Code diversity

1 Introduction

N-version programming (NVP) is a classical software fault-tolerance technique aimed at improving system reliability by developing and executing multiple independent program versions that adhere to the same specification [1]. By comparing their outputs, typically using majority voting, NVP can detect and mitigate the effects of latent software faults. The approach has been adopted in mission-critical domains, such as space shuttle flight control systems, where

© The Author(s), under exclusive license to Springer Nature Singapore Pte Ltd. 2026
Y. Chen et al. (Eds.): SFPVV 2025, LNCS 16356, pp. 1–16, 2026.
https://doi.org/10.1007/978-981-95-6032-5_1

ultra-high reliability is paramount [2,3]. Despite its conceptual appeal, the practical adoption of NVP has been limited by its prohibitively high development cost. Each version must be implemented independently, traditionally requiring multiple development teams, which significantly increases both time and labor investment compared to conventional software development.

Recent advances in generative AI, particularly in large language models (LLMs) like GPT-4, have enabled automated code generation from natural language specifications and contextual prompts. Tools such as GitHub Copilot have made AI-assisted programming increasingly accessible [4]. However, generated code is not guaranteed to be correct or reliable, raising concerns about the operational risk of integrating AI-generated code into real systems [5,6]. This motivates an important research question; that is, "Can generative AI be leveraged to automate NVP, thereby reducing development costs while retaining or even enhancing software reliability?"

In this paper, we explore this question by investigating the effectiveness of LLM-based NVP. Specifically, we propose using generative AI to automatically generate multiple independent implementations of a given specification. This approach has the potential to overcome the high-cost barrier of traditional NVP, while simultaneously using NVP's inherent fault-tolerance mechanism to improve the quality of AI-generated code. Our goal is twofold: (1) to empirically evaluate whether the reliability of generative AI-based code can be improved through NVP, and (2) to identify effective strategies for ensuring code diversity, which is critical to the success of NVP. Particularly, we explore techniques such as temperature tuning and conversational history reuse to promote diversity in generated code.

The rest of this paper is organized as follows. Section 2 provides an overview of code generation with LLMs. Section 3 describes our AI-assisted NVP framework and outlines our evaluation methodology. Section 4 presents the experimental design, results, and analysis. Finally, Sect. 5 concludes the paper and discusses future directions.

2 Code Generation with Generative AI

Generative AI refers to a class of machine learning techniques designed to produce coherent and contextually appropriate outputs from incomplete or abstract inputs. Among these, LLMs such as GPT-4 [7], Claude [8], and LLaMA [9] have demonstrated strong capabilities in generating code from natural language descriptions, partial implementations, or informal specifications. Trained on massive corpora of programming languages and natural language documents, LLMs can generate syntactically valid and semantically meaningful code fragments that match the user intent inferred from a given input prompt. A typical code generation pipeline is illustrated in Fig. 1, where the model processes a user prompt, tokenizes it, computes a distribution over possible next tokens, and samples outputs autoregressively.

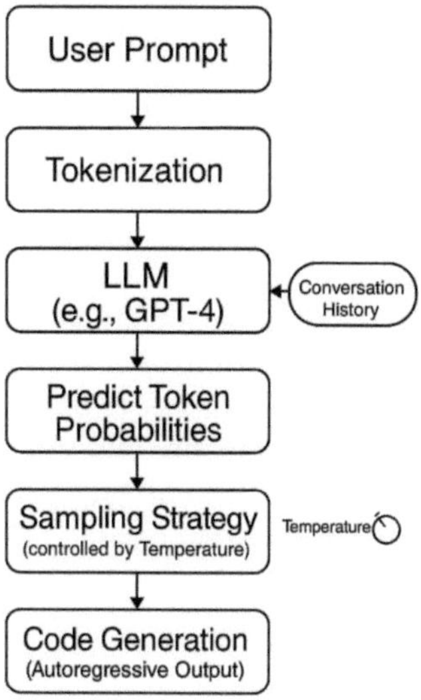

Fig. 1. Typical workflow of code generation using an LLM.

LLMs exhibit emergent capabilities when scaled, and in general, larger models tend to produce more accurate, robust, and context-aware outputs [10]. However, their behavior is inherently probabilistic and can be controlled using hyperparameters such as *temperature*. The temperature parameter ($0 \leq T \leq 1$) governs the degree of randomness in token sampling; that is, low temperature values yield more deterministic and repetitive outputs, while higher temperatures promote diversity at the cost of stability. Controlling temperature has been shown to affect not only output variability but also solution creativity [11]. Another key factor in steering LLM outputs is prompt engineering, which is the practice of crafting prompts in a way that guides the model to produce desirable behavior. Recent studies have shown that even slight changes in prompt phrasing or structure can significantly influence the correctness and style of the generated code [12,13]. In the context of NVP, where code diversity is desirable, prompt perturbation and historical context reuse can be leveraged to produce multiple distinct code variants.

Furthermore, modern APIs for LLMs, such as OpenAI's GPT API, Google's Gemini API, and Meta's LLaMA via Hugging Face, provide simple interfaces for integrating generative models into user applications. However, these APIs typically do not retain conversational state across calls. To enable multi-turn interactions, developers must manually store prior exchanges and prepend them to the current prompt. This mechanism, known as *conversation history reuse*, effectively enables continuity in multi-round programming tasks and influences the generated output's semantics and diversity.

The workflow illustrated in Fig. 1 reflects the standard pipeline adopted by modern LLMs for autoregressive code generation. This process begins with prompt tokenization, followed by context-aware inference through transformer-based architectures [14]. The model then produces a probability distribution over the vocabulary for the next token, from which a sample is selected based on a predefined sampling strategy (e.g., greedy, top-k, nucleus sampling) influenced by the temperature parameter [11]. The selected token is appended to the prompt, and the generation loop continues until a stopping condition is met. This architecture underpins many widely used LLM APIs such as OpenAI's GPT-4, Meta's LLaMA, and Anthropic's Claude [7–9], and is consistent with established literature on code generation with neural models [15]. In our context, understanding this generation process is essential, because the sampling step (and its controllability via temperature and conversational history) directly affects both the diversity and correctness of generated code, which are two key factors that influence the success of AI-assisted NVP.

3 Generative AI-Assisted NVP

3.1 Construction of N-Version Code

NVP is a classical approach to fault tolerance that achieves reliability by executing multiple independently developed implementations of the same specification [1]. Traditionally, the high cost of developing these versions has limited its practical adoption. In this work, we investigate whether modern generative AI, specifically LLMs, can be used to automatically generate diverse, functionally equivalent program versions at low cost, enabling lightweight NVP.

Previous work by Ron et al. [16] proposed a semi-automated, repair-oriented approach in which LLMs replicate or adapt a reference implementation through prompt reuse and interactive guidance. In contrast, this paper investigates a fully automated fault masking setting, where multiple program variants are generated de novo from a specification prompt, without relying on any existing codebase or iterative correction. Moreover, while both works leverage conversational history, our usage is distinct; that is, we employ it not for iterative repair, but to stimulate diversity across generations. This design enables us to assess not only the cost-saving potential of generative AI, but also its capability to improve output reliability through natural diversity and majority voting, drawing inspiration from classical NVP.

The construction process is illustrated in Fig. 2. It consists of the following steps:

1. Define function specification: A natural-language specification is written including the programing language, function name, arguments, return type, description, and preconditions.
2. Generate code using generative AI: The specification is converted into a prompt and passed to an LLM (e.g., GPT-4, Gemma). Code generation is repeated N times with varying sampling parameters (e.g., temperature, prompt phrasing, or conversation history) to produce multiple diverse implementations.

3. Save each version as a module: The generated code is validated for syntax and compiled as callable modules. Each version is stored independently and can be invoked via a central driver.

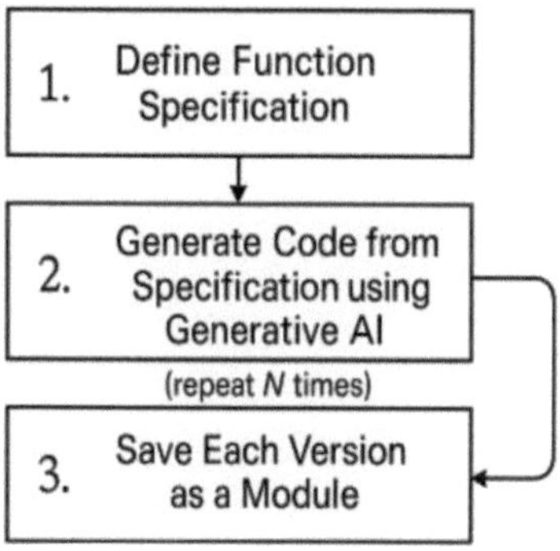

Fig. 2. Construction process of generative AI-assisted NVP.

By repeating the generation step with subtle variations in prompt structure and temperature values, we aim to induce diversity across the resulting code variants. This diversity is a prerequisite for NVP to provide resilience against common-mode failures.

3.2 Evaluation of Generated N-Version Code

To explore the reliability potential of generative AI-assisted NVP, we reference a set of evaluation perspectives drawn from both classical NVP studies and recent research on AI-based code generation [12,13,15,16]. While our focus in this paper is on automated construction and structural diversity, the following dimensions form a conceptual foundation for future empirical validation:

- Correctness: Standard correctness evaluation typically involves compilation checks, unit test validation, and, when applicable, semantic equivalence checks using formal verification tools, such as Alive2 [17] or Kani [18].
- Code diversity: Code diversity, which is critical for fault isolation in NVP, can be evaluated both statically and dynamically. Static diversity may be measured via hash comparison or abstract syntax tree (AST) structure similarity [19], while dynamic diversity involves analyzing runtime behaviors such as executed instruction traces.
- Fault masking ability: Prior work by Ron et al. [16] examined the capacity of an NVP system to suppress faults by checking whether introduced bugs in a subset of versions are masked by correct outputs from other variants under majority voting.

- Execution overhead: Measuring the runtime latency introduced by executing multiple versions is an important practical consideration. It serves to understand trade-offs between added reliability and system responsiveness.

In this work, we do not implement the full scope of these evaluations but instead propose them as key axes for future large-scale empirical studies. Our current experimental design (described in Sect. 4) focuses primarily on generating version-level diversity and verifying syntactic and basic functional correctness.

4 Numerical Experiments

4.1 Research Questions

Despite the recent advances in generative AI for code generation, it remains unclear how reliable these models are in practical software engineering tasks, especially under different prompt engineering strategies and execution paradigms. In particular, the potential of applying generative AI to NVP has not been rigorously validated. To bridge this gap, we focus on the following research questions (RQs):

- *RQ1: Can AI-assisted NVP reduce the risk of incorrect code generation?* We generate three independent program versions from the same task prompt and evaluate whether majority voting across these variants improves reliability compared to single-version generation.
- *RQ2: What strategies are effective for ensuring output diversity in code generation?* investigate two approaches for promoting code diversity: varying the temperature parameter of the language model and incorporating conversation history. We evaluate the impact of these strategies on the structural and behavioral diversity of the generated code.

These questions are rooted in both classical fault-tolerant design theory and recent empirical findings in LLM-based code synthesis. We answer them through the following experiments involving two representative tasks and a rigorous evaluation methodology.

4.2 Experimental Setup

To evaluate the feasibility and limitations of generative AI-assisted NVP, we designed a practical experiment involving two representative programming tasks: triangle classification and substring matching. The primary goal was to assess code correctness, diversity, and the effects of various generation parameters, using both cloud-hosted and locally deployed LLMs.

Models and Execution Platforms. We conducted experiments using both commercial cloud-based LLMs and locally hosted open-source models. This dual-platform approach enabled us to evaluate generation quality, control, and reproducibility across different deployment strategies.

- OpenAI GPT series (Cloud-based): We employed GPT-3.5, GPT-4o, and GPT-4o mini through the OpenAI API using the LangChain `ChatOpenAI` interface. The environment was configured with Python 3.10.14, LangChain 0.0.292, and OpenAI SDK 0.28.0. Prompt engineering and conversation state were managed using `PromptTemplate` and `ConversationBufferMemory`, supporting both one-shot and multi-turn prompt interactions. To ensure deterministic behavior, we controlled parameters such as temperature and explicitly disabled caching. All outputs were saved along with the associated prompt metadata for reproducibility.
- Gemma 2 via Ollama (Local inference): For local generation, we used Gemma 2 (27B) hosted on a university-operated server using the `ollama/ollama` Docker image. Model interaction was handled through HTTP API calls and wrapped by a custom Python module. The runtime environment consisted of Python 3.9.21 and LangChain 0.0.200. Generated outputs were captured as raw text, cleaned via regular expressions, and converted into standalone Python scripts for automated testing. This local setup allowed full control over model behavior, versioning, and memory management.

Target Programs. We selected two representative programming tasks that differ in logical complexity and required control structures. These tasks were chosen to observe how LLMs handle conditional logic and iterative structures, which are both relevant to real-world applications.

- Triangle classification: Given the (x, y) coordinates of three vertices, the function classifies the triangle into one of seven categories based on side lengths and angle types: equilateral, isosceles right, isosceles acute, isosceles obtuse, right, acute, and obtuse. The expected implementation involves conditionals and basic geometric computation.
- Substring matching: Given two strings `text` and `key`, the function returns a list of all starting indices where `key` appears exactly in `text`. If no match is found, it returns -1. This task requires a loop structure, and is representative of classic string-matching algorithms.

These tasks were chosen due to their practical relevance and contrasting logical structures, that is, conditional branching versus loop-based matching, making them suitable for evaluating both correctness and behavioral diversity in code generation.

Prompt Design and Code Generation. To instruct LLMs in generating functional code, we carefully designed structured prompts tailored to each task. The core format follows a JSON-style specification that defines the programming language, function name, input arguments with their types and descriptions, return value, task description, and preconditions. Each prompt also includes a natural-language instruction requiring the model to generate a valid, standalone Python function and to output it in Markdown format. This structure ensures

```
Please create a function based on the following specification written in JSON. The output should be in Markdown and must include only the executable function you created.

{
    "Programming language": "python",
    "Function name": "function",
    "Input arguments": {
        "ax": {"Type": "float", "Description": "X coordinate of point A"},
        "ay": {"Type": "float", "Description": "Y coordinate of point A"},
        "bx": {"Type": "float", "Description": "X coordinate of point B"},
        "by": {"Type": "float", "Description": "Y coordinate of point B"},
        "cx": {"Type": "float", "Description": "X coordinate of point C"},
        "cy": {"Type": "float", "Description": "Y coordinate of point C"}
    },
    "Result": "The function returns an integer from 0 to 6 depending on the type of triangle:
        0 = equilateral triangle,
        1 = right triangle,
        2 = isosceles right triangle,
        3 = acute triangle,
        4 = isosceles acute triangle,
        5 = obtuse triangle,
        6 = isosceles obtuse triangle.",
    "Description": "Determine which of the seven types the triangle formed by the three input points belongs to:
        equilateral triangle, right triangle, isosceles right triangle, acute triangle, isosceles acute triangle, obtuse triangle, or isosceles obtuse triangle.
        For floating-point comparisons, values are considered equal if their relative error is less than or equal to machine epsilon.",
    "Precondition": ""
}

The function must satisfy the following test cases. However, do not include the tests in your output:

function(1, 0, 2, 1.7320508075688772, 3, 0) == 0
function(0, 0, 3, 0, 0, 4) == 1
function(0, 0, 2, 0, 2, 2) == 2
function(0, 0, 3, 0, 1, 2) == 3
function(0, 0, 5, 0, 3, 4) == 4
function(0, 0, 2, 0, 4, 2) == 5
function(0, 0, 4, 0, 2, 1) == 6
```

Fig. 3. Example prompt for the triangle classification task. The prompt defines the function specification in JSON format and instructs the LLM to generate only an executable Python function in Markdown format. The function is expected to classify triangles based on the geometric properties of three input points.

```
Please create a function based on the following specification written in JSON. The output should be in Markdown and must include only the executable function you created.

{
    "Programming language": "python",
    "Function name": "function",
    "Input arguments": {
        "text": {"Type": "string", "Description": "The text to search"},
        "key": {"Type": "string", "Description": "The key to search for"}
    },
    "Result": "The function returns a list of all starting indices where the exact substring 'key' occurs in 'text'. If there is no match, the function returns -1.",
    "Description": "Find all case-sensitive occurrences of the string 'key' within 'text'. Return a list of their starting positions, or -1 if none are found.",
    "Precondition": ""
}

The function must satisfy the following test cases. However, do not include the tests in your output:

function('abcdabcd', 'ab') == [0, 4]
function('aaaaaa', 'aa') == [0, 1, 2, 3, 4]
function('abcdefg', 'z') == -1
function('abcdefg', 'efgh') == -1
function('This is a test! TEST!', 'TEST!') == [16]
```

Fig. 4. Example prompt for the substring matching task. The prompt specifies the function's input-output behavior in JSON format and instructs the LLM to generate a case-sensitive string search function that returns all match indices or -1 if none are found.

both human and model interpretability, and it supports consistent parsing for downstream post-processing. To guide correctness and reinforce expected behavior, we prepared two prompt variants per task: one without test cases, and one with appended representative test cases at the end. The intention was to evaluate whether example-based prompting would influence generation accuracy and reliability.

Figures 3 and 4 show the prompts used for the triangle classification and substring matching tasks, respectively. The prompts encode clear specifications and reflect realistic expectations for typical software development tasks. For the triangle task, geometric constraints are emphasized (e.g., relative error handling), while the substring matching task requires exact, case-sensitive occurrences. In total, each prompt was issued to the model under different temperature settings ($T = \{0.0, 0.2, 0.8, 1.0\}$), and for each configuration, three completions were collected to form the N-version ensemble. Prompt construction was kept consistent across models to ensure fair comparison.

Figures 5 and 6 present examples of the generated code for each task using GPT-4o with temperature $T = 0.0$. These outputs were further parsed and normalized for automated testing and similarity evaluation as described in later sections. The generated functions exhibit correct syntax and conform to the specification provided in the prompts. For the triangle classification task (Fig. 5), the model correctly includes helper functions (e.g., `distance()` and `is_close()`) for computing distances and comparing float values with machine epsilon, and implements logical branching for classifying triangles. For the substring matching task (Fig. 6), the function uses a loop with `str.find()` to iteratively locate all matches, and returns either a list of indices or `-1`, as instructed. In addition, we observed that the use of Markdown formatting (i.e., code blocks enclosed in triple backticks) was mostly respected, enabling easier post-processing. These code snippets were programmatically extracted, renamed to conform to testing conventions, and saved into isolated Python files. The correctness and diversity evaluations described in Sects. 4.3 and 4.4 were applied to these structured outputs.

Post-processing and Version Handling. The raw outputs generated by each LLM were post-processed to extract executable Python code. We applied regular expression-based parsing to isolate valid code blocks, typically enclosed within Markdown syntax (i.e., triple backticks). In particular, to enable consistent automated testing, all function names were normalized (e.g., renamed to `function1`) regardless of their original labels. Each versioned output was saved under a structured directory with unique file identifiers to support batch execution.

Moreover, an ensemble driver was implemented to facilitate N-version execution. This driver dynamically loaded all three versions of a function, applied the same test inputs to each, and compared their outputs. Majority voting was used to determine the final decision. In cases of disagreement or failure (e.g., syntax error or exception), fallback logic was applied to ensure fault isolation and robustness. This framework allowed us to simulate real-world NVP behavior under both ideal and degraded conditions.

4.3 Evaluation Criteria

We adopted a set of evaluation criteria to assess both the reliability and behavioral diversity of LLM-generated code in an NVP setting. These criteria reflect not only the correctness of individual outputs but also the ensemble's robustness under variability in model behavior and configuration.

Correctness. The primary criterion was functional correctness. For each generated function, we evaluated it from the following aspects; that is

````
```python
import math
import sys

def function(ax: float, ay: float, bx: float, by: float, cx: float, cy: float) -> int:
    def distance(x1, y1, x2, y2):
        return math.sqrt((x2 - x1) ** 2 + (y2 - y1) ** 2)

    def is_close(a, b, rel_tol=sys.float_info.epsilon):
        return abs(a - b) <= rel_tol * max(abs(a), abs(b))

    # Calculate the lengths of the sides of the triangle
    ab = distance(ax, ay, bx, by)
    bc = distance(bx, by, cx, cy)
    ca = distance(cx, cy, ax, ay)

    # Sort the sides so that a <= b <= c
    a, b, c = sorted([ab, bc, ca])

    # Check for equilateral triangle
    if is_close(a, b) and is_close(b, c):
        return 0

    # Check for right triangle
    if is_close(a**2 + b**2, c**2):
        # Check for right isosceles triangle
        if is_close(a, b) or is_close(b, c) or is_close(a, c):
            return 2
        return 1

    # Check for isosceles triangle
    is_isosceles = is_close(a, b) or is_close(b, c) or is_close(a, c)

    # Check for acute triangle
    if a**2 + b**2 > c**2:
        return 4 if is_isosceles else 3

    # Check for obtuse triangle
    if a**2 + b**2 < c**2:
        return 6 if is_isosceles else 5

    return -1  # Should not reach here if inputs are valid
```
````

Fig. 5. Example of generated code for the triangle classification task (GPT-4o, $T = 0.0$).

- *Compilation success:* Whether the generated Python code was syntactically valid and executable.
- *Test case passing:* Whether the implementation passed a set of manually written test cases representing core functionality.
- *Agreement in NVP ensemble:* For each 3-version group, whether all versions produced consistent outputs under identical inputs, allowing a majority vote or consensus.

Specifically, correctness was measured in two settings: individual generation (Single) and N-version ensemble (3v). Additional variations (e.g., with test cases in prompt or conversation history (3vc)) were also included to evaluate contextual robustness.

````
```python
def function(text: str, key: str) -> list:
    indices = []
    index = text.find(key)
    while index != -1:
        indices.append(index)
        index = text.find(key, index + 1)
    return indices if indices else -1
```
````

Fig. 6. Example of generated code for the substring matching task (GPT-4o, $T = 0.0$).

Diversity. To assess whether different versions were genuinely distinct, we computed the pairwise similarity among the three generated versions per task and configuration. We considered the AST-based similarity [19]; that is, we parsed each code into an AST and computed a normalized similarity score (e.g., using tree edit distance). High diversity is essential in NVP to avoid correlated failures. However, it must be balanced against correctness, as overly diverse outputs may include structural bugs.

Stability. Stability refers to how sensitive the model outputs are to changes in generation parameters. We compared results across different temperature settings ($T = 0.0, 0.2, 0.8, 1.0$)

4.4 Experimental Results

Tables 1 and 2 present the evaluation results across both tasks (triangle classification and substring matching) under different models and temperatures, without/with test cases, respectively. For each language model, we tested four temperature settings (T = 0, 0.2, 0.8, and 1.0), and evaluated three prompting conditions: single-shot (S), three-version ensemble without context (3v), and three-version ensemble with conversational context (3vc). We assessed the generated code using two primary metrics: (1) *Correctness (Correct)*, measured by the number of passed test cases; and (2) *Diversity (or Similarity (Sim))*, measured by the average pairwise AST-based similarity score within each group of three generated functions. These criteria allow us to assess not only functional validity but also structural variety of the generated implementations.

From these tables, one of the most significant findings is the effectiveness of NVP in improving output correctness, particularly in higher-performing models such as GPT-4o. Even when some individual completions failed to pass the test cases, aggregating three independent outputs via majority voting (3v) consistently achieved perfect task coverage (i.e., 100% correctness). This strongly supports the hypothesis that structural redundancy in generative outputs can effectively compensate for individual failure cases. However, this benefit was not uniformly observed across all models. Lower-end models such as GPT-3.5 and Gemma failed to benefit meaningfully from the 3v strategy, primarily due to two factors: (i) a low probability of generating correct outputs in the first place, and (ii) insufficient diversity among the generated buggy code, which rendered majority voting ineffective.

Beyond NVP, our results reveal clear trade-offs between diversity and correctness under different prompt and model configurations. Specifically, increasing the temperature parameter generally reduced similarity scores among generated outputs, thus improving diversity, but often at the cost of correctness due to

Table 1. Evaluation results of generated functions under different models and temperatures, **without test cases** (*Abbreviations:* **S**: single version; **3v**: three-version execution (NVP); **Sim**: similarity score based on AST comparison.)

Model	Temp	Correct (S)	Correct (3v)	Sim (3v)
Triangle Classification				
GPT-4o	0.0	10	10	0.33
	0.2	10	10	0.15
	0.8	10	10	0.12
	1.0	9	10	0.10
GPT-4o mini	0.0	0	0	0.46
	0.2	2	1	0.31
	0.8	2	6	0.19
	1.0	5	3	0.14
GPT-3.5	0.0	0	0	0.93
	0.2	0	0	0.48
	0.8	1	0	0.10
	1.0	1	0	0.11
Gemma 2 (27B)	–	0	2	0.21
Substring Matching				
GPT-4o	0.0	10	10	1.00
	0.2	10	10	0.95
	0.8	9	10	0.55
	1.0	8	10	0.47
GPT-4o mini	0.0	10	10	1.00
	0.2	10	10	1.00
	0.8	9	10	0.76
	1.0	8	10	0.78
GPT-3.5	0.0	0	0	1.00
	0.2	0	0	0.90
	0.8	2	2	0.25
	1.0	2	2	0.28
Gemma 2 (27B)	–	2	6	0.19

Table 2. Evaluation results of generated functions under different models and temperatures, **with test cases** (*Abbreviations:* **S**: single version; **3v**: three-version execution (NVP); **3vc**: three-version execution with conversation context; **Sim**: similarity score based on AST comparison.).

Model	Temp	Correct (S)	Correct (3v)	Correct (3vc)	Sim (3v)	Sim (3vc)
Triangle Classification						
GPT-4o	0.0	10	10	10	0.58	0.36
	0.2	10	10	10	0.34	0.29
	0.8	10	10	9	0.14	0.32
	1.0	7	10	7	0.17	0.22
GPT-4o mini	0.0	0	0	6	0.61	0.32
	0.2	0	0	5	0.38	0.38
	0.8	4	7	5	0.11	0.28
	1.0	7	4	5	0.18	0.23
GPT-3.5	0.0	0	0	0	0.73	0.03
	0.2	0	0	1	0.48	0.07
	0.8	0	0	0	0.19	0.02
	1.0	0	0	1	0.20	0.01
Gemma 2 (27B)	–	2	2	1	0.24	0.18
Substring Matching						
GPT-4o	0.0	10	10	10	1.00	0.20
	0.2	10	10	10	0.94	0.19
	0.8	10	10	10	0.52	0.16
	1.0	10	10	10	0.58	0.14
GPT-4o mini	0.0	10	10	10	1.00	0.36
	0.2	10	10	10	0.91	0.27
	0.8	10	9	10	0.73	0.13
	1.0	10	10	10	0.46	0.21
GPT-3.5	0.0	10	10	4	1.00	0.07
	0.2	10	10	4	0.99	0.05
	0.8	5	9	6	0.50	0.05
	1.0	8	7	2	0.25	0.02
Gemma 2 (27B)	–	5	4	5	0.41	0.25

higher bug rates. Conversely, temperature-induced diversity occasionally benefited correctness in GPT-4o mini by breaking deterministic generation patterns that otherwise reproduced faulty code.

Moreover, prompt augmentation strategies also influenced performance. Adding test cases consistently improved correctness for string comparison tasks across all models but had limited effect on triangle classification, possibly due to the task‘s inherent algorithmic complexity. Higher-end models such as GPT-4o performed well even under minimal prompting, while others required substantial guidance to produce usable code.

Additionally, incorporating conversation history (multi-turn prompting) had similar effects to temperature in increasing output diversity, but sometimes led to incomplete or malformed code, particularly in GPT-3.5. In some cases, the model failed to generate any code at all in follow-up completions, thus reducing overall utility.

Finally, we summarize the answers to our research questions as follows.

RQ1: Can AI-assisted NVP reduce the risk of incorrect code generation?

Yes, for high-performing models such as GPT-4o, NVP significantly reduced the risk of individual generation errors. Even when one version was faulty, majority voting successfully avoided incorrect output. However, for weaker models or difficult tasks, where the base correctness rate is low, NVP offers limited benefit and may even degrade reliability when identical bugs are shared across versions.

RQ2: What strategies are effective for ensuring output diversity in code generation?

Both temperature tuning and conversation history can enhance code diversity. However, these strategies involve trade-offs. Higher temperatures increase randomness but may reduce output quality. Conversation history can sometimes cause the model to fail entirely. As practical guidelines:

- Use temperature $T > 0.2$ when not using history, to avoid deterministic buggy code.
- Use low temperature ($T \approx 0$) when reusing history, to prevent excessive random drift.

Ultimately, the optimal choice depends on the model and task. There is no universally best configuration across all conditions.

5 Conclusion

In this paper, we implemented and evaluated the effectiveness of the NVP approach using LLMs for code generation. We also explored the impact of two diversity-enhancing strategies, i.e., temperature adjustment and conversation history reuse, on the reliability and diversity of the generated outputs. Our experiments reveal that for high-performance models such as GPT-4o, NVP significantly mitigates the risk of generating incorrect code by leveraging majority voting. However, for weaker models or inherently difficult tasks, NVP provides limited benefits and may even decrease overall reliability when similar bugs appear across multiple versions. Furthermore, we found that adjusting the temperature and incorporating conversational history can increase output diversity, but this comes with trade-offs in correctness. Specifically, higher temperatures induce randomness that can degrade output reliability, and incorporating conversation history occasionally causes the model to fail entirely. To balance diversity and correctness, we recommend using a temperature $T > 0.2$ when not reusing history and a lower temperature ($T \approx 0$) when reusing history. Importantly, combining both strategies simultaneously may introduce excessive randomness and is therefore not advisable.

As future work, we identify several limitations and directions for extension. First, our experiments demonstrated significant variation in correctness between the two evaluated tasks. In some cases, increasing temperature improved accuracy, while in others, it reduced it. This suggests that both the baseline quality of the model and the nature of the programming task strongly influence the effectiveness of NVP and diversity strategies. To derive universally effective guidelines for prompt design and parameter settings, more diverse and representative coding problems must be investigated. Second, for tasks such as triangle classification, which had very low correctness rates, even including test cases in the prompt yielded limited improvement. Consequently, we were unable to adequately assess the benefits of NVP under such challenging settings. A promising direction for future work is to explore the use of few-shot examples and error correction techniques to improve the baseline reliability of generated programs. Once a minimal accuracy threshold is achieved, the effectiveness and limitations of NVP can be more meaningfully evaluated under realistic conditions.

References

1. Chen, L., Avizienis, A.: N-version programming: a fault-tolerance approach to reliability of software operation. In: Proceedings of 8th IEEE International Symposium on Fault-Tolerant Computing (FTCS-8), vol.1, pp. 3–9 (1978)
2. Lyu, M.R.: Handbook of Software Reliability Engineering. IEEE Computer Society Press, Los Alamitos (1996)
3. Cai, X., Lyu, M.R., Vouk, M.A.: An experimental evaluation on reliability features of N-version programming. In: Proceedings of 16th IEEE International Symposium on Software Reliability Engineering (ISSRE 2005), pp. 161–170. IEEE (2005)
4. Yetiştiren, B., Özsoy, I., Tüzün, E.: Assessing the quality of GitHub copilot's code generation. In: Proceedings of the 18th International Conference on Predictive Models and Data Analytics in Software Engineering, pp. 62–71 (2022)
5. Pearce, H., Tan, B., Ahmad, B., Karri, R., Dolan-Gavitt, B.: Examining zero-shot vulnerability repair with large language models. In: Proceedings of 2023 IEEE Symposium on Security and Privacy (SP 2023), pp. 2339–2356 (2023)
6. Yetiştiren, B., Özsoy, I., Ayerdem, M., Tüzün, E.: Evaluating the code quality of AI-assisted code generation tools: An empirical study on GitHub Copilot, Amazon CodeWhisperer, and ChatGPTs. arXiv preprint arXiv:2304.10778v2 (2023)
7. Open AI: CPT-4 technical report. arXiv preprint arXiv:2303.08774v6 (2024)
8. Priyanshu, A., Maurya, Y., Hong, Z.: "AI governance and accountability: An analysis of Anthropic's Claude. arXiv preprint arXiv:2407.01557v1 (2024)

9. Touvron, H., et al.: Llama: open and efficient foundation language models. arXiv preprint arXiv:2302.13971 (2023)
10. Bubeck, S., et al.: Sparks of artificial general intelligence: Early experiments with GPT-4. arXiv preprint arXiv:2303.12712 (2023)
11. Zhang, D.: On the temperature of machine learning systems. arXiv preprint arXiv:2404.13218 (2024)
12. Si, C., Gan, Z., Yang, Z., Wang, S., Wang, J., Boyd-Graber, J., Wang, L.: Prompting GPT-3 to be reliable. arXiv preprint arXiv:2210.09150 (2022)
13. Wang, L., et al.: Prompt engineering in consistency and reliability with the evidence-based guideline for LLMs. NPJ Digital Med. **7**(1), 41 (2024)
14. Vaswani, A., et al.: Attention is all you need. Adv. Neural Inform. Process. Syst. **30** (2017)
15. Ni, A., et al.: L2CEval: Evaluating language-to-code generation capabilities of large language models. Trans. Associat. Comput. Linguist. **12**, 1311–1329 (2024)
16. Ron, J., Gaspar, D., Cabrera-Arteaga, J., Baudry, B., Monperrus, M.: Calápagos: Automated N-version programming with LLMs. arXiv preprint arXiv:2408.09536v2 (2025)
17. Lopes, N.P., Lee, J., Hur, C.K., Liu, Z., Regehr, J.: Alive2: Bounded traslation validation for LLVM. In: Proceedings of the 42nd ACM SIGPLAN International Conference on Programming Language Design and Implementation, pp. 65–79 (2021)
18. VanHattum, A., Schwartz-Narbonne, D., Chong, N., Sampson, A.: Verifying dynamic trait objects in rust. In: Proceedings of the 44th International Conference on Software Engineering: Software Engineering in Practice, pp. 321–330 (2022)
19. Salazar Paredes, P.: Comparing Python programs using abstract syntax trees. Technical Report, Uniandes (2020)

QRAT: A Reachability Analysis Tool for Quantum Programs

Canh Minh Do(✉) and Kazuhiro Ogata

Japan Advanced Institute of Science and Technology, Nomi, Japan
{canhdo,ogata}@jaist.ac.jp

Abstract. This paper introduces QRAT, the first reachability analysis tool for quantum programs, leveraging a state-of-the-art decision diagram developed in MQT Core for quantum computing. QRAT provides a novel framework for specifying quantum programs, defining their reachability properties, and searching for satisfied reachable states from an initial state, similar to the classical case. Experimental results demonstrate its effectiveness and practicality in verifying quantum programs. Since reachability analysis is a fundamental component of model-checking algorithms, QRAT represents an essential step toward the development of a full-fledged model checker for quantum programs.

Keywords: Quantum programs · Reachability analysis · Model checking

1 Introduction

Quantum computing has the potential to transform various computing applications, such as cryptography [22], deep learning [4], optimization [16], and solving linear systems [18]. It enables the solution of problems currently infeasible for classical computing, such as Shor's fast algorithm for solving the integer factoring and discrete logarithm problems [22] and Grover's fast algorithm for searching an unstructured database [17]. With exponential investments from big companies and governments, there is growing confidence that building a large-scale quantum computer is merely a matter of time and effort. However, quantum computing differs fundamentally from classical computing, making it challenging to develop efficient algorithms and increasing the likelihood of programming errors. Therefore, ensuring the correctness of quantum programs is crucial in the emerging quantum era.

In the classical domain, decision diagrams (DDs) [6] are powerful data structures that efficiently represent and manipulate Boolean functions, enabling the analysis of large state spaces in verification and optimization tasks [8,19]. Recently, several quantum decision diagrams [1,21,24,26] have been introduced to compactly represent quantum states and operations based on which efficient manipulation algorithms are developed, leading to scalable methods for quantum

© The Author(s), under exclusive license to Springer Nature Singapore Pte Ltd. 2026
Y. Chen et al. (Eds.): SFPVV 2025, LNCS 16356, pp. 17–33, 2026.
https://doi.org/10.1007/978-981-95-6032-5_2

simulation [23,30] and quantum circuit verification [7,27]. Quantum DDs provide compact, canonical representations and efficient manipulation operations, making them ideal for model-checking algorithm development. However, their potential in quantum model checking remains largely untapped, motivating our exploration of their application to quantum program verification.

In this paper, we introduce QRAT, the first reachability analysis tool for quantum programs, leveraging a state-of-the-art decision diagram developed in MQT Core[1] for quantum computing. Quantum while-programs are used as the modeling language to specify quantum systems, while reachability properties are defined using a search command that facilitates searching for satisfied reachable states from a given initial state, similar to the classical case. Reachability analysis is a fundamental component of model-checking algorithms and can be employed to verify invariant properties of systems. Therefore, we focus on the reachability analysis of quantum programs as an essential step toward the development of a full-fledged model checker for quantum programs. Additionally, we chose the DD package developed in MQT Core due to its scalability and efficiency, making it one of the most advanced quantum DDs for quantum simulation [30]. This package also effectively handles complex numbers to maintain numerical stability, enabling nodes in the decision diagrams to be efficiently stored in unique tables [29]. This ensures quantum states are uniquely represented as pointers, which is particularly well-suited for exploration-based verification, such as model checking. As a result, QRAT is scalable and has the potential to handle quantum programs with a large number of qubits. To demonstrate its effectiveness and practicality, we use QRAT to confirm the correctness of Quantum Teleportation and Grover's search algorithm as case studies. All source code and case studies are publicly available at https://github.com/canhminhdo/qrat.

The rest of the paper is organized as follows. Section 2 introduces basic notations from quantum computation. Section 3 presents the syntax and operational semantics of quantum while-programs, along with the reachability problem for quantum programs. Section 4 describes the architecture of QRAT. Section 5 details the reachability analysis algorithm in QRAT. Section 6 shows the experimental results. Section 7 mentions some existing work. Section 8 finally concludes the paper with some future directions.

2 Preliminaries

This section describes basic notations from quantum computation (refer to [20] for more details).

Quantum Bits (or Qubits). In classical computing, the fundamental unit of information is a bit whose value is either 0 or 1. In quantum computing, the counterpart is a *quantum bit* or *qubit*, which has two basis states, conventionally written in Dirac notation [12] as $|0\rangle$ and $|1\rangle$. These denote two column vectors $(1,0)^T$ and $(0,1)^T$, respectively, where ^{T} is the transpose operator. In quantum

[1] MQT Core - The Backbone of the Munich Quantum Toolkit (MQT).

computation, a general state of a quantum system is in a superposition or linear combination of basis states. A quantum state is a unit vector in a Hilbert space $\mathcal{H}$, which is a complex vector space equipped with an inner product such that each Cauchy sequence has a limit. A single-qubit state is $|\psi\rangle = \alpha|0\rangle + \beta|1\rangle$, where α and β are complex numbers and $|\psi\rangle$ is normalized such that $|\alpha|^2 + |\beta|^2 = 1$. The coefficients α and β are called the amplitudes of this quantum state. The set $\{|0\rangle, |1\rangle\}$ forms an orthonormal basis of the two-dimensional Hilbert space. States $|\psi\rangle$ can be also represented by column complex vectors as $(\alpha, \beta)^T$. The basis $\{|0\rangle, |1\rangle\}$ is called the *computational* basis besides other orthonormal bases of interest, such as *diagonal* (or *dual*, or *Hadamard*) basis consisting of two vectors $|+\rangle = \frac{1}{\sqrt{2}}(|0\rangle + |1\rangle)$ and $|-\rangle = \frac{1}{\sqrt{2}}(|0\rangle - |1\rangle)$.

Tensor Product. For multiple qubits, we use the tensor product of Hilbert spaces. Let $\mathcal{H}_1$ and $\mathcal{H}_2$ be two Hilbert spaces. Their tensor product $\mathcal{H}_1 \otimes \mathcal{H}_2$ is defined as a vector space consisting of linear combinations of the vectors $|\psi_1\psi_2\rangle = |\psi_1\rangle|\psi_2\rangle = |\psi_1\rangle \otimes |\psi_2\rangle$, where $|\psi_1\rangle \in \mathcal{H}_1$ and $|\psi_2\rangle \in \mathcal{H}_2$. Systems of two or more qubits may be in *entangled* states, meaning that states of qubits are correlated and inseparable. For instance, entanglement shows that an entangled state of two qubits cannot be expressed as a tensor product of single-qubit states.

Unitary Transformation. The evolution of a closed quantum system can be performed by a unitary transformation. If the state of a qubit is represented by a column vector, then a unitary transformation U can be represented by a complex-value matrix such that $UU^\dagger = U^\dagger U = I$ or $U^\dagger = U^{-1}$, where $U^\dagger$ is the conjugate transpose of U. U acts on the Hilbert space $\mathcal{H}$ transforming a state $|\psi\rangle$ to a state $|\psi'\rangle$ by a matrix multiplication such that $|\psi'\rangle = U|\psi\rangle$. There are some frequently used quantum gates in applications: the Hadamard gate H, the identity gate I, the Pauli gates X, Y, and Z, and the controlled-NOT gate CX. Note that the CX gate performs on two qubits, while the remaining gates perform on a single qubit. Their matrix representations are as follows:

$$I_2 = \begin{pmatrix} 1 & 0 \\ 0 & 1 \end{pmatrix}, \quad X = \begin{pmatrix} 0 & 1 \\ 1 & 0 \end{pmatrix}, \quad Y = \begin{pmatrix} 0 & -i \\ i & 0 \end{pmatrix},$$

$$Z = \begin{pmatrix} 1 & 0 \\ 0 & -1 \end{pmatrix}, H = \frac{1}{\sqrt{2}}\begin{pmatrix} 1 & 1 \\ 1 & -1 \end{pmatrix}, CX = \begin{pmatrix} 1 & 0 & 0 & 0 \\ 0 & 1 & 0 & 0 \\ 0 & 0 & 0 & 1 \\ 0 & 0 & 1 & 0 \end{pmatrix} * .$$

where i is the imaginary unit. For example, the Hadamard gate on a single qubit performs the mapping $|0\rangle \mapsto \frac{1}{\sqrt{2}}(|0\rangle + |1\rangle)$ and $|1\rangle \mapsto \frac{1}{\sqrt{2}}(|0\rangle - |1\rangle)$. The controlled-NOT gate on a pair of qubits performs the mapping $|00\rangle \mapsto |00\rangle, |01\rangle \mapsto |01\rangle, |10\rangle \mapsto |11\rangle, |11\rangle \mapsto |10\rangle$, which can be understood as inverting the second qubit (referred to as the *target*) if the first qubit (referred to as the *control*) is one.

Measurement. A quantum measurement is described as a collection $\{M_m\}$ of measurement operators, where the indices m refer to the measurement outcomes. It is required that the measurement operators satisfy the completeness relation, which is $\sum_m M_m^\dagger M_m = I$. If the state of a quantum system is $|\psi\rangle$ before the measurement, then the probability for the result m is $p(m) = \|M_m|\psi\rangle\|^2$, and the state of the quantum system after the measurement is $\frac{M_m|\psi\rangle}{\sqrt{p(m)}}$ provided that $p(m) > 0$. For instance, we consider a measurement $\{M_0 = |0\rangle\langle 0|, M_1 = |1\rangle\langle 1|\}$ that satisfies the completeness relation. Let us suppose the single-qubit state being measured is $|\psi\rangle = \alpha|0\rangle + \beta|1\rangle$ such that $|\alpha|^2 + |\beta|^2 = 1$. The result 0 will occur with probability $|\alpha|^2$ and the result 1 with probability $|\beta|^2$. Moreover, the measurement causes the quantum state to collapse to either $|0\rangle$ or $|1\rangle$ depending on the measurement result.

3 Reachability Analysis of Quantum Programs

For the convenience of the reader, we briefly review the syntax and operational semantics of quantum while-programs, as well as the reachability problem. This paper focuses on closed quantum systems, where a quantum state is represented as a pure quantum state $|\psi\rangle$ in a Hilbert space $\mathcal{H}$. Unless stated otherwise, quantum states in this paper refer specifically to pure quantum states.

3.1 Syntax of Quantum Programs

Let q and $\overline{q}$ be quantum variables that refer to a single-qubit state and a quantum register (i.e., a finite sequence of distinct quantum variables), respectively. The syntax of quantum while-programs is defined as follows:

$$\begin{aligned} S ::= \texttt{skip} \mid \overline{q} := U[\overline{q}] \mid S_1 \,;\, S_2 \\ \mid \texttt{if } M[q] = 1 \texttt{ then } S_1 \texttt{ else } S_2 \texttt{ fi} \\ \mid \texttt{while } M[q] = 1 \texttt{ do } S \texttt{ od} \end{aligned}$$

The statement `skip` does nothing and terminates. The statement $\overline{q} := U[\overline{q}]$ applies the unitary transformation U to a quantum state with respect to the quantum register $\overline{q}$. The sequential composition S_1 ; S_2 first executes S_1 and then S_2. The conditional statement `if` $M[q] = 1$ `then` S_1 `else` S_2 `fi` performs a binary projective measurement $M = \{M_0, M_1\}$ on a single-qubit q, where $M_0 = |0\rangle\langle 0|$ and $M_1 = |1\rangle\langle 1|$ are measurement operators. If the measurement result is 1, S_1 is executed; otherwise, S_2 is executed. For the while-loop statement `while` $M[q] = 1$ `do` S `od`, if the measurement result of q is 1, S is executed and the loop continues; otherwise, the loop terminates. Note that we do not provide the assignment statement $q := |\psi\rangle$ or $\overline{q} := |\psi\rangle$ because assigning q or $\overline{q}$ to a pure quantum state $|\psi\rangle$ may affect other quantum variables in general, especially in the case of entanglement.

3.2 Operational Semantics of Quantum Programs

The operational semantics of quantum while-programs is depicted in Fig. 1. Let $\mathcal{H}_S$ be the Hilbert space of quantum variables for a quantum program S. A

(SK) $\langle \mathtt{skip}, |\psi\rangle\rangle \rightarrow \langle \downarrow, |\psi\rangle\rangle$

(UT) $\langle \overline{q} := U[\overline{q}], |\psi\rangle\rangle \rightarrow \langle \downarrow, U\,|\psi\rangle\rangle$

The actual unitary matrix U applies to $|\psi\rangle$ w.r.t $\overline{q}$ on the right-hand side.

(SC) $$\frac{\langle S_1, |\psi\rangle\rangle \rightarrow \langle S_1', |\psi'\rangle\rangle}{\langle S_1 \,;\, S_2, |\psi\rangle\rangle \rightarrow \langle S_1' \,;\, S_2, |\psi'\rangle\rangle}$$

We use the convention that $\downarrow \,;\, S_2 = S_2$ and $S_2 \,;\, \downarrow = S_2$.

(IF0) $\langle \mathtt{if}\ M[q] = 1\ \mathtt{then}\ S_1\ \mathtt{else}\ S_2\ \mathtt{fi}, |\psi\rangle\rangle \rightarrow \langle S_2, \frac{M_0\,|\psi\rangle}{\|M_0\,|\psi\rangle\,\|}\rangle$

For result 0, $|\psi\rangle$ is collapsed according to M_0 of measurement $M = \{M_0, M_1\}$.

(IF1) $\langle \mathtt{if}\ M[q] = 1\ \mathtt{then}\ S_1\ \mathtt{else}\ S_2\ \mathtt{fi}, |\psi\rangle\rangle \rightarrow \langle S_1, \frac{M_1\,|\psi\rangle}{\|M_1\,|\psi\rangle\,\|}\rangle$

For result 1, $|\psi\rangle$ is collapsed according to M_1 of measurement $M = \{M_0, M_1\}$.

(L0) $\langle \mathtt{while}\ M[q] = 1\ \mathtt{do}\ S\ \mathtt{od}, |\psi\rangle\rangle \rightarrow \langle \downarrow, \frac{M_0\,|\psi\rangle}{\|M_0\,|\psi\rangle\,\|}\rangle$

For outcome 0 of measurement $M = \{M_0, M_1\}$.

(L1) $\langle \mathtt{while}\ M[q] = 1\ \mathtt{do}\ S\ \mathtt{od}, |\psi\rangle\rangle \rightarrow \langle S \,;\, \mathtt{while}\ M[q] = 1\ \mathtt{do}\ S\ \mathtt{od}, \frac{M_1\,|\psi\rangle}{\|M_1\,|\psi\rangle\,\|}\rangle$

For outcome 1 of measurement $M = \{M_0, M_1\}$.

Fig. 1. Transition rules for quantum while-programs.

configuration is a pair $\langle S, |\psi\rangle\rangle$, where S is a quantum program and $|\psi\rangle \in \mathcal{H}_S$ is a pure quantum state. Intuitively, a transition relation $\langle S, |\psi\rangle\rangle \rightarrow \langle S', |\psi'\rangle\rangle$ means that executing S for one step in a state $|\psi\rangle$ results in state $|\psi'\rangle$, with S' being the remaining program of S to be executed next. To indicate termination, we use an empty quantum program denoted by $\downarrow$ in configurations such that $S' \equiv \downarrow$, meaning that S terminates in state $|\psi'\rangle$. $\downarrow$ is an identity of ; namely that $\downarrow \,;\, S$ is the same as S and so is $S \,;\, \downarrow$. We do not explain the transition rules in Fig. 1 further because they are self-explanatory. Note that after a measurement of a quantum state, it will collapse according to the measurement result and its measurement operator. It is also important to note that $|\psi\rangle$ denotes the whole quantum state of a quantum program S, a quantum variable q refers to a specific single qubit in $|\psi\rangle$, and a quantum register $\overline{q}$ refers to multiple qubits in $|\psi\rangle$.

3.3 Reachability Problem for Quantum Programs

Given a quantum program S and an initial state $|\psi\rangle \in \mathcal{H}_S$, $\langle S', |\psi'\rangle\rangle$ is reachable from $\langle S, |\psi\rangle\rangle$ if and only if there exist configurations $\langle S_1, |\psi_1\rangle\rangle, \ldots, \langle S_n, |\psi_n\rangle\rangle$ for $n \geq 0$ such that

$$\langle S, |\psi\rangle\rangle = \langle S_1, |\psi_1\rangle\rangle \rightarrow \ldots \rightarrow \langle S_n, |\psi_n\rangle\rangle = \langle S', |\psi'\rangle\rangle$$

holds. In the case where $n = 0$, $\langle S, |\psi\rangle\rangle = \langle S', |\psi'\rangle\rangle$ holds. For each state $\langle S', |\psi'\rangle\rangle$ reachable from $\langle S, |\psi\rangle\rangle$, we are interested in checking whether the quantum state

$|\psi'\rangle_q$, referred to by a quantum variable q within the whole quantum state $|\psi'\rangle$, matches a given quantum state $|\phi\rangle$. If it does, then $\langle S', |\psi'\rangle\rangle$ is considered a satisfied state. The reachability problem is then defined to find all reachable states $\langle S', |\psi'\rangle\rangle$ from the initial state $\langle S, |\psi\rangle\rangle$ that satisfy the desired property.

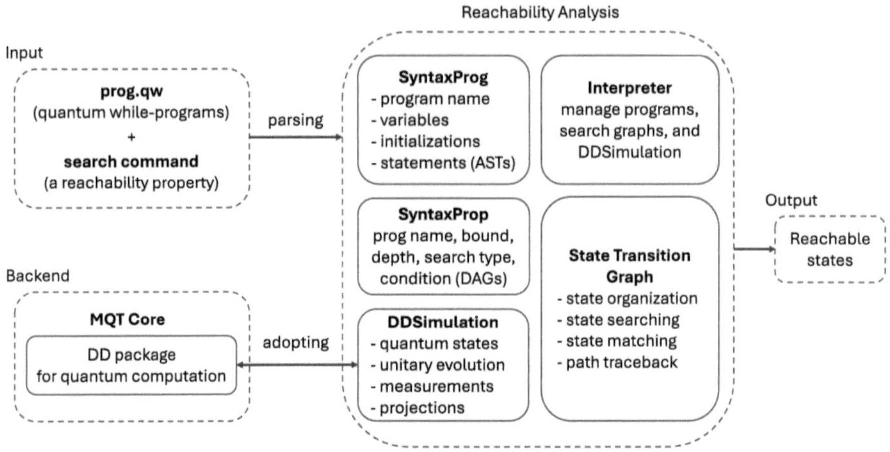

Fig. 2. Architecture of QRAT.

4 QRAT Overview

In this section, we present the architecture of QRAT in detail and the usability of the tool with interactive-mode-supported commands.

4.1 Architecture of QRAT

We present an overview of the architecture of QRAT in Fig. 2. Our reachability analysis tool for quantum programs is implemented in C++, with some key components explained as follows.

Input and Output. QRAT accepts quantum programs written within the scope of quantum while-programs described in Sect. 3.1. These programs are stored in files with the designated extension `qw`. Reachability properties are specified using search commands, which find reachable states that satisfy some conditions expressed as Boolean expressions. A quantum program is parsed into a **SyntaxProg** representation, which includes the program name, quantum variables with their initializations, and program statements represented as an abstract syntax tree (AST). ASTs allow the program counter to be uniquely represented as a pointer to the next instruction to be executed. A reachability property is parsed into a **SyntaxProp** representation, which specifies the program name, an upper bound on the number of solutions, a depth limit for the search graph, and the condition that reachable states must satisfy. The condition is represented as a directed acyclic graph (DAG), enabling the reuse of sub-expressions to prevent duplication and minimize redundant checks when verifying whether a state satisfies the condition. The output of QRAT is a finite set of reachable states that satisfy the specified condition in the search command.

Simulation. For n qubits, a quantum state is a state vector of size 2^n, and quantum operations are $2^n \times 2^n$ dimensional unitary matrices. Due to the exponential growth in size and dimension with respect to the number of qubits, it is essential to compactly represent quantum states and quantum operations and effectively simulate the execution of quantum operations on quantum states. Among several DD-based simulations for quantum computation, MQT Core provides one of the most advanced decision diagrams used for quantum simulation. It utilizes a decomposition scheme to compactly represent quantum states and quantum operations so that efficient manipulation algorithms can be developed. Rather than using decision diagrams naively, they use edge-weight decision diagrams to make representation even more compact. Moreover, they also effectively handle complex numbers to keep numerical stability so that nodes in decision diagrams are effectively stored in unique tables [29]. Many tools, such as quantum circuit simulation [30] and equivalence checking [7], have been empowered by MQT Core and natively integrated with IBM's Qiskit, demonstrating its maturity and active development. Therefore, we adopted the DD package from MQT Core for quantum simulation.

The **DDSimulation** component serves as an adapter, facilitating communication with the DD package to simulate quantum states, quantum unitary evolution, measurements, and projections. The DD package currently simulates binary projective measurements by selecting one outcome based on comparing the outcome probabilities with a threshold randomly sampled from a uniform distribution over $[0, 1)$. From a verification perspective, measurements are treated as nondeterministic choices associated with their probabilities. To support this, we have enhanced the DD package with the selection of measurement results for branching reachability analysis. Additionally, the DD package currently does not support the outer product of a state vector, which is essential for constructing projectors (or projection operators) that represent the subspaces spanned by a set of linearly independent vectors. Projectors play a crucial role in defining reachability properties through projections. To overcome this limitation, we have enhanced the DD package with the outer product of state vectors for defining reachability properties.

State Transition Graph. Given a quantum program and a desired property, the **Interpreter** component initializes both the DDSimulation and **StateTransitionGraph**, and then dynamically constructs the state transition graph by searching for reachable states that satisfy the desired property with a breadth-first search (BFS) approach. The initial state, specified in the quantum program, is set up during the initialization of the StateTransitionGraph, while the desired property, including projections, is defined during the initialization of DDSimulation. The interpreter is responsible for initializing new instances and cleaning up previous ones for DDSimulation and StateTransitionGraph each time a new reachability analysis is performed. Additionally, it keeps track of all programs that have been defined and loaded up to that point.

4.2 Usability of QRAT

When QRAT is launched from the command line, it provides an interactive mode that allows users to perform reachability analysis using the following commands:

- `load` <`progFile.qw`> .
  Loads the quantum program specified in the `progFile.qw` file. Programs and properties can also be defined together in the same file when necessary.
- `search`
  {`[bound,depth]`} `in` <`progName`> with <`searchType`> such that <`condition`>
  .
  Performs a breadth-first search for the program specified by `progName`, aiming to find reachable states that satisfy the given `condition`. The `searchType` parameter determines the type of state transitions to consider:
  `=>1` one state transition step,
  `=>+` one or more state transition steps,
  `=>*` zero or more state transition steps,
  `=>!` only final states with no further transitions are considered as solutions.
  The optional `bound` argument specifies the maximum number of solutions to find (default is infinity). The optional `depth` argument sets the maximum search depth (default is infinity). It is also possible to specify a depth bound without a solution bound by using a command of the form `search [,m] ...`.
- `show path` <`stateId`> .
  Displays the path leading to a specific state in the search graph, identified by the number `stateId`.
- `set random seed` <`number`> .
  Sets the random seed to the specified `number` to initialize a random number generator, primarily used for constructing random quantum states (default is 0).
- `quit .`
  Exit the QRAT application.

Using these commands, we illustrate how to perform the reachability analysis for Quantum Teleportation in Appendix A.

5 Reachability Analysis Algorithm

This section introduces the data structure used to represent states in the search graph, presents the reachability analysis algorithm for quantum programs, and shows how to evaluate properties that are different from classical analysis.

Algorithm 1: Reachability analysis algorithm for quantum programs

```
input  : prog – the quantum program,
         property – the reachability property.
output : a finite set of reachable states that satisfy the property.
seenStates.push(buildInitialState(prog))
results ← empty
savedStateId ← 0
while savedStateId < seenStates.size() do
    currState ← seenStates[savedStateId]
    if isEndProg(currState.pc) then
        savedStateId ← savedStateId + 1
        continue
    if isSkipStm(currState.pc) then
        procSkipStm(currState)
    else if isUnitaryStm(currState.pc) then
        procUnitaryStm(currState)
    else if isCondStm(currState.pc) then
        procCondStm(currState)
    else if isWhileStm(currState.pc) then
        procWhileStm(currState)
    savedStateId ← savedStateId + 1
return results
function procCondStm(currState) :
    (qs0, pZero, qs1, pOne) ←
      measureWithProb(currState.qs, extractTargetQubit(currState.pc))
    procBranch(currState, qs0, pZero, currState.pc.getElsePC())
    procBranch(currState, qs1, pOne, currState.pc.getThenPC())
function procBranch(currState, qs, prob, pc) :
    (newState, inCached) ← makeState(currState, qs, prob, pc)
    if not inCached then
        seenStates.push(newState)
        if checkState(newState, property) then
            results ← results ∪ {newState}
```

State Orgranization. As explained in Sect. 4, we uniquely represent the program counter as a pointer to the next instruction to be executed in the program, and the quantum state as a pointer managed by the ASTs and the DD package, respectively. These two pointers are used for hashing and uniquely identifying each state in the search graph. A state is thus defined as a tuple of the following essential components.

- `stateId` is a unique identifier for the state, assigned incrementally starting from 0 for the initial state.
- `parentId` is the ID of the parent state and is set to -1 for the initial state.
- `pc` is the pointer to the program counter.
- `qs` is the pointer to the quantum state.
- `nextIds` represents the set of IDs corresponding to successor states.

- `prob` is the probability associated with transitioning to this state. Note that this value represents only the minimum probability of first encountering this state, as probabilities from other incoming state transitions are not accumulated. Nevertheless, it remains highly useful for verification.

Algorithm. For simplicity, the reachability analysis algorithm, presented in Algorithm 1, assumes infinite solutions, unbounded depth, and includes a certain level of abstraction. In the **initialization** phase, the initial state is constructed from the program *prog* and added to the global list *seenStates*. A global set *results* is initialized as empty to store reachable states that satisfy the property. Additionally, *savedStateId* is set to 0 to track the current state being explored. During **state exploration**, while *savedStateId* remains less than the size of *seenStates*, the algorithm processes the current state. If the program counter `pc` indicates the end of the program, *savedStateId* is incremented, and the next state is processed. Otherwise, the state is processed based on the type of instruction indicated by `pc`. These include skip statements, unitary operations, conditional statements, and while loops, which are handled by corresponding functions: `procSkipStm`, `procUnitaryStm`, `procCondStm` and `procWhileStm` (lines 9–16). After processing, *savedStateId* is incremented to continue exploration.

For brevity, we present only the function `procCondStm`, which takes the current state given as input (lines 19–22). The function calls `measureWithProb` with the current quantum state `qs` and the target qubit extracted from `pc`. The function `measureWithProb` performs a binary projective measurement on the target qubit, returning two collapsed quantum states (*ps0* and *qs1*) along with their probabilities (*pZero* and *pOne*). For each measurement outcome, the function `procBranch` is invoked to handle state creation and addition. If the probability of an outcome is zero, `procBranch` is skipped for that outcome.

The function `procBranch` (lines 23–28) calls `makeState` to create a new state using the inputs: the current state ID is set as the parent ID; the quantum state and program counter are the provided values `qs` and `pc`; and the probability is calculated as the product of the current state probability and the transition probability (`prob`). If the state is new (determined by `pc` and `qs`), it is assigned a unique ID (equal to the current size of *seenStates*). The new state ID is then added to the successor states (`nextIds`) of the current state. If the state has been explored (*inCached*), no further action is taken. Otherwise, the new state is added to *seenStates* and `checkState` is invoked to verify whether the state satisfies the property; if it does, the state is added to *results*.

The algorithm explores all reachable states in the program while evaluating the property for each state. Upon completion, it returns a finite set of reachable states that satisfy the property in *results*.

Property Evaluation. We focus on properties that are expressed as whether a quantum state $|\psi\rangle_q$, referred to by a quantum variable q within the whole quantum state $|\psi\rangle$, matches a given quantum state $|\phi\rangle$. This verification can be

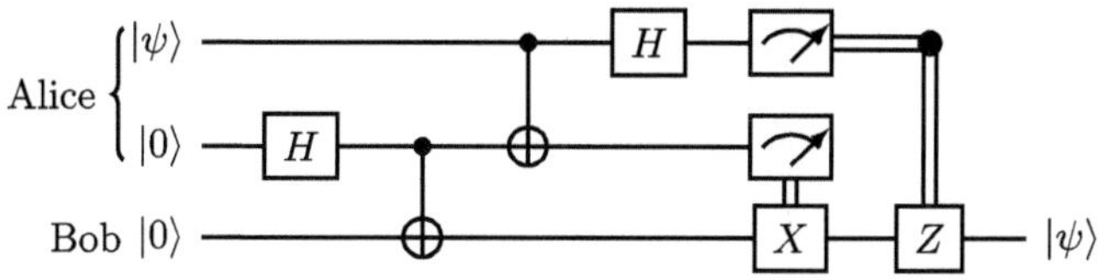

Fig. 3. Quantum Teleportation.

performed using projection. We define the property $\mathtt{P}(q, |\phi\rangle)$ as atomic propositions in Birkhoffvon Neumann quantum logic [5] to indicate whether $|\psi\rangle_q$ belongs to the subspace spanned by $|\phi\rangle$. We adopt this definition of atomic propositions because it is widely used in quantum verification [2,15,25]. To evaluate $\mathtt{P}(q, |\phi\rangle)$, we construct the projector $\mathcal{P} = |\phi\rangle\langle\phi|$ and apply it to the quantum state $|\psi\rangle_q$, resulting in

$$\mathcal{P}|\psi\rangle_q = |\phi\rangle\langle\phi||\psi\rangle_q = |\psi'\rangle_q.$$

If $|\psi'\rangle_q$ is equivalent to $|\psi\rangle_q$ up to a global phase, the property is satisfied in $|\psi\rangle$; otherwise, it is not. The equivalence can be efficiently checked by comparing their pointers, as the DD package uniquely represents quantum states as pointers.

6 Experiments

This section presents two case studies along with the experimental results obtained using QRAT for analysis. The experiments were performed on a MacPro computer equipped with a 2.5 GHz processor, 28 cores, and 1 TB of RAM.

Quantum Teleportation. [3] enables the teleportation of an arbitrary single-qubit state $|\psi\rangle$ from a sender to a receiver using only three qubits and two classical bits. The quantum circuit for this protocol is depicted in Fig 3. The protocol starts with the initial state $|\psi\rangle_{q_0} \otimes |0\rangle_{q_1} \otimes |0\rangle_{q_2}$. The goal is to verify whether $|\psi\rangle$ has been teleported correctly by checking whether the third qubit, referred to by q_2, equals $|\psi\rangle$ at the end of the protocol. We conduct multiple experiments for Quantum Teleportation, each using a different random state $|\psi\rangle$ generated by QRAT with a unique random seed.

Grover search algorithm provides a quadratic speedup for solving unstructured search problems [17]. It achieves this by iteratively amplifying the probability of the correct solution through a quantum operation known as the Grover operator. The algorithm requires $O(\sqrt{N})$ queries to locate the correct solution in a database of size N, compared to $O(N)$ in classical search methods. When the correct solution is encoded in a basis state of n qubits, the database size becomes 2^n. The goal is to verify whether the correct solution can be found with very high probability after approximately $\pi\sqrt{2^n}/4$ iterations of the Grover operator. For each configuration of n qubits, we conduct multiple experiments, each using a different correct solution selected randomly.

Table 1. Experimental results with QRAT

Program	#Qubits	#Unitary	#Meas.	#States	Time	#Exps.
Teleportation	3	8	2	17	≈ 0	100
Grover	10	1,430	10	5,503	10ms	100
	15	11,973	15	143,012	507ms	100
	20	90,108	20	4,284,369	3.9m	100

The experimental results are summarized in Table 1. The columns **#Unitary** and **#Meas.** denote the number of unitary operations and measurements in each program, respectively. The column **#Exps.** indicates the number of experiments conducted for each case, and the experiment with the longest analysis time of each case is selected to present in the column **Time** along with the total number of states explored in the column **#States**. Note that the number of unitary operations for the Grover search algorithm depends on the correct solution picked, and so the value in the column **#Unitary** corresponds to the experiment with the longest analysis time. Using QRAT, we efficiently verified the correctness of Quantum Teleportation through 100 experiments, each using a different random quantum state. Furthermore, we confirmed that the Grover search algorithm successfully identified the correct solution with nearly 100% probability for configurations of 10, 15, and 20 qubits. Each configuration involved 100 experiments, each using a different correct solution picked randomly. The 20-qubit configuration presented a significant challenge due to its complexity, involving numerous unitary operations and measurements and resulting in a reachable state space exceeding 4 million states. Nevertheless, QRAT completed the analysis in just 3.9 min. These experimental results demonstrate the effectiveness and practicality of QRAT in verifying quantum programs.

7 Related Work

QReach [11] is a reachability analysis tool for quantum Markov chains utilizing decision diagrams CFLOBDD [24]. Unlike QRAT, QReach focuses on mixed states represented as density operators, and its output identifies reachable subspaces of the Hilbert space rather than a finite set of reachable states. As noted in [28], pure states (adopted by QRAT) are more intuitive and practical for representing quantum states in applications than density operators. Consequently, the properties verified by QReach are hard to interpret regarding their meanings, and it lacks support for probabilities in reachability analysis. Moreover, QRAT allows users to work with high-level descriptions of quantum programs, rather than quantum circuits and Markov chains.

AutoQ is a tree-automata-based verification approach originally designed for quantum circuits [9] and later extended to verify quantum programs [10]. It employs Hoare triples of $\{P\}S\{Q\}$, where P and Q represent sets of pure quantum states, and S is a quantum program. AutoQ verifies whether all states in

P reach some state in Q after executing S with a deductive approach. In contrast, reachability analysis is an exploration-based approach that systematically explores all reachable states that satisfy a certain condition from an initial state. Therefore, AutoQ is not a reachability analysis tool for quantum programs like QRAT.

8 Conclusion

We have introduced QRAT, the first reachability analysis tool for quantum programs, leveraging a state-of-the-art decision diagram developed in MQT Core for quantum computing. Quantum while-programs are used as the modeling language, and the reachability properties are expressed through the `search` command. The experimental results on Quantum Teleportation and Grover's search using QRAT have demonstrated the effectiveness of our approach for reachability analysis of quantum programs. In future work, we plan to conduct additional case studies and extend our approach to symbolic reachability analysis for quantum programs, enabling handling of arbitrary quantum states as in [13,14].

Acknowledgments. The research was partially supported by JSPS KAKENHI Grant Numbers JP23K28060, JP23K19959, JP24K20757, JP24KK0185.

A Reachability Analysis of Quantum Teleportation

This section demonstrates how to use QRAT to verify that $|\psi\rangle$ is teleported correctly by checking whether the third qubit, referred to by q_2, is $|\psi\rangle$ at the end of the protocol. As shown in Fig. 3, Quantum Teleportation starts with the state $|\psi\rangle_{q_0} \otimes |0\rangle_{q_1} \otimes |0\rangle_{q_2}$. We first prepare the Quantum Teleportation program in a file named `teleport.qw` with the following content:

```
prog TELEPORT is
var q0, q1, q2 : qubit;
init
    q0 := random; // a random quantum state being teleported
    q1 := |0>;
    q2 := |0>;
begin
    q1 := H[q1];
    q1, q2 := CX[q1, q2];
    q0, q1 := CX[q0, q1];
    q0 := H[q0];
    if M[q1] = 1 then q2 := X[q2]; else skip; fi;
    if M[q0] = 1 then q2 := Z[q2]; else skip; fi;
end
```

where `TELEPORT` is the name of the program and `q0`, `q1`, and `q2` are quantum variables initialized to a random quantum state $|\psi\rangle$ (generated with a default random seed in this example), $|0\rangle$, and $|0\rangle$, respectively. The execution of the program is enclosed between `begin` and `end`.

Next, we launch QRAT from the command line where the `teleport.qw` file is located and load the program using the following command.

```
qrat> load teleport.qw .
```

We aim to conduct the reachability analysis to find all ending states where the quantum state in q_2 is the same as $|\psi\rangle$ by using the following command.

```
qrat> search in TELEPORT with =>! such that P(q2, init[q0]) .
```

where `init[q0]` is used to obtain the random quantum state $|\psi\rangle$ at the initialization and `P(q2, init[q0])` checks whether the quantum state in q_2 at the end of the program belongs to the subspace spanned by $|\psi\rangle$. In other words, this command verifies that the third qubit, referred to by q_2, is $|\psi\rangle$ at the end. QRAT returns four solutions, each with an equal probability of 0.25, as follows:

```
Solution 1 (state 13)
states: 14 in 0ms cpu (0ms real)
probability: 0.25, quantum state:
000: (0.71,-0.701)
100: (0.0446,0.0441)

Solution 2 (state 14)
states: 15 in 0ms cpu (0ms real)
probability: 0.25, quantum state:
001: (0.71,-0.701)
101: (0.0446,0.0441)

Solution 3 (state 15)
states: 16 in 0ms cpu (0ms real)
probability: 0.25, quantum state:
010: (0.71,-0.701)
110: (0.0446,0.0441)

Solution 4 (state 16)
states: 17 in 0ms cpu (0ms real)
probability: 0.25, quantum state:
011: (0.71,-0.701)
111: (0.0446,0.0441)

No more solutions.
states: 17 in 0ms cpu (0ms real)
```

We can verify that all ending states satisfy the desired property for Quantum Teleportation. For instance, in `Solution 1` with the state ID 13, we can trace the path that leads to this state from the initial state using the following command.

```
qrat> show path 13 .
```

For brevity, we do not include the verbose output here. Additionally, we can change the random quantum state used for initialization by modifying the random seed using the command described in Sect. 4. Based on the results from QRAT, we confirm the correctness of Quantum Teleportation with the random quantum state $|\psi\rangle$ teleported successfully.

References

1. Abdollahi, A., Pedram, M.: Analysis and synthesis of quantum circuits by using quantum decision diagrams. In: Proceedings of the Design Automation & Test in Europe Conference, vol. 1, pp. 1–6 (2006). https://doi.org/10.1109/DATE.2006.244176
2. Baltag, A., Smets, S.: Reasoning about quantum information: an overview of quantum dynamic logic. Appli. Sci. **12**(9) (2022). https://doi.org/10.3390/app12094458
3. Bennett, C.H., Brassard, G., Crépeau, C., Jozsa, R., Peres, A., Wootters, W.K.: Teleporting an unknown quantum state via dual classical and Einstein-Podolsky-Rosen channels. Phys. Rev. Lett. **70**, 1895–1899 (1993). https://doi.org/10.1103/PhysRevLett.70.1895
4. Biamonte, J., Wittek, P., Pancotti, N., Rebentrost, P., Wiebe, N., Lloyd, S.: Quantum machine learning. Nature **549**(7671), 195–202 (2017). https://doi.org/10.1038/nature23474
5. Birkhoff, G., von Neumann, J.: The logic of quantum mechanics. Ann. Math. **57**(4), 823–843 (1936). https://doi.org/10.2307/1968621
6. Bryant, R.E.: Binary Decision Diagrams, pp. 191–217. Springer International Publishing, Cham (2018). https://doi.org/10.1007/978-3-319-10575-8_7
7. Burgholzer, L., Wille, R.: Advanced equivalence checking for quantum circuits. IEEE Trans. Comput. Aided Des. Integr. Circuits Syst. **40**(9), 1810–1824 (2021). https://doi.org/10.1109/TCAD.2020.3032630
8. Chaki, S., Gurfinkel, A.: BDD-Based Symbolic Model Checking, pp. 219–245. Springer International Publishing, Cham (2018). https://doi.org/10.1007/978-3-319-10575-8_8
9. Chen, Y.F., Chung, K.M., Lengál, O., Lin, J.A., Tsai, W.L.: AutoQ: an automata-based quantum circuit verifier. In: Enea, C., Lal, A. (eds.) Computer Aided Verification, pp. 139–153. Springer Nature Switzerland, Cham (2023). https://doi.org/10.1007/978-3-031-37709-9_7
10. Chung, K.M., Hsieh, M.H., Huang, W.J., Lengál, O., Lin, J.A., Tsai, W.L.: AutoQ 2.0: from verification of quantum circuits to verification of quantum programs (to appear). In: Tools and Algorithms for the Construction and Analysis of Systems (2025). https://doi.org/10.48550/arXiv.2411.09121
11. Dai, A., Ying, M.: QReach: a reachability analysis tool for quantum markov chains. In: Computer Aided Verification, pp. 520–532. Springer Nature Switzerland, Cham (2024). https://doi.org/10.1007/978-3-031-65633-0_23
12. Dirac, P.A.M.: A new notation for quantum mechanics. Math. Proc. Cambridge Philos. Soc. **35**(3), 416–418 (1939). https://doi.org/10.1017/S0305004100021162
13. Do, C.M., Ogata, K.: Symbolic model checking quantum circuits in Maude. In: The 35th International Conference on Software Engineering and Knowledge Engineering, SEKE 2023, pp. 103–108 (2023). https://doi.org/10.18293/SEKE2023-014
14. Do, C.M., Ogata, K.: Symbolic model checking quantum circuits in Maude. PeerJ Comput. Sci. **10**, e2098 (2024). https://doi.org/10.7717/PEERJ-CS.2098

15. Do, C.M., Takagi, T., Ogata, K.: Automated quantum protocol verification based on concurrent dynamic quantum logic. ACM Trans. Softw. Eng. Methodol. **34**(6) (2025). https://doi.org/10.1145/3708475
16. Farhi, E., Goldstone, J., Gutmann, S., Lapan, J., Lundgren, A., Preda, D.: A quantum adiabatic evolution algorithm applied to random instances of an np-complete problem. Science **292**(5516), 472–475 (2001). https://doi.org/10.1126/science.1057726
17. Grover, L.K.: A fast quantum mechanical algorithm for database search. In: Proceedings of the Twenty-Eighth Annual ACM Symposium on Theory of Computing, STOC 1996. pp. 212–219. Association for Computing Machinery, New York (1996). https://doi.org/10.1145/237814.237866
18. Harrow, A.W., Hassidim, A., Lloyd, S.: Quantum algorithm for linear systems of equations. Phys. Rev. Lett. **103**, 150502 (2009). https://doi.org/10.1103/PhysRevLett.103.150502
19. Lozano, L., Bergman, D., Cire, A.A.: Decision Diagrams for Optimization, pp. 1–6. Springer International Publishing, Cham (2020). https://doi.org/10.1007/978-3-030-54621-2_712-1
20. Nielsen, M.A., Chuang, I.L.: Quantum Computation and Quantum Information: 10th Anniversary Edition. Cambridge University Press (2010). https://doi.org/10.1017/CBO9780511976667
21. Niemann, P., Wille, R., Miller, D.M., Thornton, M.A., Drechsler, R.: QMDDs: efficient quantum function representation and manipulation. IEEE Trans. Comput. Aided Des. Integr. Circuits Syst. **35**(1), 86–99 (2016). https://doi.org/10.1109/TCAD.2015.2459034
22. Shor, P.: Algorithms for quantum computation: discrete logarithms and factoring. In: Proceedings 35th Annual Symposium on Foundations of Computer Science, pp. 124–134 (1994). https://doi.org/10.1109/SFCS.1994.365700
23. Sistla, M., Chaudhuri, S., Reps, T.: Symbolic quantum simulation with Quasimodo. In: Computer Aided Verification, pp. 213–225. Springer Nature Switzerland, Cham (2023). https://doi.org/10.1007/978-3-031-37709-9_11
24. Sistla, M.A., Chaudhuri, S., Reps, T.: CFLOBDDs: context-free-language ordered binary decision diagrams. ACM Trans. Program. Lang. Syst. **46**(2) (2024). https://doi.org/10.1145/3651157
25. Takagi, T., Do, C.M., Ogata, K.: Automated quantum program verification in dynamic quantum logic. In: Dynamic Logic. New Trends and Applications, pp. 68–84. Springer Nature Switzerland, Cham (2024). https://doi.org/10.1007/978-3-031-51777-8_5
26. Wang, S.A., Lu, C.Y., Tsai, I.M., Kuo, S.Y.: An XQDD-based verification method for quantum circuits. IEICE Trans. **91-A**, 584–594 (02 2008). https://doi.org/10.1093/ietfec/e91-a.2.584
27. Yamashita, S., Minato, S.i., Miller, D.M.: DDMF: an efficient decision diagram structure for design verification of quantum circuits under a practical restriction. IEICE Trans. Fundamentals Electron. Commun. Comput. Sci. **E91-A**(12), 3793–3802 (2008). https://doi.org/10.1093/ietfec/e91-a.12.3793
28. Ying, M.: Foundations of Quantum Programming. Morgan Kaufmann Publishers Inc., San Francisco, CA, USA, second edition edn. (2024). https://doi.org/10.1016/C2022-0-02250-9

29. Zulehner, A., Hillmich, S., Wille, R.: How to efficiently handle complex values? implementing decision diagrams for quantum computing. In: 2019 IEEE/ACM International Conference on Computer-Aided Design (ICCAD), pp. 1–7 (2019). https://doi.org/10.1109/ICCAD45719.2019.8942057
30. Zulehner, A., Wille, R.: Advanced simulation of quantum computations. IEEE Trans. Comput. Aided Des. Integr. Circuits Syst. **38**(5), 848–859 (2019). https://doi.org/10.1109/TCAD.2018.2834427

An Empirical Study on Software Defect Prediction Based on Neural Network DeepDebugger Technique

Yuxiang Shang[1], Shaoying Liu[2(✉)], and Jin Song Dong[3]

[1] Hiroshima University, Hiroshima, Japan
[2] East China Normal University, Shanghai, China
shangyuxiang@hiroshima-u.ac.jp
[3] National University of Singapore, Singapore, Singapore

Abstract. Software engineering efforts increasingly focus on enhancing software quality by detecting, addressing, and predicting defect-prone components. This area has garnered considerable research interest due to its integral role in the software development process. Numerous methods have been proposed for software defect prediction, with recent work emphasizing data mining strategies, especially the use of neural networks, as powerful tools. Despite their effectiveness, neural networks are often criticized for their opacity, leading to doubts about the reliability of their outcomes. To address this, we use DeepDebugger, an explainable AI technique designed for defect prediction. It leverages animated visualizations composed of dynamic, color-coded elements to represent the model's learning behavior. We evaluated DeepDebugger across widely used neural network models on datasets from NASA, PROMISE, and AEEEM. Experimental findings show that this approach improves both the interpretability and the visualization of neural network training dynamics.

Keywords: Software Defect Prediction · Explainable Neural Network · Visualization

1 Introduction

In the realm of software engineering, predicting software defects (SDP) has become an essential endeavor [25]. As contemporary software systems grow in complexity and scale, maintaining quality poses a considerable challenge to both practitioners and researchers. Traditional manual debugging methods are often inefficient due to their high time and resource demands, making them unsuitable for guaranteeing software reliability [15]. This has led to a growing emphasis on the development of automated techniques for defect identification and analysis.

Artificial intelligence has become an increasingly viable approach for software defect prediction, with neural network-based models receiving particular attention due to the binary classification nature of the problem. Consequently, a vari-

© The Author(s), under exclusive license to Springer Nature Singapore Pte Ltd. 2026
Y. Chen et al. (Eds.): SFPVV 2025, LNCS 16356, pp. 34–47, 2026.
https://doi.org/10.1007/978-981-95-6032-5_3

ety of SDP techniques leveraging different neural architectures have been introduced, reflecting the growing influence of AI in this area. Notably, deep learning models such as Deep Neural Networks (DNNs) [26], Convolutional Neural Networks (CNNs) [20], Recurrent Neural Networks (RNNs) [8], Long Short-Term Memory (LSTM) networks [6], and Transformer models [38] have been applied to this task. Despite their predictive power, these models are often criticized for functioning as "black boxes" due to their intricate and non-transparent internal operations. This opacity introduces challenges in interpretability, raising valid concerns about their dependability and safety in practical applications.

Building upon recent advances, we use *DeepDebugger* [33–35], an interactive, time-travel-inspired debugging framework designed for deep learning-based software defect prediction. This approach focuses on visualizing the training behavior of neural classifiers through animated canvases composed of vibrant dots and spatial regions, aiming to make model behavior more interpretable and accessible. To assess the utility of DeepDebugger, we performed comprehensive experiments using datasets from NASA [30], PROMISE [3], and AEEEM [7]. A variety of prominent neural network models were evaluated, with empirical results detailed in Sect. 5. The principal contributions of this study include:

- The introduction of DeepDebugger into the domain of software defect prediction, accompanied by empirical validation across leading neural network architectures.
- Improved interpretability and visual transparency of binary classification models used in defect prediction.
- A comparative analysis of the performance and behavior of diverse neural network architectures applied to SDP tasks.

The remainder of this paper is organized as follows: Sect. 2 introduces the foundational concepts relevant to our research. Section 3 offers a brief survey of existing methods for visual interpretation of deep learning models. Section 4 details the design and methodology underlying the DeepDebugger framework. Section 5 presents and analyzes the experimental findings. Lastly, Sect. 6 summarizes the conclusions drawn from this study.

2 Background

2.1 Deep Classifier

In a classification task, we are given a set of input instances $S = \{s_1, s_2, ..., s_n\}$ and a corresponding set of target classes $C = \{c_1, c_2, ..., c_p\}$. The objective is to learn a classifier $m : S \rightarrow C$ that assigns each input s to a label $c_i \in C$, such that $m(s) = c_i$. Within the context of deep learning, the classifier m is generally structured as the composition of two functions: a feature extraction function $f(\cdot)$ responsible for learning representations, and a decision-making function $g(\cdot)$ that maps these representations to class labels. Hence, the overall mapping can be expressed as $m = g \circ f$, as shown in Fig. 1. For the input dataset S, this decomposition yields a set of feature representations $\mathcal{R} = \{r_1, r_2, ..., r_n\}$, where each $r_i = f(s_i)$ resides in a high-dimensional feature space. Accordingly, the classification process for an input s_i is given by $m(s_i) = g(f(s_i))$.

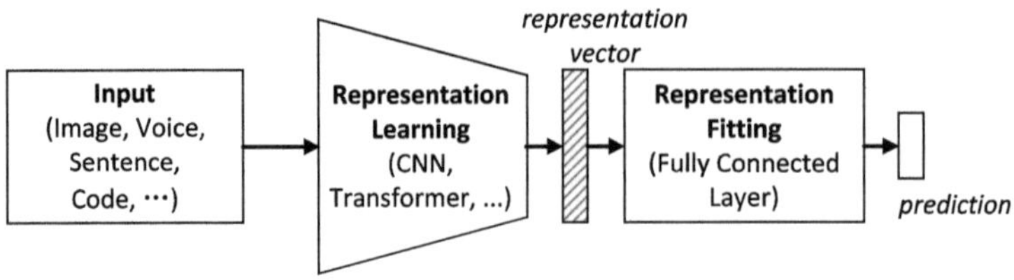

Fig. 1. Illustration of the Typical Architecture in Deep Learning Classifiers.

2.2 Time-Traveling Visualization

A time-travel visualization tool processes a dataset $\mathcal{S} = \{s_1, s_2, ..., s_n\}$ alongside a sequence of intermediate models $\mathcal{M} = \langle m_1, m_2, ..., m_k \rangle$, where each m_i corresponds to the classifier state after the *i-th* training epoch. This tool produces a series of visual frames $\mathcal{F} = \langle frm_1, frm_2, ..., frm_k \rangle$, with each frm_i depicting a 2D projection of the classification behavior in the *i-th* learned feature space $\mathcal{R}$. These visualizations capture: (1) class-specific regions within $\mathcal{R}$ and (2) the spatial variation in prediction confidence across those regions. For every pixel in frm_i, a color-mapping function $\mathbb{R}^2 \rightarrow \{0, 1, ..., 255\}^3$ assigns an RGB value, where hue encodes the predicted class and brightness reflects the classifier's confidence-lighter shades indicating lower certainty. The resulting sequence of frames reveals the evolution of decision boundaries and confidence gradients throughout training, as illustrated in Fig. 2. For instance, a pink dot appearing in a red region signals a correct prediction, whereas its presence in a blue region marks a misclassification. White areas delineate uncertain boundary zones between classes.

3 Related Work

Visual Explanation of Deep Learning Models. To improve the transparency and interpretability of deep learning systems, a wide range of visualization strategies have been proposed [5,9,28,29,31,33,34]. Grad-CAM [29] and its subsequent enhancements [5,9] are widely adopted for highlighting image regions that most influence the model's predictions. Alternatively, Seq2seq-Vis [31] caters to sequence-to-sequence architectures by visualizing influential tokens in input sentences that shape the generated outputs. Unlike these predominantly static visualization methods, our approach prioritizes dynamic interpretability and debugging. Specifically, it builds upon temporal visualization tools such as DVI [34] and TimeVis [33], allowing users to trace and analyze changes in model behavior over successive training epochs.

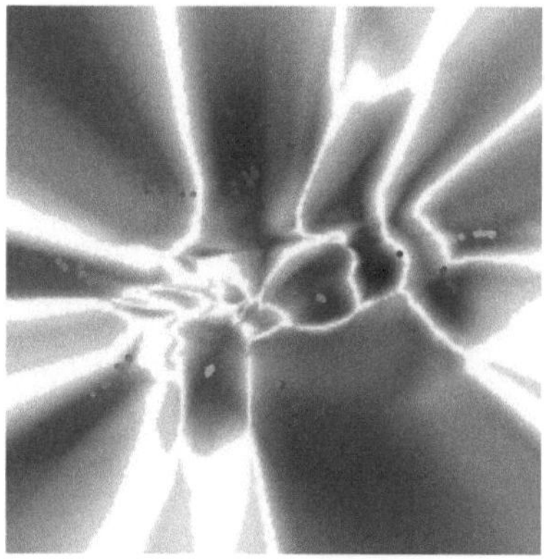

Fig. 2. Visualization of the Classification Landscape at a Single Epoch Using the TimeVis Framework.

Interactive Debugging and Fault Localization. Unlike traditional one-shot fault localization techniques such as spectrum-based methods [1,37] and delta-debugging [2,13,36], modern debugging strategies increasingly favor interactive approaches. These approaches focus on analyzing execution traces [16–19,23,24,32] and examining source code [10,12,14,21,22,27], offering developers enhanced flexibility and deeper diagnostic capabilities. Trace-centric techniques have been pivotal in advancing time-travel debugging tools. Notably, Whyline [16–19] introduced an innovative querying interface that allows developers to ask "why" and "why-not" questions regarding specific program behaviors, facilitating more intuitive fault investigation. Further enhancements include trace summarization [24], probabilistic reasoning [32], and intelligent breakpoint suggestions via machine learning [23]. Interactive approaches that center on source code have also evolved traditional fault localization. Enhancements to spectrum-based techniques [10,14,21,22] improve accuracy by involving developers directly in the fault-identification loop. Additionally, tools like VIDA [12] and

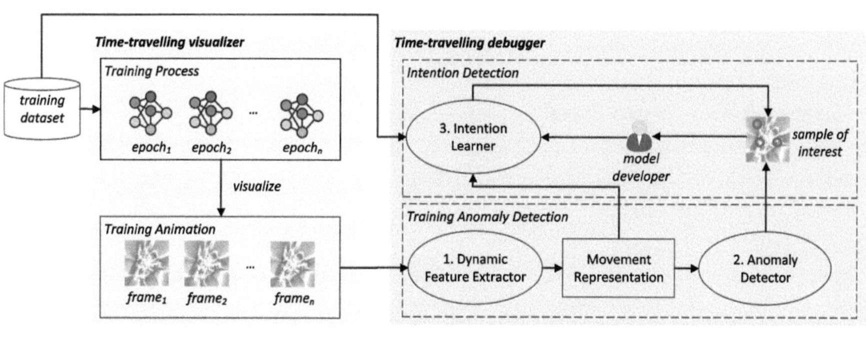

Fig. 3. Architecture of the DeepDebugger Framework.

swarm-based breakpoint recommendation systems [27] aid in determining effective debugging points. In contrast to these conventional methods, which focus on traditional software systems, *DeepDebugger* targets the unique challenges of debugging deep learning models. By building upon temporal visualization frameworks such as DVI [34] and TimeVis [33], DeepDebugger facilitates the exploration of model training dynamics. It enables users to trace model evolution, detect misclassifications, and gain interpretive insights into classifier behavior, thereby bridging the methodological gap between classic debugging practices and the intricacies of deep neural networks.

4 Approach Overview

Figure 3 presents the overall design of the DeepDebugger framework, which functions as a time-travel debugging tool for inspecting the internal dynamics of model training. This system leverages visualization components that convert the learning process into animated sequences, allowing developers to: (1) detect instances that display atypical training patterns, and (2) iteratively refine training data through interactive feedback and user-guided exploration.

To facilitate this process, the system first utilizes a Dynamic Feature Extractor (Fig. 3) to derive features that characterize the training behavior of each sample. These features are then analyzed by an Anomaly Detector (Fig. 3), which identifies unusual training patterns and proposes potentially problematic samples as initial candidates for inspection. Developers can interact with these suggestions by accepting, rejecting, or disregarding them, depending on the context of their debugging task. An integrated intention-learning module supports this interaction by (1) adapting to user feedback in real time and (2) extrapolating the limited feedback to uncover additional relevant instances. This feedback-driven loop continues until users either confirm the presence of issues such as mislabeled data or validate their debugging hypotheses, with guidance from the Intention Learner (Fig. 3).

4.1 Dynamic Feature Extraction

Each sample is characterized by dynamic features that reflect its behavior throughout training, including its movement across the visualization canvas and the progression of its predicted outputs. These are categorized as trajectory features and prediction features, respectively. Together, they represent the learning dynamics of both the representation extraction and representation fitting components, providing critical insights into the sample's evolving behavior during training (refer to Fig. 1).

Trajectory Features. The dynamic trajectory of a sample is described using three primary attributes: location, velocity, and acceleration. **Location**: This feature captures the spatial position of a sample within the classification landscape, indicating region-level behavioral patterns such as prediction similarity. For example, in Fig. 4, trajectories A, B, and C demonstrate that A and

B share closer regional proximity than either does with C, suggesting higher similarity in their learning paths. **Velocity**: Representing the first-order derivative of location, velocity measures how quickly a sample moves across the landscape. It reflects the transition pace from the sample's starting point to its current state. In Fig. 4, the velocity feature differentiates A-which follows a jagged, erratic path-from B, whose movement is smoother and more consistent. **Acceleration**: Defined as the derivative of velocity (or the second-order derivative of location), acceleration indicates changes in speed over time. As shown in Fig. 4, B and C exhibit comparable acceleration trends, with both following gradual and stable progressions. These three components are concatenated to form a comprehensive trajectory-based feature vector, denoted as $r_t = (r_{loc} \mid r_v \mid r_{ac})$.

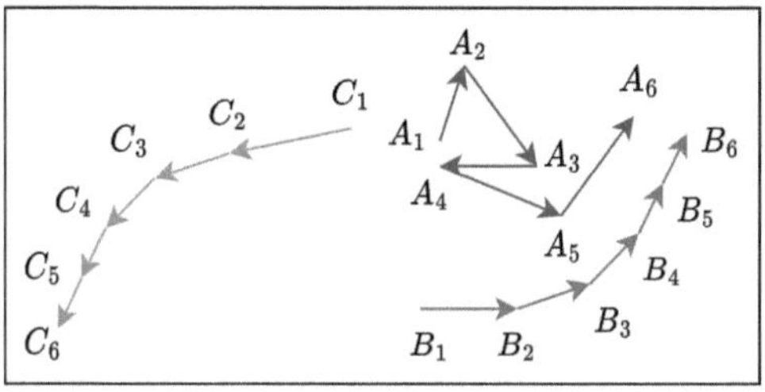

Fig. 4. Visualization of Three Learned Representation Trajectories

Prediction Feature. This study assumes that the classifier under analysis outputs a continuous confidence value for each prediction. For instance, in multiclass scenarios, the softmax function [4] yields a probability p for each class, where higher values reflect stronger confidence. In binary classification, the sigmoid function [11] outputs a score $p \in [0, 1]$, where predictions closer to 0 or 1 indicate higher certainty. Accordingly, the confidence score $\text{conf}(s)_e$ for a sample s at epoch e is computed as follows:

$$\text{conf}(s)_e = \begin{cases} p & \text{if using softmax} \\ 2 \times |p - 0.5| & \text{if using sigmoid} \end{cases} \tag{1}$$

Using this definition, the prediction-based feature vector is represented as $r_{conf} = \langle conf_1, conf_2, ..., conf_n \rangle$. Combining this with the previously defined trajectory features, we construct the full dynamic feature vector as $r_{mv} = (r_t \mid r_{conf})$.

4.2 Anomaly Detector

This module identifies anomalies by learning patterns of normal and abnormal behavior from the training data. Samples used to infer these patterns are termed "seen" data, and the learned representation is then applied to classify "unseen" instances.

To implement this, we adopt a clustering-based approach. The similarity between samples is computed using the cosine similarity metric applied to the dynamic features outlined in Sect. 4.1. An anomaly score is then assigned to each sample, inversely proportional to the size of the cluster it belongs to-samples in smaller clusters are flagged as potential anomalies.

4.3 Intention Learner

The Intention Learner is designed to meet three main objectives: (1) achieving strong performance despite limited and imbalanced user feedback, while avoiding overfitting due to the sparsity of human input; (2) ensuring real-time responsiveness for interactive debugging scenarios through computational efficiency; and (3) maintaining resilience to noisy annotations, recognizing that human feedback may contain occasional errors.

The recommendation mechanism functions through an iterative refinement process. Initially, it highlights the most anomalous training samples for user inspection, as outlined in Sect. 4.2. User responses-categorized as accepted or rejected-are then utilized as supervision signals. Each feedback instance serves as a label, and a lightweight yet resilient intention-learning algorithm leverages these inputs along with the anomaly scores from Sect. 4.2 to infer broader patterns of user interest. This results in an interest potential score for each unreviewed sample. Those with the highest scores are subsequently recommended to the user. The cycle repeats, continuously updating its suggestions based on evolving feedback.

For a more detailed explanation of the DeepDebugger framework and its components, please refer to [35].

5 Study Design

This section details the experimental setup used to assess the performance of DeepDebugger. We conduct evaluations on three benchmark datasets frequently employed in Software Defect Prediction research, and implement five popular neural network architectures to serve as classifiers.

5.1 Datasets

Our experiments utilize open-source software projects implemented in various programming languages, drawn from established datasets commonly used in defect prediction studies-NASA [30], PROMISE [3], and AEEEM [7]. These datasets contain software metric features, which we directly adopt as input representation vectors (refer to Fig. 1). Table 1 provides detailed descriptions of the associated code repositories.

To mitigate class imbalance, we apply oversampling techniques to ensure a balanced distribution of defective and non-defective instances. The resulting dataset is partitioned into 70% for training and 30% for testing. The training subset is used to learn the model parameters, while the testing subset serves to evaluate the predictive performance of the trained deep learning models.

Table 1. Project Descriptions Across Multiple Defect Prediction Datasets

Dataset	Project	Number of metrics	Number of total instances	Number of defective instances	Percentage of defective instances
NASA	CM1	22	498	49	9.84
	JM1	22	10885	8779	80.65
	KC1	22	2109	326	15.46
	KC2	22	522	105	20.11
	KC3	40	458	43	9.39
	KC4	40	125	61	48.80
	MC1	39	9466	68	0.72
	MC2	40	161	52	32.30
	MW1	40	403	61	15.14
	PC1	40	1107	76	6.87
	PC2	40	5589	23	0.41
	PC3	40	1563	160	10.24
	PC4	40	1458	178	12.21
	PC5	39	17186	516	3.00
PROMISE	ant-1.7	21	745	166	22.30
	ivy-2.0	21	352	40	11.40
	camel-1.6	21	965	188	19.50
	jedit-4.0	21	306	75	24.50
	log4j-1.2	21	109	37	33.90
	Lucene-2.4	21	195	91	46.70
	poi-2.0	21	314	37	11.80
	Synapse-1.1	21	222	60	27.00
	velocity-1.6	21	229	78	34.10
	Xerces-1.3	21	453	60	15.20
	tomcat	21	858	77	8.90
	Xalan-2.4	21	723	110	15.20
AEEEM	EQ	62	324	129	39.81
	JDT	62	997	206	20.66
	LC	62	691	64	9.26
	ML	62	1862	245	13.16
	PDE	62	1497	209	13.96

5.2 Research Models

To ensure experimental consistency in both environment and data processing, we selected a set of well-established algorithms commonly used in software defect prediction (DP) as our baseline models. These include Deep Neural Networks (DNNs) [26], Convolutional Neural Networks (CNNs) [20], Recurrent Neural Networks (RNNs) [8], Long Short-Term Memory (LSTM) networks [6], and Transformer-based models [38]. Each of these architectures was integrated with the DeepDebugger framework, enabling both detection of training anomalies and visualization of learning dynamics throughout the model's training process.

1. **DP-DNN**: This model applies traditional deep neural networks as classification tools for software defect prediction [26].
2. **DP-CNN**: DP-CNN employs convolutional neural networks to automatically extract and learn feature representations relevant to defect identification [20].
3. **DP-RNN**: Incorporating abstract syntax trees, word embeddings, and attention mechanisms, DP-RNN learns both syntactic and semantic cues essential for accurate defect detection [8].

4. **DP-LSTM**: This approach utilizes a bidirectional long short-term memory network to extract semantic-level information from source code for defect prediction tasks [6].
5. **DP-Transformer**: By capturing comprehensive syntactic and semantic structures, the DP-Transformer enhances predictive performance through deep attention-based representations [38].

5.3 Results and Discussion

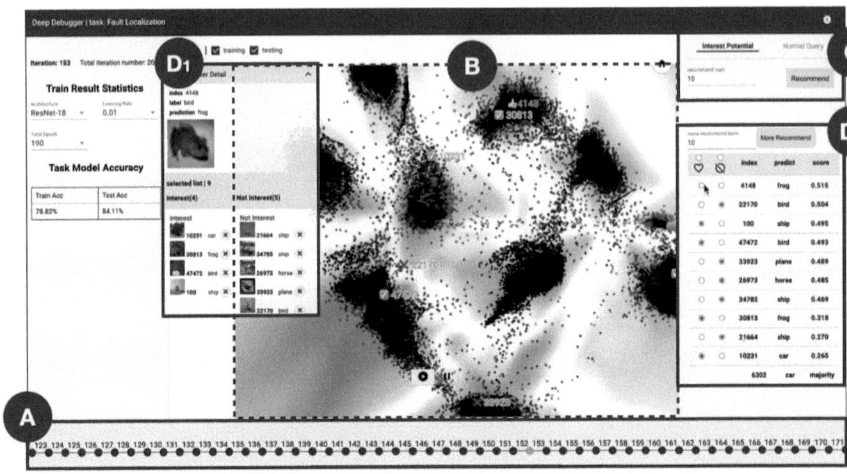

Fig. 5. Interface Snapshot of the DeepDebugger Tool.

DeepDebugger offers an intuitive visualization of the neural network training dynamics, as shown in Fig. 5 (refer to [35]). In addition to highlighting its visual analytics capabilities, this study evaluates DeepDebugger's effectiveness in identifying abnormal training behaviors within the visualization canvas. To this end, we construct ground-truth labels for both normal and anomalous trajectory patterns and assess the detection performance using standard metrics, namely precision and recall.

We initiate our study by designing training procedures tailored for visualization. In this experiment, we utilize three benchmark datasets-NASA [30], PROMISE [3], and AEEEM [7]-alongside five neural network models: DNN [26], CNN [20], RNN [8], LSTM [6], and Transformer [38]. Each model is trained on its respective dataset until convergence in training accuracy is achieved.

To visualize the training behavior, we incorporate both available time-traveling visualizers: DVI [34] and TimeVis [33]. This results in a comprehensive set of 30 visualized processes, computed as 2 (visualizers) × 3 (datasets) × 5 (models). For clarity, we define $P(dataset, visualizer, model)$ as the visualized training process corresponding to a specific combination of dataset, visualizer, and model. For instance, $P(NASA, DVI, CNN)$ refers to the visualization of the CNN model trained on the NASA dataset using DVI.

Table 2. Out-of-Distribution Dataset Selection

Dataset	NASA	PROMISE	AEEEM
OOD dataset	AEEEM	NASA	PROMISE

We define the ground-truth labels for unseen normal and abnormal sample behaviors using the following criteria: **Ground-Truth Normal Movement**: The trajectories of test samples are treated as ground-truth normal movements. These samples are excluded from the visualization process and originate from the same distribution as the training data, making them suitable baselines for normal behavior. **Synthesized Abnormal Movement**: To simulate abnormal trajectories, we manipulate both trajectory and prediction features. For the trajectory component, we generate step-wise movements that mimic the general spatial pattern of normal samples on the canvas but introduce randomized accelerations. For prediction features, we construct a sequence of confidence scores, each sampled randomly from the interval $[0, 1]$, to simulate irregular prediction behavior. **Natural Abnormal Movement**: To represent naturally occurring abnormalities, we use out-of-distribution (OOD) samples-i.e., data originating from a different dataset than the one used for training. These OOD samples are expected to deviate in behavior and appearance from in-distribution data. The corresponding OOD datasets assigned to each primary dataset are listed in Table 2.

For each visualization instance $P(dataset, visualizer, model)$, DeepDebugger detects a total of m abnormal trajectories, of which c are correctly identified. Precision is calculated as $\frac{c}{m}$, and recall is computed as $\frac{c}{n}$, where n denotes the total number of ground-truth abnormal movements. The evaluation of our anomaly detection approach is conducted using three data sources: 300 test samples representing normal behavior, 300 synthetically generated abnormal samples, and 300 out-of-distribution instances reflecting natural anomalies. As shown in Tables 3, 4, and 5, DeepDebugger achieves strong performance in detecting natural abnormal behaviors, with an average precision of 78.77% and an average recall of 79.93%. Moreover, the system maintains consistent performance across both time-travel visualizers, highlighting its robustness and reliability in identifying anomalous movement patterns.

Table 3. Evaluation Results for Identifying Out-of-Distribution Anomalies in NASA Data

Model	DNN		CNN		RNN		LSTM		Transformers	
Visualizer	DVI	TimeVis	DVI	TimeVis	DVI	TimeVis	DVI	TimeVis	DVI	TimeVis
Precision	0.7749	0.8901	0.8463	0.8197	0.7312	0.7311	0.7116	0.8732	0.8202	0.8416
Recall	0.8215	0.7341	0.7130	0.8897	0.8931	0.8616	0.7609	0.7195	0.8368	0.7880
F1 score	0.7975	0.8046	0.7739	0.8533	0.8040	0.7910	0.7354	0.7889	0.8284	0.8139

Table 4. Evaluation Results for Identifying Out-of-Distribution Anomalies in PROMISE Data

Model	DNN		CNN		RNN		LSTM		Transformers	
Visualizer	DVI	TimeVis	DVI	TimeVis	DVI	TimeVis	DVI	TimeVis	DVI	TimeVis
Precision	0.7041	0.8939	0.8664	0.7424	0.7363	0.7366	0.7608	0.8049	0.7863	0.7582
Recall	0.7244	0.7990	0.7068	0.8818	0.7517	0.8325	0.7623	0.8040	0.8093	0.7369
F1 score	0.7141	0.8438	0.7785	0.8061	0.7439	0.7816	0.7615	0.8044	0.7977	0.7474

Table 5. Evaluation of Results for Identifying Out-of-Distribution Anomalies in AEEEM Data

Model	DNN		CNN		RNN		LSTM		Transformers	
Visualizer	DVI	TimeVis	DVI	TimeVis	DVI	TimeVis	DVI	TimeVis	DVI	TimeVis
Precision	0.8223	0.7278	0.7584	0.7732	0.7912	0.8570	0.7399	0.8028	0.8184	0.7092
Recall	0.8939	0.8550	0.8878	0.8789	0.8195	0.8843	0.7176	0.7391	0.7090	0.7650
F1 score	0.8566	0.7863	0.8180	0.8227	0.8051	0.8704	0.7286	0.7697	0.7598	0.7361

6 Conclusion

This paper presents *DeepDebugger*, an innovative explainable AI framework developed to detect and visualize the training dynamics of neural networks. The system is evaluated using three benchmark datasets for software defect prediction and applied across five widely adopted deep learning architectures. Experimental findings show that DeepDebugger consistently provides meaningful visualizations of model behavior, thereby improving the interpretability of deep classifiers. It achieves strong performance metrics-including high precision, recall, and F1 scores-on the NASA, PROMISE, and AEEEM datasets. Furthermore, its effectiveness remains stable across DNN, CNN, RNN, LSTM, and Transformer architectures, underscoring the robustness and generalizability of the approach.

Acknowledgements. This research was supported by the HU SPRING Research Study Abroad Program. The completion of this paper was made possible during a visit to the laboratory of Prof. Jin Song Dong at the National University of Singapore.

The author gratefully acknowledges the support provided by Hiroshima University and sincerely thanks Prof. Jin Song Dong for the opportunity to engage in this valuable academic experience.

References

1. Abreu, R., Zoeteweij, P., Van Gemund, A.J.: On the accuracy of spectrum-based fault localization. In: Testing: Academic and industrial conference practice and research techniques-MUTATION (TAICPART-MUTATION 2007), pp. 89–98. IEEE (2007)
2. Artho, C.: Iterative delta debugging. Int. J. Softw. Tools Technol. Transfer **13**, 223–246 (2011)
3. Boetticher, G.: The promise repository of empirical software engineering data. http://promisedata.org/repository (2007)
4. Bouchard, G.: Efficient bounds for the softmax function and applications to approximate inference in hybrid models. In: NIPS 2007 workshop for approximate Bayesian inference in continuous/hybrid systems, vol. 6 (2007)
5. Chattopadhay, A., Sarkar, A., Howlader, P., Balasubramanian, V.N.: Grad-cam++: Generalized gradient-based visual explanations for deep convolutional networks. In: 2018 IEEE winter conference on applications of computer vision (WACV), pp. 839–847. IEEE (2018)
6. Deng, J., Lu, L., Qiu, S.: Software defect prediction via lstm. IET Softw. **14**(4), 443–450 (2020)
7. D'Ambros, M., Lanza, M., Robbes, R.: Evaluating defect prediction approaches: a benchmark and an extensive comparison. Empir. Softw. Eng. **17**, 531–577 (2012)
8. Fan, G., Diao, X., Yu, H., Yang, K., Chen, L.: Software defect prediction via attention-based recurrent neural network. Sci. Program. **2019**(1), 6230953 (2019)
9. Fu, R., Hu, Q., Dong, X., Guo, Y., Gao, Y., Li, B.: Axiom-based grad-cam: towards accurate visualization and explanation of cnns. arXiv preprint arXiv:2008.02312 (2020)
10. Gong, L., Lo, D., Jiang, L., Zhang, H.: Interactive fault localization leveraging simple user feedback. In: 2012 28th IEEE International Conference on Software Maintenance (ICSM), pp. 67–76. IEEE (2012)
11. Han, J., Moraga, C.: The influence of the sigmoid function parameters on the speed of backpropagation learning. In: International Workshop on Artificial Neural Networks, pp. 195–201. Springer (1995)
12. Hao, D., Zhang, L., Zhang, L., Sun, J., Mei, H.: Vida: Visual interactive debugging. In: 2009 IEEE 31st International Conference on Software Engineering, pp. 583–586. IEEE (2009)
13. Hodován, R., Kiss, Á.: Modernizing hierarchical delta debugging. In: Proceedings of the 7th International Workshop on Automating Test Case Design, Selection, and Evaluation, pp. 31–37 (2016)
14. Horváth, F., Beszédes, Á., Vancsics, B., Balogh, G., Vidács, L., Gyimóthy, T.: Using contextual knowledge in interactive fault localization. Empir. Softw. Eng. **27**(6), 150 (2022)
15. Jiang, Y., Cukic, B., Ma, Y.: Techniques for evaluating fault prediction models. Empir. Softw. Eng. **13**, 561–595 (2008)

16. Ko, A.J., Myers, B.A.: Debugging reinvented: asking and answering why and why not questions about program behavior. In: Proceedings of the 30th International Conference on Software Engineering, pp. 301–310 (2008)
17. Ko, A.J., Myers, B.A.: Source-level debugging with the whyline. In: Proceedings of the 2008 International Workshop on Cooperative and Human Aspects of Software Engineering, pp. 69–72 (2008)
18. Ko, A.J., Myers, B.A.: Finding causes of program output with the java whyline. In: Proceedings of the SIGCHI Conference on Human Factors in Computing Systems, pp. 1569–1578 (2009)
19. Ko, A.J., Myers, B.A.: Extracting and answering why and why not questions about java program output. ACM Trans. Softw. Eng. Methodol. (TOSEM) **20**(2), 1–36 (2010)
20. Li, J., He, P., Zhu, J., Lyu, M.R.: Software defect prediction via convolutional neural network. In: 2017 IEEE International Conference on Software Quality, Reliability and Security (QRS), pp. 318–328. IEEE (2017)
21. Li, X., Zhu, S., d'Amorim, M., Orso, A.: Enlightened debugging. In: Proceedings of the 40th International Conference on Software Engineering. pp. 82–92 (2018)
22. Liang, J., Ji, R., Jiang, J., Zhou, S., Lou, Y., Xiong, Y., Huang, G.: Interactive patch filtering as debugging aid. In: 2021 IEEE International Conference on Software Maintenance and Evolution (ICSME). pp. 239–250. IEEE (2021)
23. Lin, Y., Sun, J., Tran, L., Bai, G., Wang, H., Dong, J.: Break the dead end of dynamic slicing: Localizing data and control omission bug. In: Proceedings of the 33rd ACM/IEEE international conference on automated software engineering. pp. 509–519 (2018)
24. Lin, Y., Sun, J., Xue, Y., Liu, Y., Dong, J.: Feedback-based debugging. In: 2017 IEEE/ACM 39th International Conference on Software Engineering (ICSE). pp. 393–403. IEEE (2017)
25. Menzies, T., Greenwald, J., Frank, A.: Data mining static code attributes to learn defect predictors. IEEE Trans. Software Eng. **33**(1), 2–13 (2006)
26. Nevendra, M., Singh, P.: Software defect prediction using deep learning. Acta Polytechnica Hungarica **18**(10), 173–189 (2021)
27. Petrillo, F., Guéhéneuc, Y.G., Pimenta, M., Freitas, C.D.S., Khomh, F.: Swarm debugging: The collective intelligence on interactive debugging. J. Syst. Softw. **153**, 152–174 (2019)
28. Schneider, F., Dangel, F., Hennig, P.: Cockpit: A practical debugging tool for the training of deep neural networks. Adv. Neural. Inf. Process. Syst. **34**, 20825–20837 (2021)
29. Selvaraju, R.R., Cogswell, M., Das, A., Vedantam, R., Parikh, D., Batra, D.: Grad-cam: Visual explanations from deep networks via gradient-based localization. In: Proceedings of the IEEE international conference on computer vision. pp. 618–626 (2017)
30. Shepperd, M., Song, Q., Sun, Z., Mair, C.: Data quality: Some comments on the nasa software defect datasets. IEEE Trans. Software Eng. **39**(9), 1208–1215 (2013)
31. Strobelt, H., Gehrmann, S., Behrisch, M., Perer, A., Pfister, H., Rush, A.M.: S eq 2s eq-v is: A visual debugging tool for sequence-to-sequence models. IEEE Trans. Visual Comput. Graphics **25**(1), 353–363 (2018)
32. Xu, Z., Ma, S., Zhang, X., Zhu, S., Xu, B.: Debugging with intelligence via probabilistic inference. In: Proceedings of the 40th International Conference on Software Engineering. pp. 1171–1181 (2018)

33. Yang, X., Lin, Y., Liu, R., Dong, J.S.: Temporality spatialization: A scalable and faithful time-travelling visualization for deep classifier training. In: Proceedings of the Thirty-First International Joint Conference on Artificial Intelligence, IJCAI-22 (2022)
34. Yang, X., Lin, Y., Liu, R., He, Z., Wang, C., Dong, J.S., Mei, H.: Deepvisualinsight: Time-travelling visualization for spatio-temporal causality of deep classification training. In: The Thirty-Sixth AAAI Conference on Artificial Intelligence (AAAI) (2022)
35. Yang, X., Lin, Y., Zhang, Y., Huang, L., Dong, J.S., Mei, H.: Deepdebugger: An interactive time-travelling debugging approach for deep classifiers. In: Proceedings of the 31st ACM Joint European Software Engineering Conference and Symposium on the Foundations of Software Engineering. pp. 973–985 (2023)
36. Zeller, A.: Yesterday, my program worked. today, it does not. why? ACM SIGSOFT Software engineering notes **24**(6), 253–267 (1999)
37. Zhang, M., Li, Y., Li, X., Chen, L., Zhang, Y., Zhang, L., Khurshid, S.: An empirical study of boosting spectrum-based fault localization via pagerank. IEEE Trans. Software Eng. **47**(6), 1089–1113 (2019)
38. Zhang, Q., Wu, B.: Software defect prediction via transformer. In: 2020 IEEE 4th Information Technology, Networking, Electronic and Automation Control Conference (ITNEC). vol. 1, pp. 874–879. IEEE (2020)

Fuzzing the Solidity Compiler Solc with Fuzz4All

Haruto Igaki(✉) and Tatsuhiro Tsuchiya

Graduate School of Information Science and Technology, The University of Osaka, Osaka, Japan

u588267e@ecs.osaka-u.ac.jp, t-tutiya@ist.osaka-u.ac.jp

Abstract. Fuzz testing (fuzzing) is an established technique for identifying software vulnerabilities by automatically generating a large volume of test inputs to uncover bugs. However, traditional compiler fuzzers are often designed for a specific language, making them difficult to adapt to others. To address this challenge, fuzzers that use Large Language Models (LLMs) to generate inputs for a wide variety of languages have emerged. This research aims to evaluate the effectiveness of Fuzz4All, an LLM-based universal compiler fuzzer, by applying it to Solc, the compiler for the smart contract language Solidity. Specifically, we selected five distinct features of Solidity as fuzzing targets, implemented a script to enable testing of these features, and generated 10,000 fuzzing inputs for each. The experimental results show that while the validity rate of the generated code was low, a substantial code coverage of approximately 47% was achieved. This suggests that Fuzz4All can generate high-quality test inputs that cover complex execution paths of the compiler, even for a novel language like Solidity.

Keywords: Compiler fuzzing · LLM · Solc · Solidity

1 Introduction

Fuzz testing, or fuzzing, is a powerful technique for discovering unknown bugs and vulnerabilities by automatically generating a large number of test inputs and feeding them to a System Under Test (SUT) [2,7,13]. Systems that interpret and execute programming languages, such as compilers and runtime environments, are foundational to modern software development, making their reliability critically important. Therefore, fuzzers for these systems have attracted considerable attention as a means of realizing reliable software systems.

However, conventional compiler fuzzers [5] are often designed for a single, specific language, which makes it challenging to adapt them to other languages or even different versions of the same language. This limitation means that the generated inputs tend to focus on specific features of the target language, restricting their ability to find bugs related to other or newly introduced features.

To overcome this issue, fuzzing techniques leveraging Large Language Models (LLMs) have recently gained attention. Fuzz4All [10], used in this study, is

© The Author(s), under exclusive license to Springer Nature Singapore Pte Ltd. 2026
Y. Chen et al. (Eds.): SFPVV 2025, LNCS 16356, pp. 48–58, 2026.
https://doi.org/10.1007/978-981-95-6032-5_4

a fuzzer that achieves exceptional versatility by utilizing an LLM as its input generation and mutation engine. By providing Fuzz4All with hints such as documentation and example inputs for a target language, it can, in theory, generate diverse and realistic test inputs for any programming language.

The developers of Fuzz4All reported promising results from applying it to several major programming languages, such as C and Java [10]. However, the applicability and effectiveness of the tool for systems that process other languages remain unclear.

The objective of this study is to explore the applicability of the universal fuzzer Fuzz4All to languages that have not yet been targeted. To address this, the study applies Fuzz4All to Solc, the compiler for the Solidity language. Solidity plays a central role in the Ethereum blockchain, serving as the de facto standard for programming smart contracts. In this study, we selected several fundamental features of Solidity and instrumented Fuzz4All to generate fuzz inputs tailored to each feature. We then used the fuzzer to test these features, demonstrating Fuzz4All's adaptability and effectiveness for this new language.

The remainder of this paper is organized as follows. Section 2 describes the background of this research. Section 3 explains the proposed approach and experimental design. Section 4 presents the experimental results and discussion. Finally, Sect. 5 concludes the paper.

2 Background

2.1 Fuzz4All

Fuzz4All [10] is a universal fuzzer that generates test inputs using a novel two-stage Large Language Model (LLM) pipeline. Its main feature is its language-agnostic nature, allowing it to target a wide variety of compilers and interpreters with minimal human effort. Instead of relying on traditional mutation or grammar-based generation, Fuzz4All leverages LLMs to produce syntactically and semantically complex inputs based on natural language descriptions and documentation of a target feature.

The first stage of the pipeline, called "autoprompting," uses GPT-4 to automate prompt engineering. A user provides high-level materials about a target feature, such as official documentation, code examples, or specifications, along with a simple natural language trigger (e.g., /* Please create a short program that combines goto with new C features in a complex way */). GPT-4 processes this verbose information and distills it into a concise, optimized prompt that is specifically engineered to guide a code-generation model effectively.

The second stage is the fuzzing loop, which uses StarCoder, an LLM specifically trained for code generation. The optimized prompt created by GPT-4 is fed to StarCoder, which then generates a batch of fuzzing inputs (i.e., source code). These inputs are compiled and executed, and the results are used to provide feedback for subsequent generation cycles. This mechanism allows Fuzz4All to generate syntactically and semantically complex programs that are more likely to exercise obscure edge cases in a compiler, potentially uncovering bugs that are difficult for traditional fuzzers to find.

2.2 Solidity and Solc

Solidity is a statically-typed, object-oriented programming language designed for implementing smart contracts on blockchain platforms, most notably Ethereum [1]. Since smart contracts are difficult to modify once deployed, the reliability of their compiler, Solc, is of utmost importance. Solc is responsible for compiling Solidity source code into bytecode that can be executed by the Ethereum Virtual Machine (EVM). In this study, Solc is the SUT for our fuzzing campaign.

2.3 Related Work

The integration of LLMs into fuzzing frameworks has led to improvements in test case generation across multiple domains. LLMs have been used to generate diverse and valid inputs for REST API fuzzing [12], deep learning library testing [3], and JavaScript interpreter fuzzing [4]. [6] discusses the challenges of using LLMs in fuzzing, such as ensuring syntactic validity and improving test case diversity, while WhiteFox [11] proposes a white-box LLM-based compiler fuzzer that leverages source code analysis to guide test generation.

For Solidity-specific fuzzing, existing tools such as sFuzz [8] and SynTest-Solidity [9] focus on fuzzing smart contracts rather than the Solidity compiler itself. These tools aim to detect vulnerabilities in contract logic before deployment but do not target compiler correctness.

3 Proposed Approach

3.1 Approach

The overall approach of our study is illustrated in Fig. 1. To instrument Fuzz4All for generating Solidity test inputs, we developed a new Python program, `SOL.py`, and modified an existing one, `make_target.py`. These scripts work in conjunction with two user-provided configuration files: `config.yaml`, which specifies parameters like the target compiler path and trigger prompts, and a document file containing the standard specification or examples of the targeted feature. In this study, we used materials provided on the official Solidity website for the document file.

To make Fuzz4All compatible with the Solidity compiler (Solc), we first implemented `SOL.py`. This file serves as a new target module within the Fuzz4All framework. Its primary responsibilities are to handle the compilation of the LLM-generated Solidity code using Solc and to analyze and classify the outcome. The results are categorized as valid (compilation successful), invalid (compilation failed), or a crash (abnormal termination of the compiler).

To integrate our custom Solidity module into Fuzz4All's execution flow, we modified the existing `make_target.py` script. Our additions enable this script to read the `config.yaml` file, recognize that Solc is the designated target, and, based on this configuration, invoke our newly developed `SOL.py` module to manage the fuzzing process.

Consequently, with our custom scripts configured, Fuzz4All is able to generate random Solidity programs. Its internal LLMs use the provided documentation to create test cases. Each generated program is then fed to Solc via our `SOL.py` module. If the generated code causes Solc to terminate abnormally, a potential bug is detected and reported. This process is repeated to continuously discover new bugs in the Solidity compiler.

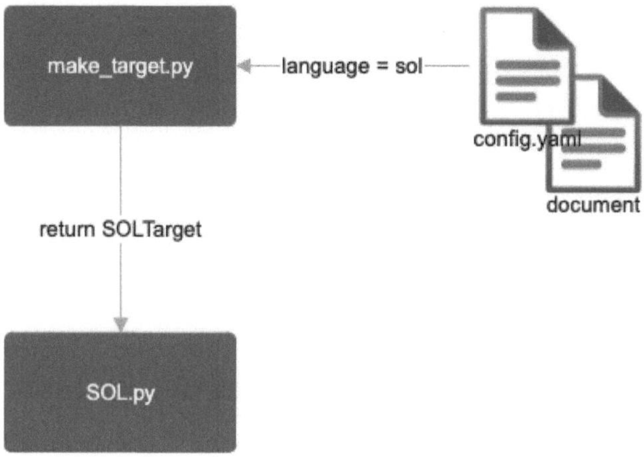

Fig. 1. Overview of the Research Approach.

3.2 Targets

To comprehensively test the various functionalities of Solc, we conducted fuzzing on five specific features of Solidity.

- **Target 1 (Dynamic Array):** Arrays that can be resized at runtime. This is an essential feature for handling variable-length data whose size is not known at compile time.
- **Target 2 (Fallback Function):** A special default function that is executed when a contract receives Ether directly or when a called function does not exist. It plays a crucial role in handling Ether payments.
- **Target 3 (Inline Assembly):** A feature that allows writing low-level assembly language (Yul) directly within Solidity code. It is used for gas optimization and fine-grained control not possible in standard Solidity.
- **Target 4 (Standard Libraries):** Importing and using commonly used standard libraries, such as OpenZeppelin. This tests common patterns for enhancing code reusability and security.

- **Target 5 (New Features):** The latest features introduced in new versions of Solidity. This aims to discover bugs in the implementation of new functionalities and their interaction with existing ones.

3.3 Document and Configuration File

To guide the LLM-based input generation process of Fuzz4All, two primary files were created for each of the five fuzzing targets: a documentation file and a configuration file. The documentation file provides Fuzz4All with the necessary context about a specific language feature, while the config.yaml file sets the parameters for the fuzzing campaign.

Take Target 5 (New Features) as an example. To facilitate the fuzzer's understanding of this target, we used the official Solidity documentation that explains the new features of Solidity. A snippet of this documentation is shown in Fig. 2.

```
The following code, for example, will trigger such an error:

contract C {
    function f() public pure {
        uint x = 0;
        x--;
    }
}
The checks are based on the actual type of the variable, so even if the result
would fit on EVM word of 256 bits, if your type is uint8 and if the result is
larger than 255, it will trigger a Panic.
We did not introduce checks for explicit type conversions from larger to smaller
types, because we think that such checks might be unexpected. We would love to
get your input on that matter!
```

Fig. 2. Snippet from the official Solidity documentation used for Target 5 (New Features).

```
target:
 language: sol
 path_to_documentation: config/documentations/sol/sol_new_features.md
 trigger_to_generate_input: "/* Please create a short program which uses
                              new Solidity features in a complex way. */"
 input_hint: "pragma solidity ^0.8.0;"
```

Fig. 3. Snippet from the `config.yaml` file for Target 5.

Based on this documentation, the config.yaml file was set up to instruct Fuzz4All on how to generate relevant inputs. As shown in Fig. 3, the configuration specifies the language, the path to the documentation file, a natural language "trigger" to prompt the LLM, and an "input hint" to provide a starting point for the generated code. These two files work in tandem to ensure that the generated fuzzing inputs are highly relevant to the targeted feature.

4 Experimental Evaluation

4.1 Environment and Metrics

The experiments were conducted on an AWS instance (g4dn.4xlarge) running Ubuntu 24.04 LTS. The SUT was Solc version 0.8.28, built from source to enable code coverage measurement. For each target, we generated 10,000 fuzzing inputs.

We used the following two metrics for evaluation:

- **Validity Rate:** The percentage of all generated inputs that were successfully compiled by Solc. This indicates the LLM's ability to generate syntactically correct code.
- **Code Coverage:** The percentage of lines in the Solc source code executed by the valid inputs. Measured using the lcov tool, higher code coverage implies a more comprehensive test.

4.2 Enabling Code Coverage for Solc

As the official Solc binary does not include coverage instrumentation, we built it from the v0.8.28 source. The build process was configured using CMake with the `-DENABLE_COVERAGE=ON` flag to include the necessary gcov profiling hooks. The Z3 solver dependency was disabled to prevent potential warnings during the build. This custom build allowed us to generate `.gcda` files during compilation, from which line coverage data could be extracted using `lcov`.

4.3 Experimental Results

The fuzzing results for each target are summarized in Table 1.

Table 1. Validity Rate and Code Coverage for Each Target

Target	Validity Rate (%)	Code Coverage (%)
1. Dynamic Array	38.81	47.8
2. Fallback Function	31.16	47.6
3. Inline Assembly	35.81	47.5
4. Standard Libraries	41.86	47.6
5. New Features	36.86	47.8

The key findings are as follows:

- **Low Validity Rate:** For all targets, the validity rate was relatively low, ranging from approximately 30% to 40%.
- **Substantial Code Coverage:** In contrast, the code coverage reached around 47% for all targets. This indicates that the small number of valid inputs generated by Fuzz4All were high-quality tests that executed a wide range of Solc's internal logic.

Figure 4 shows an example of a valid code snippet generated for Target 1.

4.4 Discussion

Our experiment reveals a pattern of low validity rates (30–41%) paired with substantial code coverage (approx. 47%). While 47% does not represent exhaustive testing, achieving this level of coverage on a complex, novel compiler using a universal fuzzer with minimal setup is a noteworthy outcome. It suggests that the LLM, despite generating many invalid inputs, successfully produced a small subset of syntactically and semantically complex programs. These valid inputs were able to exercise deep and diverse execution paths within the Solc compiler, which traditional fuzzers might only reach with extensive, language-specific grammar and rule definitions.

Although this campaign did not uncover new bugs in Solc, it successfully demonstrated Fuzz4All's capability to generate effective inputs for testing the deeper parts of a compiler, even for an unknown language like Solidity. This is a significant finding that showcases the versatility and effectiveness of Fuzz4All.

It is important to note that this study did not compare Fuzz4All's performance against a baseline, such as a traditional grammar-based fuzzer for Solidity. Such a comparison would provide clearer context for these coverage numbers and remains an area for future work.

4.5 Code Coverage Measurement with Echidna

To further analyze the quality of the valid inputs generated by Fuzz4All, we also measured the code coverage of the generated smart contracts themselves using Echidna, a property-based fuzzer. The goal here was to determine if the generated code was trivial or contained meaningful, executable logic. As shown in Table 2, the inputs achieved high execution counts across their source lines. This indicates that Fuzz4All did not merely generate simple, syntactically-correct declarations; it produced functional contracts with executable paths. This inherent complexity in the valid test inputs helps explain how a relatively small set of programs was sufficient to exercise nearly half of the Solc compiler's source code.

Figure 5 is one of the test inputs generated using dynamic arrays. "*" is marked if an execution ended with STOP, and "r" is marked if it ended with REVERT.

Figure 6 shows how many times each line of the input code was executed during fuzzing.

```
contract B {
        function x() public pure returns(bytes memory) {
        bytes memory res = new bytes(1);
        res[0] = 'a';
        return res;
    }
    function z() public pure returns (uint256) {
        uint256x = 1 / 0;
        uint256[] memory a =[1,2,3];
        uint256 y = x * 10;
        require( y > x, "error here");
        return y;
    }
    function f() external returns(bytes memory) {
        uint256 x = 1 / 0;
        uint256[] memory a =[1,2,3];
        uint256 y = x * 10;
        require( y > x, "error here" );
        require( a[0] <= 7, "error here" );
        bytes memory res = new bytes(1);
        res[0] = 'a';
        return res;
    }
    function bar() public pure returns (uint256) {
        uint256 x = 1 / 0;
        uint256[] memory a = [1,2,3];
        uint256 y = x * 10;
        require( y > x, "error here" );
        require( a[0] <= 7, "error here" );
        (uint256[] memory a, bool bl) = (a, true);
        return y;
    }

    uint x = 1 / 0;
    function zer() public {
        require(x == 0, "error here");
        uint256 x=10;
        uint y = 1 / 0;
        uint256[] memory ba = [1,2,3];
        uint256 z = [1,3,5][1];
        require(y + x==z + ba.length, "error here");
        if (x < z) {
            (bool b, uint x)=(b, x);
        }

        require(x==1, "error here");
        address a = msg.sender;
        uint s = a.send(1);
    }
}
```

Fig. 4. Example of Generated Code Using Dynamic Array.

Table 2. Code Coverage for Each Case Measured by Echidna

Target	Code Coverage (lines)
Dynamic Array	384119
Fallback Function	198409
Inline Assembly	363654
Standard Libraries	238068
New Features	259218

```
|   | pragma solidity ^0.8.0;
|*r| contract SemanticTest11
|*r|     uint[] public array;
|   |     uint x;
|   |     uint y;
|*  |     constructor () public {
|*  |         x = 0;
|*  |         y = 0;
|*  |         for(uint i = 0; i < 2; i++) {
|*  |             array.push(i + 1);
|   |         }
|   |     }
|*  |     function add() public {
|*  |         y += array[x];
|*  |         x += 1;
|   |     }
|   | }
```

Fig. 5. Echidna coverage results for a generated program using a dynamic array.

This outcome demonstrates that the generated Solidity programs contain a substantial number of lines executed during runtime, suggesting that the generated inputs are applicable not only to testing string-based processing features, such as compiler parsing, but also to testing runtime systems. Thus, the generated valid code could potentially be applied not only to testing Solc but also to testing EVM clients that execute the resulting EVM bytecode, indicating a direction for future research.

```
TN:
SF:/home/Fuzz4All/outputs/fuzzing_outputs_sol/9997.sol
DA:2,51
DA:3,63
DA:6,7
DA:7,6
DA:8,6
DA:9,22
DA:10,41
DA:13,8
DA:14,39
DA:15,19
end_of_record
```

Fig. 6. Line-by-Line Execution Count.

5 Conclusion

In this research, we applied the LLM-based universal fuzzer Fuzz4All to test the Solidity compiler, Solc, and evaluated its effectiveness. By fuzzing five targets covering diverse features of Solc, we achieved a high code coverage of approximately 47%, despite the low validity rate of the generated code.

These results confirm that Fuzz4All can generate high-quality test inputs for effective fuzzing, even for a complex language like Solidity that it has not previously targeted. The findings of this study demonstrate the versatility and future potential of LLM-based fuzzing technology and are expected to contribute to its application in testing other programming languages and complex software systems.

This study, however, has several limitations. Our evaluation relied on line coverage and did not analyze more fine-grained metrics such as path diversity, which would offer deeper insight into the quality of the test cases. Furthermore, we did not measure efficiency metrics, such as the time required to generate a valid input, nor did we compare Fuzz4All against a language-specific baseline fuzzer for Solc. Addressing these points would provide a more complete picture of the practical trade-offs of using LLM-based fuzzers and are promising directions for future research.

Future work also includes improving the validity rate through further optimization of prompt engineering and establishing methods for analyzing discovered vulnerabilities.

References

1. https://docs.soliditylang.org/en/v0.8.30/
2. Boehme, M., Cadar, C., Roychoudhury, A.: Fuzzing: challenges and reflections. IEEE Softw. **38**(3), 79–86 (2021). https://doi.org/10.1109/MS.2020.3016773

3. Deng, Y., Xia, C.S., Yang, C., Zhang, S.D., Yang, S., Zhang, L.: Large language models are edge-case generators: crafting unusual programs for fuzzing deep learning libraries. In: Proceedings of the IEEE/ACM 46th International Conference on Software Engineering. ICSE 2024, Association for Computing Machinery, New York (2024). https://doi.org/10.1145/3597503.3623343
4. Eom, J., Jeong, S., Kwon, T.: Fuzzing javascript interpreters with coverage-guided reinforcement learning for LLM-based mutation. In: Proceedings of the 33rd ACM SIGSOFT International Symposium on Software Testing and Analysis, pp. 1656–1668. ISSTA 2024, Association for Computing Machinery, New York (2024). https://doi.org/10.1145/3650212.3680389
5. Even-Mendoza, K., Sharma, A., Donaldson, A.F., Cadar, C.: Grayc: greybox fuzzing of compilers and analysers for c. In: Proceedings of the 32nd ACM SIGSOFT International Symposium on Software Testing and Analysis, pp. 1219–1231. ISSTA 2023, Association for Computing Machinery, New York (2023). https://doi.org/10.1145/3597926.3598130
6. Jiang, Y., et al.: When fuzzing meets LLMS: challenges and opportunities. In: Companion Proceedings of the 32nd ACM International Conference on the Foundations of Software Engineering, pp. 492–496. FSE 2024, Association for Computing Machinery, New York (2024). https://doi.org/10.1145/3663529.3663784
7. Liang, H., Pei, X., Jia, X., Shen, W., Zhang, J.: Fuzzing: state of the art. IEEE Trans. Reliab. **67**(3), 1199–1218 (2018). https://doi.org/10.1109/TR.2018.2834476
8. Nguyen, T.D., Pham, L.H., Sun, J., Lin, Y., Minh, Q.T.: sfuzz: an efficient adaptive fuzzer for solidity smart contracts. In: Proceedings of the ACM/IEEE 42nd International Conference on Software Engineering, pp. 778–788. ICSE 2020, Association for Computing Machinery, New York (2020). https://doi.org/10.1145/3377811.3380334
9. Olsthoorn, M., Stallenberg, D., van Deursen, A., Panichella, A.: Syntest-solidity: automated test case generation and fuzzing for smart contracts. In: Proceedings of the ACM/IEEE 44th International Conference on Software Engineering: Companion Proceedings, pp. 202–206. ICSE 2022, Association for Computing Machinery, New York (2022). https://doi.org/10.1145/3510454.3516869
10. Xia, C.S., Paltenghi, M., Le Tian, J., Pradel, M., Zhang, L.: Fuzz4all: universal fuzzing with large language models. In: Proceedings of the IEEE/ACM 46th International Conference on Software Engineering. ICSE 2024, Association for Computing Machinery, New York (2024). https://doi.org/10.1145/3597503.3639121
11. Yang, C., et al.: Whitefox: white-box compiler fuzzing empowered by large language models. Proc. ACM Program. Lang. **8**(OOPSLA2) (2024). https://doi.org/10.1145/3689736
12. Zheng, T., Shao, J., Dai, J., Jiang, S., Chen, X., Shen, C.: Restless: enhancing state-of-the-art rest API fuzzing with LLMS in cloud service computing. IEEE Trans. Serv. Comput. **17**(6), 4225–4238 (2024). https://doi.org/10.1109/TSC.2024.3489441
13. Zhu, X., Wen, S., Camtepe, S., Xiang, Y.: Fuzzing: a survey for roadmap. ACM Comput. Surv. **54**(11s) (2022). https://doi.org/10.1145/3512345

Diagnosing and Repairing Field Access Hallucinations in LLM-Based Test Generation

Xiujing Guo(✉) and Tatsuhiro Tsuchiya

The University of Osaka, Suita, Osaka, Japan
{guoxiujing,t-tutiya}@ist.osaka-u.ac.jp

Abstract. Large language models (LLMs) are increasingly used to generate unit tests directly from source code. However, their generated test cases often fail due to hallucinated references to non-existent class fields, a phenomenon we term *Field Access Hallucination (FAH)*. Despite its frequency and impact on test executability, FAH has not been systematically studied in prior work. This paper presents the first framework that uses static guidance to diagnose and correct FAH in LLM-generated test code. We begin by analyzing the prevalence and patterns of FAH errors under minimal prompt settings, revealing that they account for a substantial proportion of test failures. To mitigate FAH, we propose a repair pipeline that combines static analysis, hallucination detection, and prompt rewriting. Our approach statically analyzes attribute access paths in the target function and selectively injects only the necessary field initialization logic into the prompt, improving test reliability without overwhelming the LLM with irrelevant context. We evaluate our method on seven real-world Python modules spanning multiple projects. Experimental results show that our approach increases test execution success rates compared to naive prompting and outperforms full-context prompting strategies in mitigating FAH. Furthermore, our method maintains prompt conciseness while achieving targeted error reduction. These findings suggest that addressing FAH is essential for practical and scalable LLM-based test generation, and that static guidance offers an effective path forward.

Keywords: Test Case Generation · Large Language Models · Field Access Hallucination · Prompt Engineering

1 Introduction

Automated test generation is a long-standing topic in software testing research, aiming to reduce the manual effort of writing test cases and improve testing effectiveness. Traditional approaches, such as fuzzing testing [1], symbolic execution [2], and search-based software testing (SBST) [3], have achieved significant progress in improving code coverage and fault detection. However, these

© The Author(s), under exclusive license to Springer Nature Singapore Pte Ltd. 2026
Y. Chen et al. (Eds.): SFPVV 2025, LNCS 16356, pp. 59–77, 2026.
https://doi.org/10.1007/978-981-95-6032-5_5

methods often struggle with handling dynamic language features, complex object hierarchies, or codebases with limited formal specifications.

In recent years, Large Language Models (LLMs) have emerged as a new paradigm for code understanding and generation. When guided with appropriate prompts, these models are capable of generating function-level unit tests that are syntactically correct and contextually relevant, often without the need for instrumentation or execution feedback. As a result, LLM-based test generation has been increasingly explored as a promising complement to traditional techniques, particularly in developer productivity tools and continuous integration pipelines.

Despite these promising capabilities, a major gap remains in the reliability of LLM-generated tests. While such tests may appear plausible, they frequently suffer from semantic errors that prevent execution or result in incorrect behavior. A particularly pervasive and under-recognized issue is what we term Field Access Hallucination (FAH)'a phenomenon where the LLM-generated test case attempts to access an attribute or field that does not exist in the corresponding class or object. For example, given only a partially visible class definition, an LLM may generate a test asserting that obj.name exists, even though the name attribute is never defined in the constructor or class body. These hallucinated accesses typically lead to runtime exceptions such as AttributeError: 'Foo' object has no attribute 'name', rendering the test invalid and often misleading.

We argue that FAH is not merely a generation artifact, but often arises from insufficient or noisy contextual cues that hinder the LLM's ability to infer object state and initialization semantics. Crucially, these failures cannot be reliably resolved by the LLM alone without structural guidance.

This motivates us to systematically investigate FAH: to formally define the phenomenon, measure its prevalence across LLM-generated test suites, and develop practical methods to detect and mitigate such errors. Our ultimate goal is to improve the executability, reliability, and trustworthiness of LLM-based unit test generation in real-world scenarios.

To address this gap, we conduct a systematic study of field access hallucination in LLM-generated test cases. This paper makes the following contributions:

- **We formally define and detect FAH**, a recurring and impactful failure mode in LLM-generated unit tests, where the model fabricates nonexistent fields or misuses uninitialized attributes. We provide concrete examples and a lightweight static analysis method to detect such hallucinations.
- **We propose a static analysis-driven repair framework** that diagnoses FAH failures in generated tests and automatically rewrites prompts with precise field usage guidance. This approach introduces minimal but targeted structural hints without overwhelming the LLM with excessive context.
- **We conduct an empirical evaluation across 8 real-world Python modules**, comparing four prompting strategies. Our results demonstrate that the proposed repair method improves test executability and reduces hallucination-related failures, outperforming both naive prompting and full-context baselines.

The rest of this paper is organized as follows: Sect. 2 reviews related work on LLM-based test generation, test executability challenges, and prompt engineering strategies. Section 3 provides a diagnostic study of FAH through real-world examples. Section 4 presents our proposed FAH detection and prompt repair methodology. Section 5 describes our experimental setup, evaluation metrics, and results across multiple Python projects. Section 6 discusses the implications, limitations, and threats to validity. Finally, Sect. 7 concludes the paper and outlines directions for future work.

2 Related Work

Traditional program analysis-based testing techniques have shown success but often struggle with scalability and integration challenges in complex or dynamic codebases. With the advent of LLMs, recent research has shifted toward leveraging pretrained generative models to synthesize test inputs and test functions directly from source code. These LLM-based methods typically rely on prompt engineering [4], code summarization [5], or documentation alignment [6] to guide the generation process. Unlike symbolic or search-based methods, LLMs benefit from vast training corpora and are capable of generating test code without requiring concrete execution or compilation of the target program.

While LLMs have shown promising capabilities in generating syntactically correct test cases, ensuring their semantic validity and executability remains a significant challenge. A major class of failures arises from hallucinated imports, nonexistent methods, and incorrect assumptions about object structure or initialization. These issues often lead to runtime exceptions such as TypeError or AttributeError, especially when test code assumes a class is instantiable without parameters, even though its constructor requires complex arguments.

Even when prompted with documentation, function signatures, or code examples, LLMs frequently fail to infer the correct initialization logic or capture the stateful dependencies required for successful execution [7]. These issues are particularly pronounced in object-oriented Python programs that feature dynamic behaviors—such as decorators, metaclasses, or dynamic attribute access. Recent benchmarks have shown that LLM-generated tests often fail or become unexecutable in such scenarios due to an inability to reconstruct object lifecycles or mock complex internal dependencies [8].

To address these limitations, some prior works have attempted to enhance prompt quality using retrieval-augmented generation (RAG) [9] or reinforcement learning techniques [10]. However, these approaches still fall short in mitigating core execution failures, especially in black-box or partially observable settings. Notably, they often lack mechanisms to accurately model field availability, initialization order, or object state.

Among the most recurring and persistent failure patterns is FAH-where the generated test code accesses object attributes that do not exist at runtime. This issue is exacerbated by insufficient prompt context, including the omission of relevant initializers and internal field declarations. As a result, the LLM is forced to guess the existence of fields based on patterns learned from unrelated training data, rather than actual program structure.

Recent studies have explored structured prompts and context enrichment to improve the reliability of LLM-based code and test generation. For example, Li et al. proposed Structured Chain-of-Thoughts (SCoTs), which integrate program structures such as sequences, branches, and loops into prompting to enhance code synthesis accuracy [11]. Similarly, Ryan et al. introduced SymPrompt, a stage-wise prompting strategy that explicitly incorporates contextual dependencies to boost test coverage and correctness [12]. While these approaches demonstrate the benefits of organizing or enriching prompt context, they typically treat all retrieved information as equally important and lack mechanisms to prioritize initializer logic or filter out unrelated details. More critically, they do not reason about which fields must exist at runtime versus those that are conditionally initialized, leaving models prone to persistent FAH.

In contrast, our work introduces a static analysis-driven prompt construction approach. It systematically identifies the fields accessed by the function under test, verifies their initialization paths, and embeds this information into the prompt to guide LLM generation. This not only improves field-level accuracy but also resolves a key blind spot in existing prompt design strategies, leading to significantly improved test executability.

3 Diagnostic Study of Field Access Hallucination

Despite the recent advances in unit test generation using LLMs, a recurring failure pattern undermines the executability of generated tests: accessing non-existent or incorrectly interpreted object fields. We refer to this phenomenon as FAH. This section presents representative examples of FAH, followed by its formal definition and a static method for detecting such errors.

3.1 Motivating Example

To illustrate the nature of FAH, consider the following real-world example extracted from a widely-used Python codebase employing object-oriented design:

Listing 1.1. Illustrative Example

```
class QueryBase:
    def __init__(self, test_func, hashval: Tuple):
        self.test_func = test_func
        self.hashval = hashval

class Query(QueryBase):
    def __init__(self):
        self._path: Tuple[str, ...] = ()
        def notest(_):
            raise RuntimeError("Empty query was evaluated")
        super().__init__(notest, (None,))
```

```
def _generate_test(self, test: Callable[[Any], bool],
        hashval: Tuple) -> "QueryBase":
        return QueryBase(test, hashval)

def __eq__(self, rhs: Any):
        return self._generate_test(lambda value: value == rhs
            , ('==',␣self._path,␣rhs))
```

Suppose the LLM is prompted to generate a test case for the _generate_test method, but is only provided with the method's source code and minimal class context (e.g., class name and method signature). This often occurs in prompt construction strategies that limit the code window for simplicity or retrieval cost. Without awareness of the QueryBase class and its field test_func, the model generates the following test case:

Listing 1.2. Hallucinated Attribute in Generated Test

```
query = Query()
result = query._generate_test(lambda x: x > 0, (1,))
assert result.test == ...
```

This test triggers an AttributeError, as the attribute test does not exist. The correct field is test_func. The hallucination arises because the model attempts to guess the field name based on learned patterns or semantic cues, without grounding it in the actual object definition.

3.2 Formal Definition of FAH

We define FAH as follows:

Definition. A field access hallucination occurs when a generated test case attempts to access an attribute obj.x, where:

- obj is an instance of a known class C at generation time,
- x is not among the declared or dynamically assigned fields of C or its superclasses under any valid execution path,
- and the hallucinated field is not imported or mock-injected elsewhere in the test.

Unlike general test failures such as TypeError due to misused arguments or ImportError due to missing dependencies, FAH reflects a misalignment between the generated test and the target program's field structure. FAH is commonly observed when an LLM is used to generate tests for object-oriented Python code, where attribute initialization may depend on runtime conditions, complex constructors, or inheritance hierarchies.

In the next section, we propose a lightweight static analysis method to identify FAH from failed test cases, enabling both diagnostic analysis and prompt-level repair.

4 Methodology: Detecting and Mitigating FAH

As demonstrated in our diagnostic study (Sect. 3), naively generated test cases often suffer from FAHs-a class of errors where the model fabricates or misuses field accesses, leading to runtime failures. These hallucinations are not merely syntactic issues, but reflect a lack of type awareness and contextual grounding in LLM-generated code.

To tackle this problem, we introduce a framework that not only diagnoses FAH errors but also actively mitigates them through targeted prompt repair. Our approach is organized into three main phases: (1) generating test code using minimal prompts, (2) detecting hallucinated field accesses via static analysis, and (3) repairing the prompt to suppress such hallucinations in regenerated code.

We begin this section by presenting a high-level overview of our pipeline and its components.

4.1 Overview

To address the challenge of FAH in LLM-generated test cases, we propose a three-phase methodology: **Naive Test Synthesis**, **FAH Diagnosis**, and **Prompt Repair**. This pipeline is designed to not only expose hallucinated field usages but also actively suppress them in subsequent generations by refining the prompts based on static analysis feedback.

The overall workflow is illustrated in Fig. 1.

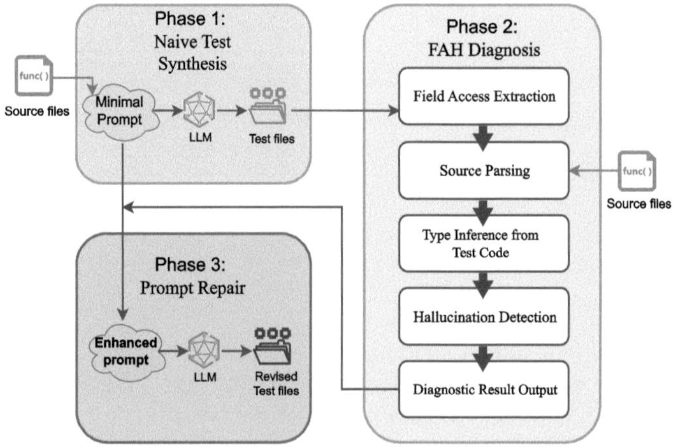

Fig. 1. Overview of FAH detection and repair pipeline.

Phase 1: Naive Test Synthesis. In the first phase, we prompt an LLM to generate test cases given a minimal, structure-agnostic description of the target function or class. These prompts include only the target function and its containing class's __init__ method, but exclude unrelated class definitions, type annotations, and field constraints. This phase simulates a realistic use case where developers rely on LLMs to infer object structures implicitly. The generated tests in this stage often contain hallucinated field accesses.

Phase 2: FAH Diagnosis. The second phase performs static and semantic analysis on the generated test code to detect hallucinated attribute accesses. Specifically, we trace expressions in the form of `variable.field` and verify whether the referenced fields are valid given the variable's inferred type. The diagnosis process involves four analytical sub-steps:

- **Source Parsing:** Extracts return types of functions and initialized fields of classes.
- **Field Access Extraction:** Extracts all expressions of the form `var.field` from the test code.
- **Type Inference from Test Code:** Determines the types of variables based on their assignment or constructor usage.
- **Hallucination Detection:** Compares accessed attributes against registered fields to identify inconsistencies and outputs a list of hallucinated field usages.

Phase 3: Prompt Repair. In the final phase, we synthesize an enhanced prompt by incorporating type-level field constraints. For each hallucinated attribute access, the prompt explicitly informs the LLM of the valid and invalid fields associated with the object type. This corrected prompt is then fed back into the LLM, enabling the generation of a revised test case with reduced or eliminated hallucinations.

4.2 Naive Test Synthesis

Prompt Design. We formulate a standard prompt template that instructs the LLM to generate a `pytest`-style unit test for a given target function. The prompt consists of the following components:

- **Role instruction:** A system-level instruction such as "You are a Python unit test generator. Generate a test file in pytest style for the target function."
- **Code context:** The full class containing the target function is provided, including the `__init__` method and the function under test.
- **Import restrictions:** An explicit directive stating that only top-level classes or functions from the `target module path` are allowed to be imported. This discourages redefinition or implicit corrections by the model.

An example prompt is shown below:

Listing 1.3. Naive prompt used to generate test cases for the example in Listing 1.1.

```
You are a Python unit test generator.
Generate a test file in pytest style for the '_generate_test'
     function.

Function to test:
'''python
class Query:
    def __init__(self):
        self._path: Tuple[str, ...] = ()
        ...
    def _generate_test(self, test: Callable[[Any], bool],
        hashval: Tuple) -> 'QueryBase':
        return QueryBase(test, hashval)

Do NOT redefine the function.
You must only import top-level classes or functions from
Program.source.query_module.
```

Design Rationale. This prompt design reflects a common practice in unit testing, where test generators are provided only with the function or class under test, without full program context. While the prompt is semantically sufficient for generating executable code, it lacks explicit type or structural annotations. As a result, the generated tests may be prone to type-related errors, including FAHs.

These naively generated tests are then passed to the diagnosis module in the next phase.

4.3 Source Parsing

The first step in our FAH diagnosis process focuses on analyzing the source code under test to extract type-level structural information. This step focuses on two key aspects:

- **Function return types:** For each function or method, we extract its explicitly declared return type annotation (e.g., `def f(...)` $\rightarrow$ `ClassName`).
- **Declared class fields:** For each class, we collect fields that are either initialized in the `__init__` method (e.g., `self.xxx = ...`) or defined at the class level (e.g., `xxx: int = 42`).

The output of this phase is a mapping from:

- Function signature $\rightarrow$ return type
- Class name $\rightarrow$ set of valid attribute names

For example, in the case of the `Query` and `QueryBase` classes shown in Listing 1.1, the extracted result may be:

```
function_return_types = {
  ('Query',␣'_generate_test'): 'QueryBase'
}

class_fields␣=␣{
␣␣'Query':␣{'_path'},
␣␣'QueryBase':␣{'test_func',␣'hashval'}
}
```

This structural information serves as the semantic ground truth for validating field accesses during hallucination detection.

4.4 Field Access Extraction

The next step is to identify all attribute access expressions in the failed test cases. These expressions typically take the form `variable.field` (e.g., `result.test`, `query._path`) and may correspond to either valid or hallucinated field references.

Target Scope. Rather than analyzing all generated test code, we restrict our diagnosis to test files that are known to have failed during execution. This design focuses our effort on high-risk test cases and improves analysis efficiency.

Extraction Procedure. For each failed test file, we statically parse its abstract syntax tree (AST) to extract all field access expressions. We recursively traverse the AST to identify all `Attribute` nodes and represent each access path as a list of strings. For example, the expression `result.test` would be represented as `["result", "test"]`.

Output Format. The result of this phase is a mapping from test filenames to sets of extracted field access paths, such as:

```
{"test_2.py": [["result", "test"], ["query", "_path"]]}
```

These paths are passed to subsequent stages to determine whether the accessed fields are valid for the inferred object types.

4.5 Type Inference from Test Code

To validate field accesses in LLM-generated test cases, we must first infer the types of intermediate variables. Since test code often lacks explicit type annotations, we leverage available source information to infer types based on constructor calls and method return types.

We formalize the inference process as follows:

1. **Constructor-based inference:** For any assignment of the form `v = C(...)` where `C` is a known class name from the source code, we infer that variable v has type `C`.

2. **Call-chain-based inference:** For any assignment `v = u.m(...)` where the type of `u` has previously been inferred (say, type T), and where `m` is a method defined in class T with known return type T', we infer that variable `v` has type T'.

We recursively apply this inference to propagate type information through the test file f. The output is a variable-to-type mapping of the form:

$V_f =$ {"v1": "T1", "v2": "T2", ...}

Example. Consider the following test code in Listing 1.2:

```
query = Query()
result = query._generate_test(...)
```

Assuming `Query._generate_test` returns a `QueryBase` instance, we infer the mapping:

{"query": "Query", "result": "QueryBase"}

This type mapping is used in the next validation phase to verify whether field accesses such as `result.test` are consistent with the declared fields in the source code.

4.6 Hallucination Detection

With both the field access paths (extracted from test code) and the type information (parsed from source code) available, we now perform the core FAH diagnosis. The goal is to identify attribute access expressions where the accessed field does not exist in the corresponding object type.

Detection Logic. For each field access expression `var.field`, we look up the type of the variable `var` using the variable-to-type mapping produced during type inference. We then retrieve the set of known valid fields (class_fields) associated with that type. If the accessed `field` is not in the set, the expression is flagged as a hallucination.

This comparison is repeated for each access path in each test file. The process ignores expressions that cannot be typed (i.e., when `var` has no known type).

Output Format. The final output is a mapping from test filenames to lists of hallucinated attribute accesses. Each hallucination is recorded as a pair `(variable, field)`. For example:

```
{
  "test_2.py": [("result", "test")]
}
```

This indicates that the test file `test_2.py` attempted to access a nonexistent field `test` on the variable `result`. These results are passed to the prompt repair phase for mitigation.

The overall FAH diagnosis process described in Sects. 4.3 to 4.6 is summarized in Algorithm 1. Each attribute access in the test code is represented as a pair (`var, field`), where `var` is a variable name and `field` is the accessed attribute. These pairs are derived from AST-level analysis of the test code.

Algorithm 1: FAH Diagnosis

Input: Test directory T, execution log directory L, source code file S
Output: FAH report R mapping test files to hallucinated accesses

$F \leftarrow$ failed test files in T (based on execution logs in L);
$R \leftarrow$ empty mapping;
$S_{\text{types}}, S_{\text{fields}} \leftarrow$ parse S to extract function return types and class fields;
; `// Source Parsing`
foreach $f \in F$ **do**
    $A_f \leftarrow$ list of field accesses `var.field` extracted from test file f;
    ; `// Field Access Extraction`
    $V_f \leftarrow$ infer variable types in f using S_{types};
    ; `// Type Inference`
    foreach $(var, field) \in A_f$ **do**
        if $var \in V_f$ ***and*** $field \notin S_{\textit{fields}}[V_f[var]]$ **then**
            $R[f] \leftarrow R[f] \cup \{(var, field)\}$; `// FAH Detected`
return R

4.7 Prompt Repair

Once hallucinated field accesses have been diagnosed, we proceed to mitigate them by modifying the test generation prompt. The goal of this phase is to proactively inform the LLM about valid and invalid attribute accesses, thereby suppressing the likelihood of repeating the same hallucinations in regenerated test cases.

We retain the original structure of the prompt, which includes:

- A role instruction that tells the LLM to generate a test file in `pytest` style.
- The source code of the function under test, including the surrounding class and its `__init__` method.
- Explicit constraints on allowed import paths (to prevent redefinition).

On top of this base, we append a structured repair section labeled as `Additional Notes`. This section includes guidance based on the output of the FAH diagnosis phase, detailing:

- The valid fields associated with each object type involved in hallucinated accesses.

– Explicit instructions to avoid accessing specific invalid fields, with reference to the variable names involved.

Example Output. A repaired prompt may include the following suffix:

```
Additional Notes:
Object(s) of type ‘QueryBase‘ have the following valid
fields: hashval, test_func.
Do not access ‘result.test‘, as ‘test‘ is not a valid
attribute of ‘QueryBase‘.
```

This information is synthesized from the known class fields and the specific hallucinated accesses detected earlier. The resulting prompt is then reused as input for the LLM to regenerate the test code with hallucinations suppressed. In our implementation, the revised prompt is submitted in a new session rather than appended to the prior conversation history, ensuring that the regeneration is influenced solely by the repaired context. This design decision avoids potential bias from earlier hallucinated outputs, though alternative implementations could incorporate session continuity if desired. Listing 1.4 shows an example test case generated by the LLM for the `_generate_test` method of the `query_module` program introduced in Listing 1.1.

Listing 1.4. Example test case generated by the LLM for the `_generate_test` method.

```
import pytest
from Program.source.query_module import Query, QueryBase

def test_generate_test():
    query_instance = Query()

    def sample_test(x):
        return x > 0

    sample_hashval = (42,)
    result = query_instance._generate_test(sample_test,
        sample_hashval)
    assert isinstance(result, QueryBase), "Result␣should␣be␣
        an␣instance␣of␣QueryBase"
    assert result.test_func(sample_hashval[0]), "Test␣
        function␣should␣return␣True␣for␣input␣42"
    assert result.hashval == sample_hashval, "Hash␣value␣
        should␣match␣the␣input␣hash␣value"
if __name__ == "__main__":
    pytest.main()
```

5 Evaluation

To assess the effectiveness of our approach in mitigating FAH and improving the executability of LLM-generated test cases, we conduct a set of controlled experiments across multiple real-world Python modules. Our evaluation aims to answer the research questions posed in Sect. 5.2, focusing on FAH frequency, repair effectiveness, and comparisons with alternative prompting strategies. The remainder of this section details our experimental setup, subject programs, evaluation metrics, and key findings.

5.1 Experimental Setup

We evaluate the effectiveness of our proposed pipeline across three real-world Python projects: TinyDB [13], Arrow [14], and SQLAlchemy [15]. For each project, we select representative source files containing complex class definitions and object interactions. In total, we evaluate our method on seven Python modules, as summarized in Table 1, which also includes the number of lines of code and functions for each module. For each function, we generate a separate test file, resulting in the same number of test files as functions per module. The number of test cases within each test file is determined by the LLM itself.

Table 1. Overview of Experimental Subjects

Project	Module	Description	No. of LOC	No.of functions (No.of Total generated test files)
TinyDB	`queries.py`	Implements predicate logic and query operators.	185	35
	`table.py`	Manages basic table-level operations and data access.	293	23
Arrow	`arrow.py`	Provides the main interface for date-time manipulation.	868	70
SQLAlchemy	`orm/session.py`	Controls ORM session and transaction behavior.	2547	158
	`engine/base.py`	Manages core engine and DB connection logic.	1721	131
	`pool/base.py`	Implements connection pool management.	824	77
	`sql/type_api.py`	Declares SQL type abstractions and metadata.	811	92

We use the `GPT-4o` model via the OpenAI API [16] with a temperature of 0.2 to generate test code. Each prompt produces a single test file. Test cases are executed using `pytest`. To isolate issues caused by faulty test generation rather than bugs in the software under test (SUT), we assume that the SUT is correct and contains no defects. Under this assumption, any test file that raises an exception (e.g., `AttributeError`, `TypeError`) or results in at least one failed or errored test is considered **non-executable**, indicating that the generated test code is semantically invalid or incorrectly structured.

We evaluate four distinct prompt strategies to examine the effectiveness of our FAH-aware repair mechanism and to explore the trade-offs between minimal, targeted, and full-context prompting:

1. **Naive Prompt**: This serves as a realistic baseline in which the prompt contains only the target function, its enclosing class name, and the `__init__`

method. No type or structural context is provided, simulating how developers typically request unit tests for isolated functions.
2. **Repaired Prompt**: Starting from a naive prompt, we apply our FAH diagnosis to the initial generated test, then regenerate a new test using a revised prompt that includes minimal but precise repair instructions-such as valid field lists and hallucination warnings. This setting tests whether targeted, test-specific feedback is sufficient to suppress hallucinations.
3. **Full Source Prompt**: The entire source file containing the target function is included in the prompt. This setting evaluates whether a large, unpruned context can naturally prevent hallucinations by exposing the LLM to all possible definitions, despite the risk of overwhelming it with irrelevant information.
4. **Full Static Info Prompt**: This setting directly injects all statically extracted function return types and class fields from the entire source file into the initial prompt-without filtering by relevance to the generated test. This allows us to compare our repair-after-failure strategy against an approach that front-loads all available structural information.

Together, these four strategies allow us to investigate whether hallucination mitigation is better achieved through minimal, context-aware guidance or maximal, information-rich prompting.

5.2 Research Questions

To evaluate the effectiveness of our proposed FAH diagnosis and prompt repair framework, we aim to answer the following research questions:

- **RQ1:** *How frequently do field access hallucinations occur in LLM-generated test cases under minimal prompting?*
  This question investigates the prevalence of FAH errors when only minimal context (i.e., class and target method) is provided to the LLM. It helps establish the necessity of mitigation mechanisms.
- **RQ2:** *Can our FAH diagnosis and repair mechanism improve the execution success rate of LLM-generated test cases?*
  We assess whether the repaired prompts-generated after identifying and correcting hallucinated field accesses-lead to more executable and reliable test cases.
- **RQ3:** *How does our method compare to other context-enhancing strategies?*
  This question explores whether our proposed repair strategy is more effective than providing the LLM with the full source code or all static information at once.

These questions collectively assess both the frequency and severity of FAH, and the trade-offs between minimal prompting, targeted repair, and full-context prompting strategies.

5.3 Evaluation Metrics

To answer the above research questions, we define the following evaluation metrics based on function-level test file execution results:

- **Execution Success Rate:** The rate of generated test files that run successfully under `pytest` without any errors or failures. It reflects the overall executability of generated tests.

$$\text{Execution Success Rate} = \frac{\text{No. of Passed test files}}{\text{No. of Total test files}}$$

- **FAH Fail Rate:** The rate of test files that fail specifically due to field access hallucination (e.g., `AttributeError` caused by accessing undefined fields).

$$\text{FAH Fail Rate} = \frac{\text{No. of FAH-related failures}}{\text{No. of Total test files}}$$

- **FAH Rate among Failures:** The rate of FAH-related failures among all failed test files, reflecting the relative contribution of FAH to test generation failure.

$$\text{FAH Rate} = \frac{\text{No. of FAH-related failures}}{\text{No. of Failed test files}}$$

- **Fix Success Rate (only applicable to Repaired method):** The rate of FAH-induced failures that are successfully repaired by our diagnosis-and-prompt-repair mechanism.

$$\text{Fix Success Rate} = \frac{\text{No. of FAH failures fixed}}{\text{No. of FAH-related failures}}$$

These metrics allow us to quantify both the severity of FAH in baseline test generation and the effectiveness of various strategies-including our proposed repair method-in improving test executability.

5.4 Results and Analysis

In this section, we present a detailed analysis of the experimental results to answer the three research questions posed in Sect. 5.2. We compare the effectiveness of different prompt strategies in terms of execution success, failure causes, and repair outcomes. The findings are discussed in the context of FAH and the impact of our proposed mitigation technique.

RQ1: How Frequently Do Field Access hallucinations Occur in LLM-Generated Test Cases Under Minimal prompting? To assess the prevalence of FAH, we analyze the test failures generated using four types of prompts. As shown in Fig. 3, a substantial number of failures can be attributed to FAH errors.

In larger modules such as `orm/session`, `engine/base`, and `sql/type_api`, the number of FAH-induced failures dominates the overall failure cases. For example, in `orm/session`, 54 out of 77 failed tests (70.1%) are due to FAH under the naive prompt. These numbers confirm that FAH is a widespread and critical failure mode under minimal prompting. Even in smaller modules like `queries` and `table`, FAH-related issues are non-negligible, with FAH rates reaching 50% or higher in the naive setting (see Fig. 4).

Fig. 2. Execution success rate for each prompt method across all modules.

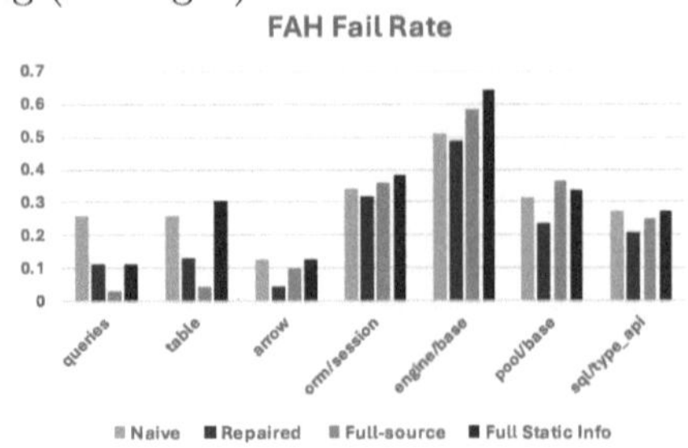

Fig. 3. FAH-induced failure rate among all test files per method.

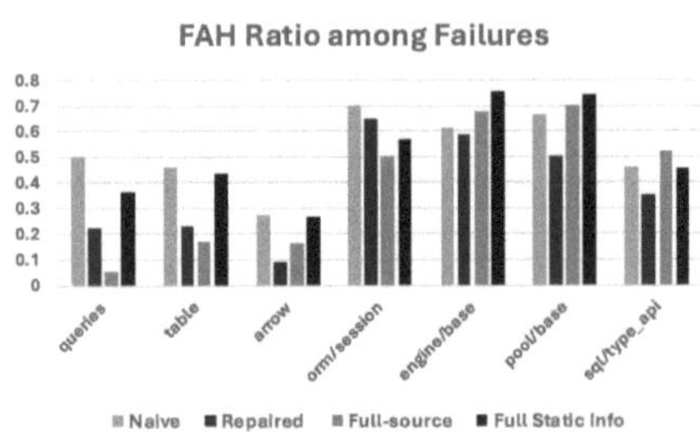

Fig. 4. FAH rate: rate of FAH errors among all observed errors for each prompt method.

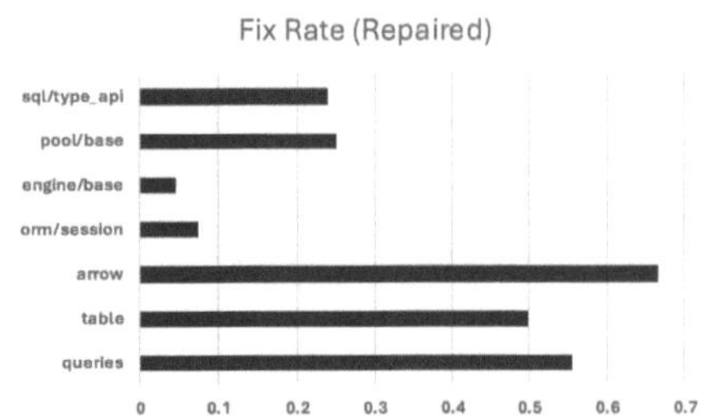

Fig. 5. FAH fix success rate: rate of FAH errors successfully resolved using repair mechanism.

RQ2: Can Our FAH Diagnosis and Repair Mechanism improve the Execution Success Rate of LLM-Generated Test Cases? We now examine the effectiveness of our FAH repair method by comparing the execution success rate of test cases before and after prompt repair. As shown in Fig. 2, our method (Repaired) consistently improves execution success rate compared to the baseline across most modules, despite not having access to the full source context.

Furthermore, Fig. 5 reports the rate of FAH-induced failures successfully fixed by our method. For instance, in the `arrow` module, 6 out of 9 FAH-induced failures are resolved, yielding a fix rate of 66.7%. Similarly, in the `queries` and `table` modules, the fix rate exceeds 50%, demonstrating the efficacy of prompt-level repair guided by static FAH detection.

While some modules such as `engine/base` exhibit lower fix rates, this may be attributed to the complexity and depth of attribute chains, which present challenges for both hallucination detection and mock suggestion. Nonetheless, even modest improvements in such modules translate to significant execution gains, as seen in the increased number of final passed test cases.

These results indicate that prompt repair based on static hallucination detection is an effective strategy to enhance test reliability, particularly in scenarios where full source context is unavailable.

RQ3: How Does Our Method Compare to Other context-Enhancing Strategies? To evaluate the benefit of context control, we compare our method with two alternative strategies: (1) *Full-source*, which provides the entire source file, and (2) *Full Static Info*, which injects global type and field annotations at prompt time. As shown in Fig. 2, the Full-source strategy does not consistently outperform our method. In some modules, such as `table` and `sql/type_api`, Full-source achieves slightly higher success rates, but this advantage diminishes in more complex modules.

More importantly, Fig. 4 shows that Full-source and Full Static Info still suffer from high FAH rates, indicating that providing more context does not necessarily resolve hallucinations. On the contrary, excessive or irrelevant context may confuse the LLM and lead to new failure modes unrelated to FAH.

Our method strikes a balance by providing only contextually relevant field information inferred from static analysis. This targeted repair reduces noise and avoids overwhelming the model, making it particularly effective for pinpointing and resolving hallucination-related errors.

6 Threats to Validity

We identify the following potential threats to the validity of our evaluation.

Internal Validity. Implementation bugs or misconfigurations in our pipeline (e.g., static analysis, FAH detection, or prompt generation) may affect the accuracy of diagnosis or repairs. To reduce this risk, we manually inspected a subset of test files and confirmed the correctness of mock injection and FAH error detection. Additionally, we fixed several false positives during iterative validation.

External Validity. Our evaluation is limited to three popular Python libraries (TinyDB, Arrow, and SQLAlchemy). While these projects cover a range of sizes and domains, the generalizability of results to other languages, codebases, or testing styles (e.g., integration testing) is not guaranteed. Further studies on diverse real-world projects would strengthen the applicability of our findings.

Construct Validity. We rely on observable execution failures (e.g., `AttributeError`, `TypeError`) to identify FAH instances. This may miss some subtle semantic issues that do not raise immediate exceptions. In addition, the success of a test file is defined by whether it passes `pytest` without errors, which may not reflect deeper correctness issues or assertion quality.

Conclusion Validity. Our analysis is based on a single round of test generation per prompt due to cost and reproducibility constraints. While this avoids sampling bias, it may underrepresent variance in LLM output. We also focus on pass/fail outcomes rather than assertion richness or fault detection power, which limits the strength of conclusions about test quality.

7 Conclusion and Future Work

This paper presents a systematic study of FAH errors in LLM-generated test code and proposes a static-analysis-driven repair framework to mitigate them. Through experiments on real-world Python modules, we demonstrate that FAH errors are highly prevalent under minimal prompting and often responsible for execution failures. Our proposed diagnosis and repair mechanism improves the test file execution rate by injecting targeted field initialization instructions while preserving prompt minimalism. Compared to full-source and full-static-info prompting strategies, our approach achieves a favorable balance between precision and context size, leading to more reliable and executable test code in practice.

While our repair strategy shows promising results, several limitations remain. First, our method primarily focuses on resolving detectable FAH symptoms and does not address other forms of semantic hallucinations or incorrect mocking logic. Second, although effective in many cases, our repair strategy may struggle with complex internal object structures and dynamic behaviors, especially in deeply nested or highly stateful programs. Finally, our evaluation is currently limited to Python and method-level unit testing scenarios. In future work, we plan to enhance the robustness of our approach for handling structurally complex programs, extend our techniques to other programming languages, and integrate fault-detection metrics to assess test effectiveness beyond execution success.

References

1. Manès, V.J., et al.: The art, science, and engineering of fuzzing: a survey. IEEE Trans. Softw. Eng. **47**(11), 2312–2331 (2019)
2. King, J.C.: Symbolic execution and program testing. Commun. ACM **19**(7), 385–394 (1976)
3. Harman, M., Jones, B.F.: Search-based software engineering. Inf. Softw. Technol. **43**(14), 833–839 (2001)
4. Austin, J., et al.: Program synthesis with large language models. *arXiv preprint*arXiv:2108.07732 (2021)
5. Wang, Y., Wang, W., Joty, S., Hoi, S.C.: CodeT5: identifier-aware unified pre-trained encoder-decoder models for code understanding and generation. In: Proceedings of the 2021 Conference on Empirical Methods in Natural Language Processing, pp. 8696–8708. Association for Computational Linguistics (2021)
6. Schäfer, M., Nadi, S., Eghbali, A., Tip, F.: An empirical evaluation of using large language models for automated unit test generation. IEEE Trans. Software Eng. **50**(1), 85–105 (2023)

7. Wang, S., Wei, Z., Choi, Y., Ren, X.: Can LLMS reason with rules? logic scaffolding for stress-testing and improving LLMS. *arXiv preprint*arXiv:2402.11442 (2024)
8. Liu, R., Zhang, Z., Hu, Y., Lin, Y., Gao, X., Sun, H.: LLM-based unit test generation for dynamically-typed programs. *arXiv preprint*arXiv:2503.14000 (2025)
9. Shin, J., Aleithan, R., Hemmati, H., Wang, S.: Retrieval-augmented test generation: how far are we? *arXiv preprint*arXiv:2409.12682 (2024)
10. Chen, C.-Y., Huang, J.-L.: Reinforcement-learning-based test program generation for software-based self-test. In: IEEE 28th Asian Test Symposium (ATS), pp. 73–735. IEEE (2019)
11. Li, J., Li, G., Li, Y., Jin, Z.: Structured chain-of-thought prompting for code generation. ACM Trans. Softw. Eng. Methodol. **34**(2), 1–23 (2025)
12. Ryan, G., et al.: Code-aware prompting: a study of coverage-guided test generation in regression setting using LLM. In: Proceedings of the ACM on Software Engineering, vol. 1, no. FSE, pp. 951–971 (2024)
13. Tinydb: A lightweight document oriented database. https://tinydb.readthedocs.io
14. Arrow: Better dates and times for python. https://arrow.readthedocs.io
15. Sqlalchemy: The python SQL toolkit and object relational mapper. https://www.sqlalchemy.org
16. OpenAI, Model release blog: Gpt-4o (2024). https://openai.com/index/hello-gpt-4o/

Data-Driven and Scenario-Based Risk Analysis Considering Uncertainty in Machine Learning Systems

Toshiya Okubo[1(✉)], Hironori Washizaki[1], Naoyasu Ubayashi[1], Nobukazu Yoshioka[2], Hironori Takeuchi[3], and Truong Vinh Truong Duy[4]

[1] Waseda University, Tokyo, Japan
toshiya.o@fuji.waseda.jp, washizaki@waseda.jp, ubayashi@aoni.waseda.jp
[2] QAML Inc., Tokyo, Japan
nobukazuy@acm.org
[3] Musashi University, Tokyo, Japan
h.takeuchi@cc.musashi.ac.jp
[4] Aisin Corporation, Tokyo, Japan
duy.truong@aisin.co.jp

Abstract. Safety-critical systems that integrate machine learning (ML) components have gained significant traction in recent years. However, current safety analysis methods lack a systematic approach to address the uncertainty inherent in ML system decision-making. Consequently, performing thorough risk analysis for ML systems with these methods is often time-consuming and makes it difficult to identify risks associated with uncertainty. In this study, we introduce a novel risk analysis method called eAI-Risk, designed for complex ML systems comprising multiple ML components. This method employs a data-driven and scenario-based approach, providing a structured framework for systematically identifying factors that contribute to high risks in ML systems and for evaluating potential countermeasures. A key feature of eAI-Risk is its capacity to identify risks within ML systems based on the classification patterns of the ML components and the action patterns defined by the system, while considering the uncertainty that characterizes ML systems. In addition, risks are quantitatively assessed from two perspectives: severity and likelihood. The product of these values generates a risk score, facilitating the prioritization of risks to address. This study illustrates the effectiveness of eAI-Risk by applying it to an automated driving system. Through the eAI-Risk process cycle, we anticipate that optimal risk mitigation strategies can be effectively identified and implemented.

Keywords: Risk assessment · Safety · Machine learning · AI

1 Introduction

Recent years have seen a notable increase in the prevalence of systems that incorporate machine learning (ML) components, collectively referred to as ML sys-

© The Author(s), under exclusive license to Springer Nature Singapore Pte Ltd. 2026
Y. Chen et al. (Eds.): SFPVV 2025, LNCS 16356, pp. 78–97, 2026.
https://doi.org/10.1007/978-981-95-6032-5_6

tems, particularly in safety-critical systems. Examples of these types of ML systems in which safety assurance is crucial include automated driving systems and medical diagnostic systems utilizing image recognition [9] [11] [10]. This is particularly evident in the automotive industry, where automated driving systems are developed. The analysis of the safety risks associated with integrating multiple ML components, such as object detection, road sign recognition, and path planning, is critical. Our industrial partner has observed that current safety analysis methods struggle to systematically assess the inherent uncertainties in ML systems. Cai et al. [1] experimentally demonstrated, through a case study involving a CNN-based handwritten character recognition system, that modern deep learning models are particularly vulnerable to "environmental changes" and "extreme inputs." Given this context, the need to analyze the safety risks associated with ML systems is becoming increasingly critical. Effectively addressing ML uncertainty is essential to prevent unexpected accidents and losses [24]. In addition, a systematic literature review by Wang et al. [26] highlighted that the application of AI technologies in safety-critical domains remains in an exploratory stage, with significant verification and validation challenges arising from "black-box characteristics" and "uncertainty." In practice, ensuring the safety of advanced AI technologies such as deep learning and reinforcement learning requires careful consideration before their deployment in real-world operations.

However, existing methods are insufficient for detailed analyses of the risks unique to ML systems. For example, systems-theoretic process analysis (STPA) [13], which evaluates system hazard factors based on the systems-theoretic analysis model and processes (STAMP) accident model, can be applied to ML systems. Nevertheless, STPA does not systematically support the analysis of risks associated with the classification results of ML components or the dangers in system decision-making based on those results. Moreover, STPA does not provide a quantitative risk evaluation. To provide a more detailed analysis of risks caused by ML components, such as classification models, classification failure mode and effects analysis (CFMEA) [17] has been proposed. Although CFMEA is designed for classification tasks in the perception components of automated driving systems (ADSs), its core concept can be extended to other ML systems. Furthermore, we have developed classification uncertainty risk analysis (CURA) [15], a safety analysis method that integrates these approaches while considering uncertainty in ML systems. However, CURA faces challenges when dealing with multiple ML components or when the outputs of ML components do not correspond one-to-one with system actions.

In this study, we propose eAI-Risk, a method that provides safety analysis of various ML systems by leveraging the strengths of existing methods, such as STPA and CFMEA, and simultaneously addressing the limitations of CURA. As a case study, we applied eAI-Risk to a virtual ADS and discussed its applicability to industrial examples.

The contributions of this study are as follows:

- We present a comprehensive process for eAI-Risk, which addresses the safety risk analysis challenges faced by ML systems in industry.

- We explain how eAI-Risk surpasses existing methods and validate its practicality through evaluations conducted with an industrial partner.
- We demonstrate an efficient cycle that spans from risk identification to improvement, illustrated through a road sign recognition task, an essential component in the development of automated driving systems.

The remainder of this paper is organized as follows. Section 2 reviews related work. Section 3 outlines the research challenges and objectives. Section 4 details the proposed method. Section 5 demonstrates the practicality of this method through a case study. Section 6 discusses the results of the case study, highlighting how eAI-Risk addresses the identified challenges. Section 7 concludes the paper.

2 Related Work

Research on risk assessment for ML systems has progressed with the introduction of systematic classification frameworks. Tan et al. [22] proposed the machine learning system risk framework, which organizes risks into primary and secondary categories. Varshney et al. [23] emphasized the necessity of reducing uncertainty to ensure the safety of ML systems. Grey and Segerie [6] systematized AI safety evaluation along three axes: capabilities, propensities, and control. Our method focuses specifically on the control axis, prioritizing the quantification of ML-specific risks.

In RQ3 of Salhab et al. [18], the main concerns regarding safe AI include "robustness," "reliability," "fairness and bias," "explainability (XAI)," and "monitoring." eAI-Risk directly addresses these concerns as follows:

- **Robustness**: By quantifying the uncertainty of classification results and action patterns, eAI-Risk aides in identifying and mitigating vulnerabilities to adversarial attacks and out-of-distribution data.
- **Reliability**: Risks are quantified based on severity and likelihood, facilitating the evaluation of consistent and accurate outputs from ML systems.
- **Explainability**: Risk factors are explicitly presented for each classification and action pattern, offering interpretable explanations for decision rationales and the mechanisms behind risk occurrence.
- **Monitoring**: Quantified risk indicators are employed to continuously monitor for anomalies and risk changes during operation, enabling timely countermeasures.

In this manner, eAI-Risk enhances the safety of ML systems by providing concrete evaluation and management strategies for each of the concerns identified by Salhab et al.

We compare eAI-Risk with existing methods for safety and security analysis in general ML systems, ADSs, and connected cars. Table 1 summarizes the key characteristics of these methods. Traditional engineering safety methods such as failure mode and effects analysis (FMEA) [4], fault tree analysis (FTA) [19],

Table 1. Comparison of Safety Analysis Methods

Method	Description	Year	Qual/ Quant	Assessment type	Operation and ML-component risk analysis	Metrics	Uncertainty assessment
FMEA [4]	Failure Mode and Effects Analysis	-	Qual Quant	Component	No	Occurrence Severity Detectability Risk Priority Number	No
FTA [19]	Fault Tree Analysis	-	Qual Quant	Component	No	Occurrence probability	No
STPA [13]	System-Theoretic Process Analysis	2013	Qual	Scenario	Partially Yes	Safety constraint Unsafe control action Hazard causal factor Loss scenario	No
CFMEA [17]	Classification Failure Mode and Effects Analysis	2019	Quant	Data Simulation	No	Occurrence probability Severity	Yes
Vogt et al. [25]	Comprehensive Risk Management for Intelligent Transport Systems	2021	Qual Quant	Scenario	No	Severity Failure Probability	No
PIER [16]	Probability, Impact, Exposure, and Recovery (PIER) Iterative scenario-based risk assessment	2022	Quant	Scenario	No	Probability Impact Exposure Recovery	No
ISDS [12]	Integrated System Design and Safety Framework	2022	Qual Quant	Model Simulation	No	FMEA: Failure Mode, Severity, Occurrence FTA: Fault Tree, Minimal Cut Sets Verification: Missed Warning Rate, Collision Rate	No
RAM [2]	Reliability Assessment Model for ML Components	2023	Quant	Data Scenario	No	Probability of Misclassification (pmi) Reliability Bound Robustness Metric	Yes
StreetWise [5]	Data-Driven Scenario-Based Assessment Method for Automated Driving Systems	2024	Qual Quant	Data Scenario Simulation	No	Exposure Collision probability Injury probability Risk Controllability	No
eAI-Risk	Data-driven Scenario-based Engineerable-AI Risk Analysis	2025	Qual Quant	Data Scenario	Yes	Severity Value Occurrence Value Accident Occurrence Risk Value	Yes

and hazard and operability studies (HAZOP) [3] focus on component failures or deviations. However, these methods neither account for ML-specific uncertainty nor provide an integrated quantitative view of operational and component risks. STPA [13] adds system-theoretic, scenario-based causal reasoning and can identify unsafe control actions, but it still lacks a quantitative approach to ML classification uncertainty.

CFMEA [17] offers a quantitative evaluation of severity and occurrence for classification tasks and partially addresses uncertainty at the ML component level. However, it fails to consider operational decision risks or interactions between multiple components. Vogt et al. [25] and probability, impact, exposure, and recovery (PIER) [16] expand on scenario-based or iterative assessments but omit explicit uncertainty propagation across ML components. Integrated system design and safety (ISDS) framework [12] combines model-based design, traditional safety analysis (FMEA/FTA), and simulation/fault injection (e.g., CARLA) to automate feedback. Still, it does not account for learning-induced uncertainty or provide a unified ranking that encompasses both action decisions and misclassification scenarios. Reliability assessment model for ML components (RAM) [2] provides statistically grounded reliability indicators (such as pmi and robustness evidence) for classifier components under operational profiles, but it remains limited to single-component reliability and does not link to system action consequences. StreetWise [5] offers an iterative scenario-based ADS evaluation, featuring comprehensive metrics on exposure, collisions, and injuries; however, it does not quantify ML classification uncertainty or connect misclassification patterns with operational risk rankings.

In summary, no existing method simultaneously (i) unifies operation-level and ML component-level risk analysis, (ii) quantifies and ranks risks while incorporating classification uncertainty, and (iii) integrates these elements into a cyclic mitigation-improvement process. eAI-Risk addresses this gap by providing a two-layer, uncertainty-aware, data- and scenario-based framework that produces comparable ranked risk indicators across decision-making and classification scenarios, thereby directly aiding in the prioritization of mitigation measures.

3 Research Challenges and Objectives

This section identifies the key challenges in the safety analysis of ML systems that motivate our research and outlines the objectives that eAI-Risk aims to achieve.

3.1 Current Challenges in Safety Evaluation of ML Systems

Recently, ML systems have been deployed across various sectors, including automated driving, healthcare, and finance. However, traditional safety analysis methods fall short in addressing the unique challenges posed by ML, such as uncertainty, data dependency, black-box characteristics, and adaptability to dynamic environments. Based on the gaps identified in Sect. 2 and industrial requirements, we distill the following three fundamental research challenges:

C1: Methodological integration gaps: Existing methods such as STPA focus on system-level analysis, whereas CFMEA targets component-level analysis. However, no method exists that systematically integrates operation-level (action decision) and ML component-level (classification) risks within a coherent framework. Current safety analysis methods also fail to systematically capture and utilize ML classification uncertainty and decision uncertainty in risk assessment, particularly using empirical evidence like confusion matrices.

C2: Analytical capability limitations: Existing approaches do not make risk factors and their propagation from misclassification to unsafe system actions transparent and traceable for stakeholders. Furthermore, existing methods lack comparable and rankable risk scores that encompass both operation and component layers, making it difficult to prioritize mitigation efforts.

C3: Practical deployment barriers: Many methods fail to integrate into existing engineering workflows and collaboration mechanisms with practitioners, hindering timely decision support. Additionally, insufficient alignment with safety standards (e.g., ISO 26262) and limited capabilities for comprehensive analysis of rare scenarios represent significant obstacles to industrial adoption.

3.2 Research Objectives

eAI-Risk seeks to address these challenges through the following research objectives:

O1: Develop a unified framework that systematically integrates operation-level and ML component-level risk analysis while incorporating systematic uncertainty assessment using confusion matrices and empirical data (addressing C1).
O2: Provide transparent and traceable mechanisms for identifying risk factors and their propagation, enable quantitative risk scoring and ranking across multiple layers to facilitate prioritization, and establish an iterative cycle for continuous risk mitigation and improvement (addressing C2).
O3: Ensure practical applicability through industrial collaboration and workflow integration, and lay the groundwork for future alignment with safety standards and comprehensive scenario analysis (addressing C3).

3.3 Collaboration with Industry and Standards

A key goal of this research is to establish a practical framework for safety evaluation and risk management through collaboration with industry and standards organizations is a key goal of this research. This effort contributes to the social implementation and widespread adoption of ML systems.

4 Data-Driven and Scenario-Based Risk Analysis Method Considering Uncertainty in ML Systems (eAI-Risk)

4.1 Overview

Figure 1 presents an overview of eAI-Risk. Step 1 involves confirming the fundamental information of the target ML system for analysis. This information includes the system's actions, components, and algorithms for decision-making, which are essential for the subsequent safety analysis process. Step 2 focuses on risk analysis at the operational level, where risks associated with specific system actions are quantified, and their underlying causes are identified and estimated. Step 3 moves to risk analysis at the ML component level, quantifying risks related to classification results of ML components involved in system action selection and considering risk mitigation measures. In Step 4, the risk mitigation measures identified in Step 3 are implemented. The eAI-Risk framework comprises these four steps as one continuous cycle, with the aim of analyzing and mitigating risks through repeated execution of the cycle. The following sections detail the eAI-Risk process.

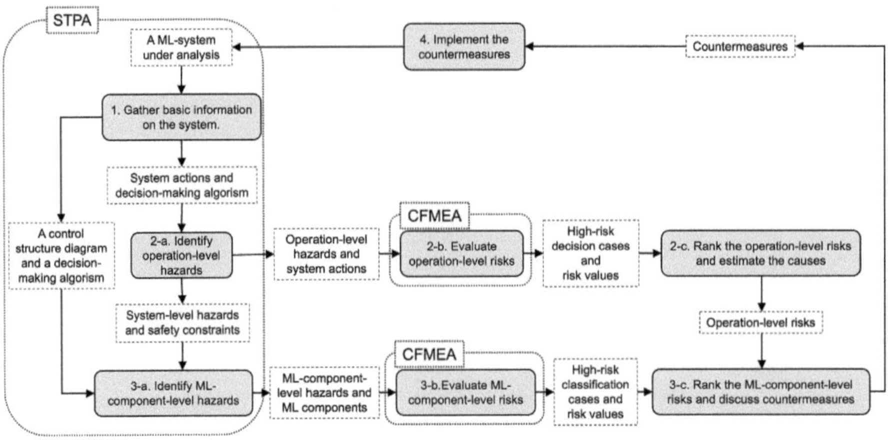

Fig. 1. Overview of eAI-Risk.

4.2 Step 1: Organizing Basic Information

First, the basic information necessary for analyzing the safety of the ML system is organized. Managing all information at the beginning of the study is not required; only the essential assumptions should be clarified, with additional details supplemented as needed during the analysis. Examples of basic system information include the following three points:

- Control structure
- Actions to be taken by the system
- Classes to be classified by ML components

The control structure is a diagram developed during the safety analysis process using STPA, visualizing the components within the system and their interactions. These interactions encompass control process outputs (control actions) directed toward the controlled process, as well as feedback from uncontrolled processes to control actions. For example, Fig. 2 illustrates the control structure of a virtual ADS. As the figure shows, this ADS contains a classification model as an ML component, which influences the determination of the system's actions. Examples of ADS actions are summarized in Table 2, based on the application case of CFMEA [17].

4.3 Step 2: Operation-Level Risk Analysis

Operation-level risk analysis examines the risks associated with the system's action decisions. This process consists of the following three sub-processes:

1. Identification of operation-level hazards
2. Evaluation of operation-level risks
3. Rankings and cause estimation of operation-level risks

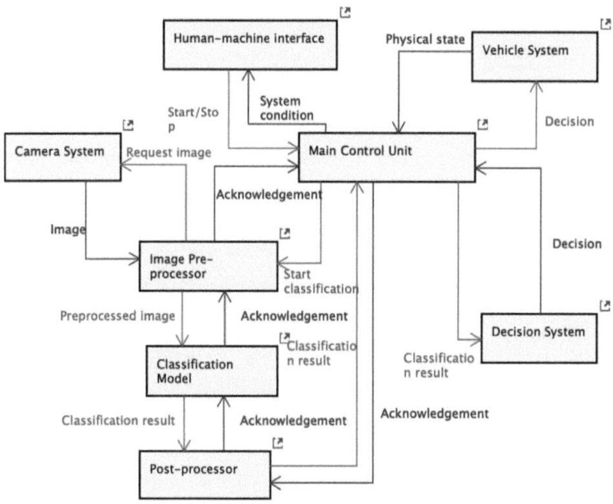

Fig. 2. Control structure of ADS.

Table 2. Examples of ADS actions

Action	Description
Stop	The vehicle stops safely.
Follow	If there is an obstacle ahead (up to *Cruise* speed), the vehicle matches its speed; otherwise, it stops.
Creep	The vehicle moves at a safe low speed and passes around slow or stationary obstacles.
Slowdown	The vehicle slows down below *Cruise* speed to avoid slow or stationary obstacles.
Cruise	The vehicle travels at the optimal speed up to the legal speed limit.

4.3.1 Identification of Operation-Level Hazards The first step involves identifying accidents and operation-level hazards within the target ML system. The goal is to recognize scenarios in which operation-level risks may arise and to understand the hazards that will inform the detailed risk evaluations that follow. An accident is defined as an undesirable event that results in some form of loss, including unacceptable damage to stakeholders, such as loss of life, injury, or property damage. Operation-level hazards represent a set of system states or conditions that, combined with specific worst-case environmental factors, can lead to these types of loss. For example, an accident resulting in loss of life might occur from a collision between a car and a pedestrian. Hazards could include a vehicle failing to slow down in high pedestrian traffic areas or neglecting to reduce speed when approaching sidewalks. Furthermore, safety constraints based on these hazards are defined. Safety constraints are measures put in place to prevent hazards and ensure safety. In the car example, safety constraints would mandate that the vehicle must slow down when operating in areas with a high concentration of pedestrians or near sidewalks. These identified safety constraints will be utilized in the ML component-level risk analysis.

4.3.2 Evaluation of Operation-Level Risks Evaluation of operation-level risks quantifies the hazards associated with improper action decisions made by the system.

First, the severity value S_{action} for accidents resulting from each decision case is calculated. A decision case refers to a situation where the system must choose a specific action a_t but selects action a_r, denoted as (a_t, a_r). Severity can be assessed from multiple perspectives, such as safety and progress, which often have a trade-off relationship in ADS. The severity of each evaluation metric is assigned discrete values across several levels on a 11-point scale ranging from 0 to 10. When multiple evaluation metrics (denoted as set M) are used to determine severity, the weighted average of the severity evaluation value $sev_k(a_t, a_r)$ for each metric $k \in M$ in each decision case is calculated, and this value is designated as S_{action}. The calculation formula for S_{action} is expressed by Eq. 1.

The severity $sev_k(a_t, a_r)$ is assessed on a 11-point scale, with values ranging from 0 to 10. The weighted average value is then rounded up to obtain $S_{action}(a_t, a_r)$, also represented as a 11-point scale from 0 to 10:

$$S_{action}(a_t, a_r) = \left\lceil \sum_{k \in M} \omega_k \cdot sev_k(a_t, a_r) \right\rceil \tag{1}$$

The occurrence value O_{action} for accidents attributed to each decision case is evaluated using the conditional probability derived from statistical data obtained during system operation tests. Specifically, for a given correct action a_t, the conditional probability $\text{prob}(a_r|a_t)$ represents the likelihood of the system selecting action a_r. This conditional probability is then converted to a discrete scale from 0 to 10 using a problem-specific mapping function f_{action}:

$$O_{action}(a_t, a_r) = f_{action}(\text{prob}(a_r|a_t)) \tag{2}$$

Following the calculation of S_{action} and O_{action} for all decision cases, the risk value R_{action} for each decision case is determined. R_{action} is computed as the product of S_{action} and O_{action}, with the calculation formula given as Eq. 2. Since both S_{action} and O_{action} are on a 11-point scale from 0 to 10, R_{action} becomes a 101-point scale from 0 to 100:

$$R_{action}(a_t, a_r) = S_{action}(a_t, a_r) \cdot O_{action}(a_t, a_r) \tag{3}$$

4.3.3 Ranking and Cause Estimation of Operation-Level Risks Decision cases are ranked in descending order based on the calculated R_{action}. This ranking enables the identification of high-risk decision cases, which are prioritized for countermeasures. In addition, the causes of accidents associated with these decision cases are estimated. The information gathered in this subprocess informs the selection of risk mitigation measures during the ML component-level risk analysis.

4.4 Step 3: ML Component-Level Risk Analysis

Operation-level risk analysis evaluates the risks related to the system's action decisions. This process is composed of the following three sub-processes:

1. Identification of ML component-level hazards
2. Evaluation of ML component-level risks
3. Ranking and consideration of risk mitigation measures at the ML component level

4.4.1 Identification of ML Component-Level Hazards In this phase, ML components included in the system are identified from the control structure. Furthermore, unsafe control actions (UCA) executed by these ML components are extracted as ML component-level hazards. For instance, in the control actions illustrated in Fig. 2, this ADS incorporates a classification model. As part of its control actions, the classification model sends its classification results to the central control unit; thus, UCAs correspond to scenarios in which incorrect classifications occur.

4.4.2 Evaluation of ML Component-Level Risks The evaluation of ML component-level risks quantifies the dangers posed by incorrect classification results produced by ML components.

First, a control policy is established to govern the system's actions based on the classification results from the classification model. This control policy, as used in CFMEA, defines the relationship between classes identified by the classification model and the corresponding actions of the system.

Then, utilizing the control policy, the severity value (S_{model}) for accidents resulting from each classification case is calculated. A classification case is defined as a pair (c_t, c_r) where, in a situation in which a class c_t should be assigned to a specific environment or object, it is assigned to class c_r. S_{model}, like S_{action}, can be evaluated based on multiple criteria. Each evaluation metric's severity is rated using discrete values across several levels, typically on a scale from 0 to 10. When evaluation metrics from the set M are used to evaluate severity, the weighted average of the severity evaluation value $sev_k(c_t, c_r)$ for each metric $k \in M$ in each decision case is calculated, and this value is used as S_{model}. Therefore, the calculation formula for S_{model} is given as Eq. 4.

The severity $sev_k(c_t, c_r)$ is evaluated on a 11-point scale from 0 to 10. The weighted average value is rounded up to obtain $S_{model}(c_t, c_r)$, which also becomes a 11-point scale from 0 to 10:

$$S_{model}(c_t, c_r) = \left\lceil \sum_{k \in M} \omega_k \cdot sev_k(c_t, c_r) \right\rceil \tag{4}$$

The occurrence value O_{model} for accidents derived from each classification case is evaluated based on the conditional probability derived from the statistical data of estimation results produced by ML components. Specifically, for a given ground truth class c_t, the conditional probability $\text{prob}(c_r|c_t)$ represents the likelihood that the ML component classifying it is class c_r. This conditional probability is converted to a discrete scale from 0 to 10 using a problem-specific mapping function f_{model}:

$$O_{model}(c_t, c_r) = f_{model}(\text{prob}(c_r|c_t)) \tag{5}$$

After S_{model} and O_{model} are calculated for all classification cases, the risk value R_{model} for each classification case is calculated. R_{model} is computed as the product of S_{model} and O_{model}, and the calculation formula is given as Eq. 6. Because both S_{model} and O_{model} are on a 11-point scale from 0 to 10, R_{model} becomes a 101-point scale from 0 to 100:

$$R_{model}(c_t, c_r) = S_{model}(c_t, c_r) \cdot O_{model}(c_t, c_r) \tag{6}$$

4.4.3 Ranking and Consideration of Risk Mitigation Measures at the ML Component Level Classification cases are ranked in descending order based on the calculated R_{model}. This prioritization allows for the identification of high-risk classification cases, facilitating the consideration of targeted risk mitigation measures. Although mitigation efforts may address individual classification cases, when multiple cases exhibit similarly high R_{model} values, countermeasures can be considered for them collectively. In addition, ensuring that mitigation measures do not inadvertently increase the risk of cases in which R_{model} is already sufficiently low is essential.

4.5 Step 4: Implementation of Risk Mitigation Measures

The risk mitigation measures identified during the ML component-level risk analysis are implemented. Following implementation, a comparison is made between the operation-level risk (R_{action}) and ML component-level risk (R_{model}) before and after the measures are applied to evaluate their effectiveness. If multiple countermeasures are considered, the eAI-Risk process cycle is repeated to assess their individual effects and identify the most effective risk mitigation strategy. The outcomes of applying the eAI-Risk framework, which encompasses these processes, to a virtual ADS are discussed in the following section.

5 Case Study

This section presents the results from applying eAI-Risk to a“speed limit sign classification” task, simulating challenges encountered by our industrial partner, an automated driving system development company. The selection of this topic is motivated by the following: (1) road sign recognition is a crucial ML component directly linked to safety in the automated driving systems developed by our industrial partner; (2) using a relatively easy-to-understand subject clarifies the effectiveness of the method and facilitates efficient execution of the improvement cycle; (3) the demand from industry is high for risk analysis methods applicable to systems with multiple ML components. Note that in our study, actual company data could not be used due to confidentiality. Therefore, a virtual ADS with equivalent complexity was analyzed. Our industrial partner positively evaluated the usefulness of risk identification and the improvement cycle provided by this method.

5.1 Basic Information of the Target System

The target system analyzed in this case study is a virtual ADS, where the control structure is shown in Fig. 2. Because the focus of this case study is on the classification of speed limit signs, Table 3 lists the system actions related to this scenario. Three actions are defined: *LowSpeed*, *MiddleSpeed*, and *HighSpeed*.

Table 3. ADS Actions Related to Speed Limit Sign Classification

Action	Description
LowSpeed	Driving at speeds below 30 km/h
MiddleSpeed	Driving at speeds between 30 km/h and 70 km/h
HighSpeed	Driving at speeds above 70 km/h

5.2 Operation-Level Risk Analysis Results

As previously mentioned, detailed risk evaluation cannot be performed on the target ADS due to the inability to conduct actual operation tests. Therefore, this section focuses on identifying operation-level hazards. Table 4 defines the accidents and hazards related to speed limit sign classification in ADS, where three accidents and their corresponding hazards are described. If operation tests were conducted, quantitatively analyzing and evaluating risks for more detailed decision cases, including these hazards, would be possible.

Table 4. Accidents and Hazards in ADS

Accident	Hazard
Collision between ADS and pedestrian	ADS does not slow down when approaching areas with many pedestrians
Collision between ADS and bicycle	ADS does not slow down when approaching areas with many bicycles
Collision between ADS and another vehicle	ADS drives at speeds exceeding the speed limit

5.3 ML Component-Level Risk Analysis Results

This section presents the results of risk analysis at the ML component level. Based on the control structure shown in Fig. 2, this ADS includes a classification model as an ML component. Accordingly, we extracted UCAs related to the classification of road signs by the model. Among these, UCAs related to speed limit signs include instances such as "the classification model incorrectly classifies a speed limit sign as a sign indicating a higher speed."

Next, the dataset used for training the classification model was GTSRB [21], which contains over 50,000 images of 43 types of German road signs. In this study, we conducted a risk analysis with a focus on the classification of eight types of maximum speed limit signs included in the GTSRB. A CNN-based ML model was trained on this dataset, and a confusion matrix of prediction results for each test data sample was prepared in advance using the trained model.

In addition, a control policy was defined to map each class to the corresponding ADS actions listed in Table 3. Specifically, *LowSpeed* was assigned to 20 km/h and 30 km/h, *MiddleSpeed* to 50 km/h, 60 km/h, and 70 km/h, and *HighSpeed* to 80 km/h, 100 km/h, and 120 km/h.

Next, Safety and Progress were set as risk evaluation metrics, collectively denoted as M. For each metric $k \in M$, the severity of risk for each class-action pair was evaluated on a 11-point scale from 0 to 10. The weighted average of the evaluation values $sev_k(c_t, c_r)$ for each classification case was calculated with a ratio of Safety: Progress = 3:1, resulting in S_{model}. Table 5 lists the S_{model} values for all classification cases.

In this case study, f_{model} used 0.05 intervals with probabilities exceeding 0.45 assigned the maximum score (10).

We computed O_{model} for each classification case based on Eq. 4. We then calculated R_{model} for each classification case based on Eq. 5 (Table 7). Furthermore, by extracting classification cases with the high R_{model} values shown in Table 7 and summarizing them in Table 8, we found that the classification case with the maximum risk value was the one that incorrectly classified 20 km/h as 70 km/h, as shown in Fig. 3.

Table 5. Calculation results of S_{model}

		Predicted Class							
		20km/h	30km/h	50km/h	60km/h	70km/h	80km/h	100km/h	120km/h
Ground Truth	20km/h	–	4	8	9	10	10	10	10
	30km/h	1	–	6	8	9	10	10	10
	50km/h	2	1	–	4	6	8	10	10
	60km/h	2	2	1	–	4	6	9	10
	70km/h	3	2	2	1	–	4	8	10
	80km/h	3	3	2	2	1	–	6	9
	100km/h	4	3	3	2	1	1	–	4
	120km/h	4	4	4	3	3	2	2	–

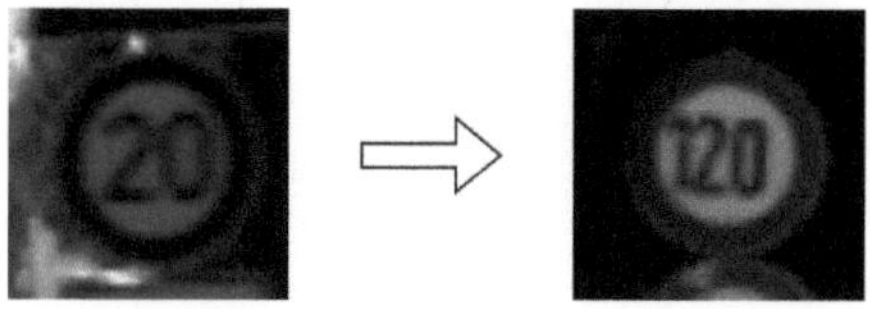

Fig. 3. Image example of the classification case with the maximum Risk Value.

Table 6. Calculation results of O_{model}

		Predicted Class							
		20km/h	30km/h	50km/h	60km/h	70km/h	80km/h	100km/h	120km/h
Ground Truth	20km/h	–	1	1	1	7	2	1	6
	30km/h	1	–	3	1	2	2	1	1
	50km/h	1	1	–	1	1	2	1	1
	60km/h	1	1	1	–	1	5	1	1
	70km/h	5	1	1	1	–	1	1	1
	80km/h	1	2	1	2	1	–	1	1
	100km/h	1	1	1	1	1	1	–	1
	120km/h	1	1	1	1	1	1	1	–

Table 7. Calculation results of R_{model}

		Predicted Class							
		20km/h	30km/h	50km/h	60km/h	70km/h	80km/h	100km/h	120km/h
Ground Truth	20km/h	–	4	8	9	70	20	10	60
	30km/h	1	–	18	8	18	20	10	10
	50km/h	2	1	–	4	6	16	10	10
	60km/h	2	2	1	–	4	30	9	10
	70km/h	15	2	2	1	–	4	8	10
	80km/h	3	6	2	4	1	–	6	9
	100km/h	4	3	3	2	1	1	–	4
	120km/h	4	4	4	3	3	2	2	–

We extracted high-risk classification cases as UCAs using the classification model. Figure 3 presents an actual image example of the UCA with the maximum risk value.

5.4 Consideration and Implementation of Risk Mitigation Measures and Re-Analysis of Risks

To mitigate the risks associated with the identified classification cases, we employed various deep-learning-based model repair methods [20]. Specifically,

Table 8. High-risk classification cases

High-risk classification cases	R_{model}
Classification model misclassified 20 km/h as 70 km/h	70
Classification model misclassified 20 km/h as 120 km/h	60
Classification model misclassified 60 km/h as 80 km/h	30
Classification model misclassified 30 km/h as 80 km/h	20
Classification model misclassified 30 km/h as 50 km/h	18
Classification model misclassified 50 km/h as 80 km/h	16

Table 9. High-risk classification cases after classification model repair

High-risk classification cases	R_{model}
Classification model misclassified 60 km/h as 80 km/h	18
Classification model misclassified 80 km/h as 30 km/h	12
Classification model misclassified 120 km/h as 20 km/h	12
Classification model misclassified 80 km/h as 60 km/h	6
Classification model misclassified 120 km/h as 60 km/h	6
Classification model misclassified 100 km/h as 30 km/h	6

based on the magnitude of R_{model} as listed in Table 8, we set priorities for the 20 km/h and 60 km/h classes in this order to achieve local improvements of the classification model. In addition, after implementing the classification model repair, we recalculated R_{model} for each classification case and re-extracted high-risk classification cases (Table 9). We discuss the results of this case study in the next section.

6 Discussion

In this section, we present the results of our case study. Building on the discussion of eAI-Risk in Sect. 4 and the risk analysis example provided in Sect. 5, we identified three key properties of eAI-Risk: (i) systematic integration of operation-level and ML component-level risk analysis with uncertainty quantification, (ii) transparent and traceable risk factor identification with quantitative ranking capabilities, and (iii) practical integration with existing engineering workflows.

(i) eAI-Risk systematically integrates operation-level (action decision) and ML component-level (classification) risk analysis within a coherent framework, distinguishing between "operation level" and "ML component level" for independent risk assessments. By incorporating uncertainty quantification through confusion matrices, eAI-Risk systematically accounts for both ML classification uncertainty and decision uncertainty using empirical evidence while enabling risk analysis independent of the dependency relationships among actions and classes.

This approach comprehensively addresses the methodological integration gaps (C1).

(ii) eAI-Risk provides transparent and traceable mechanisms for identifying risk factors and their propagation from misclassification to unsafe system actions. The method enables quantitative risk scoring and ranking that encompasses both operation and component layers, facilitating effective prioritization of mitigation efforts based on comparable risk values across various decision and classification scenarios. These features comprehensively address the analytical capability limitations (C2).

(iii) The method's integration with existing engineering workflows and provision of timely decision support demonstrate progress toward addressing practical deployment barriers (C3). The industrial partner has positively assessed the method's practical applicability, though further development of application support tools and comprehensive evaluation across diverse ML system types remains necessary for full deployment.

These features of eAI-Risk facilitate the analysis of safety risks associated with the uncertainties present in ML systems.

6.1 Effectiveness of Risk Mitigation Measures

We evaluate the utility of eAI-Risk by examining the effectiveness of the implemented risk mitigation measures. In the case study, ML model repairs were executed for high-risk classification cases. As Tables 8 and 9 show, R_{model} was reduced overall following classification model repair. Particularly for 20 km/h and 60 km/h classification cases, which were prioritized during model repair, R_{model} decreased in all cases. This outcome indicates that eAI-Risk effectively identifies high-risk cases and supports the implementation of comprehensive risk mitigation strategies.

6.2 Industrial Value and Evaluation

From an industrial value perspective, our industrial partner has provided the following feedback evaluating eAI-Risk's practical contributions.

- The framework supports multi-component ML systems, making it especially valuable for domains like autonomous driving, where interdependencies between components are complex.
- It provides a structured pathway for integrating safety analysis into development pipelines, enhancing decision support and risk governance.

These evaluations confirm that eAI-Risk offers significant practical value by providing systematic risk analysis capabilities that are essential for safe ML system deployment in industrial settings. The positive industry feedback validates the method's potential for real-world application and its alignment with practical safety engineering needs.

6.3 Current Limitations and Challenges

Based on feedback from our industrial partner, eAI-Risk faces several challenges that require further attention.

First, the improvement cycle currently focuses on classification tasks; extending it to other ML paradigms (e.g., regression or reinforcement learning) may require additional adaptation.

Second, the method currently lacks full integration with safety standards like ISO 26262, which could limit its adoption in regulated industries. While eAI-Risk provides a systematic framework for risk analysis, establishing formal mappings between its risk metrics and standardized safety integrity levels remains an open challenge that requires collaboration with regulatory bodies.

Third, the current severity and occurrence scales, while intuitive, lack empirical validation across different application domains, potentially leading to inconsistent risk assessments when applied to diverse ML systems.

Fourth, there is no mention of integration with cost models or metrics, which are often essential for enterprise-level resource planning. Industrial deployment requires consideration of the economic trade-offs between risk mitigation measures and their implementation costs, an aspect not currently addressed by the framework.

Finally, full deployment in industry will require tool support and broader validation across diverse ML system types. The manual nature of the current process limits scalability, and comprehensive validation across various ML architectures and application domains is necessary to establish the method's generalizability.

These limitations highlight the need for continued development to enhance the method's applicability and ensure its alignment with industrial requirements and regulatory frameworks.

6.4 Future Research Directions

Several future research directions are motivated by the current challenges and limitations identified in eAI-Risk. First, to address the current focus on classification tasks, future work should extend the framework to other ML paradigms such as regression and reinforcement learning. This will require adapting risk quantification and mitigation strategies to accommodate different output types and decision-making processes.

Second, integration with established safety standards such as ISO 26262 and SOTIF is essential for industrial adoption. Future research should focus on mapping eAI-Risk's risk metrics to standardized safety integrity levels and developing formal processes that align with regulatory requirements. This will facilitate broader acceptance and deployment in safety-critical domains. However, Henriksson et al. [7] points out that current ISO 26262 standards present difficulties for direct application to ML systems. Therfore, the development of novel approaches are required to functional safety that are specifically designed to accommodate ML systems' unique characteristics.

Third, to improve scalability and consistency, it is necessary to develop tool support for automating the risk analysis process and to empirically validate severity and occurrence scales across diverse application domains. Incorporating cost-benefit analysis into the framework will also enable more informed decision-making regarding risk mitigation measures in industrial settings.

7 Conclusion

This study proposed eAI-Risk, a data-driven, scenario-based risk analysis method for ML systems. Through case studies with our industrial partner, we demonstrated the effectiveness of this method in addressing safety risk analysis challenges. The key contributions of this research are summarized as follows:

- We provided a detailed process for eAI-Risk, tackling the safety risk analysis challenges faced by ML systems in industry.
- We illustrated how eAI-Risk outperforms existing methods and validated its practicality through evaluations conducted with an industrial partner.
- We showcased an efficient cycle from risk identification to improvement using a road sign recognition task, which is essential for developing automated driving systems.

Despite the promise eAI-Risk holds for industrial applications, several challenges remain, including the need for standardized evaluation scales and objective criteria for assessing risk values. Future work will focus on developing application support tools, establishing connections with safety standards such as SIL and ASIL [14], and integrating eAI-Risk into comprehensive frameworks for ML system development, such as M^3S [8]. By continuing collaboration with the industrial partner, we aim to expand the practical application of our method to more extensive and complex ML systems.

Acknowledgement. This work was supported in part by the Japan Society for the Promotion of Science (JSPS) KAKENHI Program under Grant 21KK0179 and Grant 23K18470, and in part by the Japan Science and Technology Agency (JST)-Mirai Program under Grant JPMJMI20B8.

References

1. Cai, Y.: Safety analytics for AI systems. In: International Conference on Human-Computer Interaction, pp. 434–448. Springer (2020)
2. Dong, Y., et al.: Reliability assessment and safety arguments for machine learning components in system assurance. ACM Trans. Embedded Comput. Syst. **22**(3), 1–48 (2023)
3. Earthy, J.: Hazard and operability study as an approach to software safety assessment. In: IEE Colloquium on Hazard Analysis, pp. 5–1. IET (1992)
4. Frankel, E.G., Frankel, E.G.: Failure mode and effects analysis—fault tree analysis. Systems Reliability and Risk Analysis, pp. 64–82 (1988)

5. de Gelder, E., et al.: Scenario-based safety assessment of automated driving systems. Tech. rep., Nederlandse Organisatie voor Toegepast Natuurwetenschappelijk Onderzoek (TNO) (2024)
6. Grey, M., Segerie, C.R.: Safety by measurement: a systematic literature review of AI safety evaluation methods. arXiv preprint arXiv:2505.05541 (2025)
7. Henriksson, J., Borg, M., Englund, C.: Automotive safety and machine learning: Initial results from a study on how to adapt the ISO 26262 safety standard. In: Proceedings of the 1st International Workshop on Software Engineering for AI in Autonomous Systems, pp. 47–49 (2018)
8. Husen, J.H., et al.: Integrated multi-view modeling for reliable machine learning-intensive software engineering. Software Qual. J. **32**(3), 1239–1285 (2024)
9. Jordan, M.I., Mitchell, T.M.: Machine learning: trends, perspectives, and prospects. Science **349**(6245), 255–260 (2015)
10. Kononenko, I.: Machine learning for medical diagnosis: history, state of the art and perspective. Artif. Intell. Med. **23**(1), 89–109 (2001)
11. Koopman, P., Wagner, M.: Challenges in autonomous vehicle testing and validation. SAE Int. J. Transp. Safety **4**(1), 15–24 (2016)
12. Krishnan, R., Bhada, S.V.: Integrated system design and safety framework for model-based safety assessment. IEEE Access **10**, 79311–79334 (2022)
13. Leveson, N.G., Thomas, J.P.: STPA handbook (2018)
14. Nouri, A., Warmuth, J.: IEC 61508 and ISO 26262 – a comparison study. In: Proceedings of the 5th International Conference on System Reliability and Safety (ICSRS), pp. 138–142 (2021)
15. Okubo, T., Husen, J.H., Washizaki, H., Yoshioka, N., Fukazawa, Y.: Safety analysis and risk quantification method for machine learning systems (in japanese). In: Technical Report on Software Engineering (SE), pp. 1–8. Information Processing Society of Japan (IPSJ) (2024)
16. Park, S., Park, H.: Pier: cyber-resilient risk assessment model for connected and autonomous vehicles. Wireless Netw. **30**(5), 4591–4605 (2022)
17. Salay, R., Angus, M., Czarnecki, K.: A safety analysis method for perceptual components in automated driving. In: Proceedings of the 30th IEEE International Symposium on Software Reliability Engineering (ISSRE), pp. 24–34 (2019)
18. Salhab, W., Ameyed, D., Jaafar, F., Mcheick, H.: A systematic literature review on AI safety: identifying trends, challenges and future directions. IEEE Access (2024)
19. Sharma, P., Singh, A.: Overview of fault tree analysis. Int. J. Eng. Res. Technol. **4**(3), 337–340 (2015)
20. Sohn, J., Kang, S., Yoo, S.: Arachne: search-based repair of deep neural networks. ACM Trans. Softw. Eng. Methodol. **32**(4), 1–26 (2023)
21. Stallkamp, J., Schlipsing, M., Salmen, J., Igel, C.: Man vs. computer: benchmarking machine learning algorithms for traffic sign recognition. Neural Netw. **32**, 323–332 (2012)
22. Tan, S., Taeihagh, A., Baxter, K.: The risks of machine learning systems. arXiv preprint arXiv:2204.09852 (2022)
23. Varshney, K.R.: Engineering safety in machine learning. In: 2016 Information Theory and Applications Workshop (ITA), pp. 1–5. IEEE (2016)
24. Varshney, K.R., Alemzadeh, H.: On the safety of machine learning: cyber-physical systems, decision sciences, and data products. Big Data **5**(3), 246–255 (2017)

25. Vogt, T., et al.: A comprehensive risk management approach to information security in intelligent transport systems. SAE Int. J. Transp. Cybersecur. Privacy **4**(1), 39–58 (2021)
26. Wang, Y., Chung, S.H.: Artificial intelligence in safety-critical systems: a systematic review. Industr. Manag. Data Syst. **122**(2), 442–470 (2022)

Similarity Evaluation Between Queries and Chunks in RAG Systems

Shun Noguchi[1(✉)], Kozo Okano[1], Shipei Ogata[1], and Shin Nakajima[2]

[1] Shinshu University, 4–17–1 Wakasato, Nagano-shi, Nagano 380–8553, Japan
25w6074a@shinshu-u.ac.jp, {okano,ogata}@cs.shinshu-u.ac.jp
[2] National Institute of Informatics, 2–1–2 Hitotsubashi, Chiyoda-ku, Tokyo 101–8430, Japan
nkjm@nii.ac.jp

Abstract. While Large Language Models (LLMs) demonstrate excellent performance, their output depends on pre-trained knowledge. It has been pointed out that LLMs have various problems, such as generating outdated or incorrect information and they cannot always generate accurate answers. Retrieval-Augmented Generation (RAG) is a technical means that can mitigate the aforementioned problems by connecting an external database to LLM and retrieving relevant information from it, thereby making it possible to utilize a piece of information not learnt. However, it is difficult to always obtain expected answers even with RAG, and one of the reasons for this is the inability to obtain chunks that contain correct answers to user questions or requests, that is, queries. We consider it important to quantitatively evaluate the effect of structure inside the obtained chunks. In this paper, we focus on the similarity between queries and chunks in RAG architecture. The experiments use three embedding models for validation, and the results show that some models tend to increase the cosine similarity when the relevant words of the query are located at the beginning of the chunks. On the other hand, no such tendency was observed when the related words were placed near the end of the chunk, suggesting that the location of the related words influences the accuracy of acquiring chunks.

Keywords: LLM · RAG · readout performance · embedding · Wilcoxon signed-rank test

1 Introduction

Large Language Models (LLMs) demonstrate excellent performance; however, their knowledge depends on pre-trained data. Therefore, they cannot reflect new facts or information and may generate content based on outdated knowledge [1]. Additionally, despite the increased model and data scale of recent LLMs [2], the issue of generating incorrect answers as if they were facts (hallucination) still occurs [3]. This phenomenon can occur even with general questions; however, it is known to be more pronounced in fields requiring specialized knowledge

© The Author(s), under exclusive license to Springer Nature Singapore Pte Ltd. 2026
Y. Chen et al. (Eds.): SFPVV 2025, LNCS 16356, pp. 98–111, 2026.
https://doi.org/10.1007/978-981-95-6032-5_7

[4]. In application domains such as medicine or law, it is essential to adopt an approach that combines LLMs with other methods and information sources to improve response accuracy.

Retrieval-Augmented Generation (RAG) is a technology that incorporates external knowledge into an LLM, enabling it to search that external data for highly relevant text to the user's query and generate the latest, most reliable information. RAG is expected to reduce the aforementioned issues [2] and be practicalized in various applications, such as chatbot systems using internal documents within companies. However, even with RAG, it is difficult to always obtain accurate answers, and various studies are being conducted to improve accuracy of RAG systems. Many of these studies aim to improve RAG performance by developing enhanced architectures such as Self-RAG [5] and CRAG [6], and evaluating their precision. On the other hand, no studies have investigated the factors affecting the chunks acquired by RAG systems. Since the content generated by the LLM depends on the chunks obtained, obtaining appropriate chunks has a significant impact on the final response accuracy.

Therefore, in this paper, we quantitatively evaluate how the position of query-related words within a chunk affects the similarity between the query and the chunk. We evaluate multiple embedding models using medical data, assuming that RAG is used in medical chatbots. When a query-related word appears at the beginning or end of a chunk, we calculate the difference in similarity between the preceding and subsequent chunk groups using that chunk as a reference. By conducting statistical analysis and effect size evaluation on these differences, we investigate the impact of related word position on similarity. Additionally, we examine whether the presence or absence of an answer within a chunk influences this effect.

This paper is structured as follows: Sect. 2 provides a review of related work. Section 3 provides explanations of key terms in preparation for the study. Section 4 describes experimental methods. Section 5 presents the results, and Sect. 6 discusses them. Finally, Sect. 7 summarizes the study.

2 Related Work

The relationship between word position and LLM performance has been experimentally investigated for some time. Liu et al. [7] systematically varied the position of relevant information within a prompt and demonstrated that LLMs struggle to effectively utilize information appearing in the middle of the input, while relying more heavily on information located at the beginning or the end. This phenomenon, known as "Lost in the Middle," becomes more pronounced as the input length increases. The authors also investigated whether instruction fine-tuning could mitigate this position dependence and found that it slightly reduced the performance gap across positions. Nevertheless, the Lost in the Middle phenomenon persisted, indicating that position bias remained even after the tuning process.

RAG is important for developing practical systems because it improves the factual accuracy and transparency of models, enabling them to generate verifiable, knowledge-based, and trustworthy responses. Existing research on RAG has primarily focused on enhancing the reliability of retrieved information and the factual consistency of generated outputs. For instance, Self-RAG (Self-Reflective Retrieval-Augmented Generation) [5] integrates a self-reflection mechanism into the RAG framework to enhance the quality of retrieval and generation. Unlike standard RAG, Self-RAG performs retrieval on demand and evaluates the relevance and factual consistency of the retrieved passages during generation. Similarly, CRAG (Corrective Retrieval-Augmented Generation) [6] extends the RAG framework by incorporating a retrieval evaluator that assesses the quality of the retrieved evidence prior to generation. Based on this evaluation, the model takes corrective action, such as refining or replacing unreliable sections, to improve the reliability of the generated output. However, these frameworks lack a mechanism to control word positions within the retrieved context and may therefore exhibit a similar problem to that discussed in [7].

In the case of RAG, since text is pre-split into chunks, performance may vary depending on the boundaries of these chunks. Following the perspective discussed in [7], it is therefore necessary to investigate RAG's behavior while considering its characteristics, such as how it identifies key information from the input prompt and selects relevant chunks.

3 Preliminaries

This section describes the terminology related to experiments.

3.1 RAG

RAG is a technology to address the issues of outdated knowledge and hallucinations in LLMs. Figure 1 shows the basic architecture of a RAG system. In RAG, documents used as external knowledge are divided into chunks before being stored in a vector database. The vector database stores document embedding vectors, enabling efficient and fast retrieval [10]. The RAG process consists of two stages, implemented as the retriever and generator.

Retriever. The retriever first converts user queries into embedding vectors. It then uses these embeddings to calculate the similarity to chunks stored in the vector database. The top-k most relevant chunks are retrieved from the vector database based on their similarity to the query and passed to subsequent processing. The role of the retriever is to identify relevant context for the query and provide the necessary information to answer it.

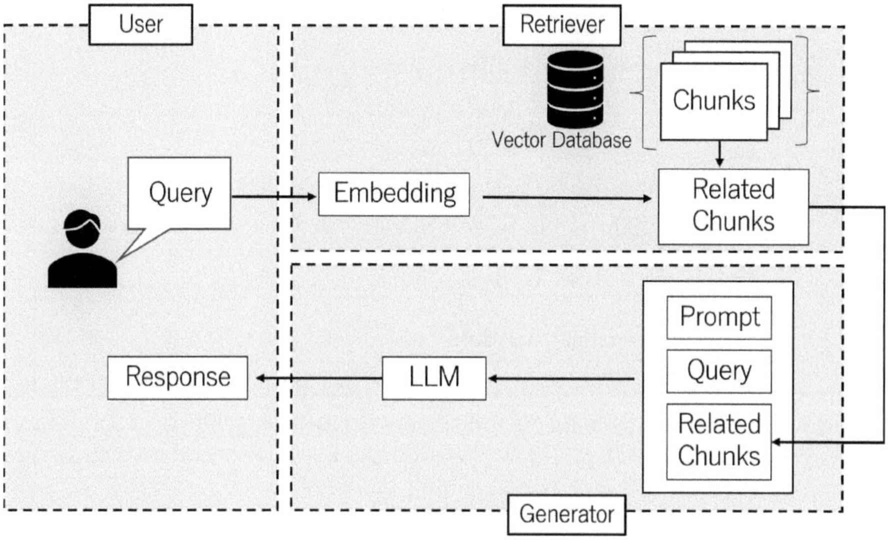

Fig. 1. RAG architecture.

Generator. The generator combines three types of input—the relevant chunks retrieved by the retriever, the user's question, and a system prompt that provides the LLM with a role and instructions—and passes them to the LLM. The generator's role is to generate a response to the user's query with the LLM based on this information.

3.2 Embedding

Embedding is the process of converting data, such as text, audio, and images, into numerical vectors. Embedding spaces are characterized by their ability to place semantically similar data close to each other, and they are widely used in natural language processing and information retrieval [8,9].

3.3 Cosine Similarity

In this study, we use cosine similarity to evaluate the similarity between queries and chunks. Existing studies on RAG often use cosine similarity to calculate similarities [11,12]. This approach is also considered one of the most effective for measuring similarity in RAG. Cosine similarity is calculated as the scalar product of two vectors divided by the product of their magnitudes, thereby measuring only the similarity in direction without being affected by vector length. Cosine similarity takes values in the range of -1 to 1, with values closer to 1 indicating greater similarity. The calculation of cosine similarity is expressed by Eq. (1) when two vectors are denoted as $\mathbf{A} = (a_1, a_2, \ldots, a_n)$ and $\mathbf{B} = (b_1, b_2, \ldots, b_n)$.

$$\textbf{Cosine similarity} = \frac{\mathbf{A} \cdot \mathbf{B}}{\|\mathbf{A}\| \, \|\mathbf{B}\|} \tag{1}$$

4 Experiments

In this section, we explain the data and models used, define the research questions, and describe the experimental procedure.

4.1 Data and Embedding Models

For this experiment, we use rare disease data provided by the Ministry of Health, Labour and Welfare [14]. These documents are divided into chunks of 300 characters. We also use OpenAI's [13] text-embedding-3-small, text-embedding-3-large, and text-embedding-ada-002 as embedding models to vectorize the documents and analyze how the pattern of similarity differs among the models.

4.2 Research Questions

The aim of this study is to answer research questions with respect to query-related words, where a query-related word is a piece of information primarily concerned with the user query. However, it is not clear which words are considered related when calculating similarity. In this study, therefore, query-related words are defined as words that either fully or partially match words within the query. Furthermore, ten queries were manually created based on the content of the rare disease dataset, to ensure that each had a corresponding answer included within it.

Based on these definitions and experimental conditions, the following research questions (RQs) are defined in this study.

RQ1: Does the position of query-related words within a chunk affect the similarity scores?
RQ2: Does the presence or absence of answers to queries within chunks affect the similarity scores?

4.3 Experimental Setup

We explain the experimental setup for RQ1 and RQ2. When a query-related word appears at the beginning or end of a chunk, that chunk is denoted as C. With respect to C, the sets of the preceding n chunks and succeeding n chunks are denoted as $\mathcal{P}_n$ and $\mathcal{N}_n$, respectively. Here, $n \in \{7, 10, 15, 30\}$. Cosine similarity is represented by $s(\cdot)$. The medians of $\mathcal{P}_n$ and $\mathcal{N}_n$ are denoted as P_n and N_n, respectively. The difference between the similarity of chunk C and these medians is denoted as Δ, that is, $\Delta^{(n)}_{\text{prev}} = s(C) - P_n$ and $\Delta^{(n)}_{\text{next}} = s(C) - N_n$.

Query : 天疱瘡の原因は何ですか?
(What are the causes of pemphigus?)

	chunks	Cosine Similarity	
$\mathcal{P}_7$	られる。 2．原因 天疱瘡の基本的…	0.569499945	
$\mathcal{P}_7$	れる。 2．原因 天疱瘡の基本的な …	0.571372206	P_7
$\mathcal{P}_7$	る。 2．原因 天疱瘡の基本的な病…	0.571870775	
$\mathcal{P}_7$	。 2．原因 天疱瘡の基本的な病態…	0.555627154	
$\mathcal{P}_7$	2．原因 天疱瘡の基本的な病態生…	0.56262654	
$\mathcal{P}_7$	2．原因 天疱瘡の基本的な病態生理…	0.575420039	
$\mathcal{P}_7$	．原因 天疱瘡の基本的な病態生理は…	0.576904729	
C	原因 (cause) 天疱瘡 (pemphigus) の基本的な病態生理は、…	0.575007728	
$\mathcal{N}_7$	因 天疱瘡の基本的な病態生理は、I…	0.555059241	
$\mathcal{N}_7$	天疱瘡の基本的な病態生理は、Ig…	0.523006575	
$\mathcal{N}_7$	天疱瘡の基本的な病態生理は、IgG…	0.532921712	N_7
$\mathcal{N}_7$	天疱瘡の基本的な病態生理は、IgG自…	0.577180145	
$\mathcal{N}_7$	疱瘡の基本的な病態生理は、IgG自己…	0.531692427	
$\mathcal{N}_7$	瘡の基本的な病態生理は、IgG自己抗…	0.54008526	
$\mathcal{N}_7$	の基本的な病態生理は、IgG自己抗体…	0.516331225	

	chunks	Cosine Similarity	
$\mathcal{P}_7$	…剤誘発性天疱瘡などが知られる。 2．	0.582084416	
$\mathcal{P}_7$	…誘発性天疱瘡などが知られる。 2．原	0.565316731	
$\mathcal{P}_7$	…発性天疱瘡などが知られる。 2．原因	0.598915926	P_7
$\mathcal{P}_7$	…性天疱瘡などが知られる。 2．原因	0.604957113	
$\mathcal{P}_7$	…天疱瘡などが知られる。 2．原因	0.599216915	
$\mathcal{P}_7$	…疱瘡などが知られる。 2．原因 天	0.604775418	
$\mathcal{P}_7$	…瘡などが知られる。 2．原因 天疱	0.582853958	
C	…などが知られる。 2．原因 (cause) 天疱瘡 (pemphigus)	0.589864642	
$\mathcal{N}_7$	…どが知られる。 2．原因 天疱瘡の	0.597387003	
$\mathcal{N}_7$	…が知られる。 2．原因 天疱瘡の基	0.592462256	
$\mathcal{N}_7$	…知られる。 2．原因 天疱瘡の基本	0.599089248	
$\mathcal{N}_7$	…られる。 2．原因 天疱瘡の基本的	0.596512102	N_7
$\mathcal{N}_7$	…れる。 2．原因 天疱瘡の基本的な	0.597434101	
$\mathcal{N}_7$	…る。 2．原因 天疱瘡の基本的な病	0.594444885	
$\mathcal{N}_7$	…。 2．原因 天疱瘡の基本的な病態	0.590303417	

Fig. 2. An example of the experimental setup for the case that n = 7, where a query-related word (in red) appears at the **beginning** of the chunk (*upper figure*) or at the **end** of the chunk (*lower figure*).

Figure 2 shows a schematic example. In the figure, the chunk sets $\mathcal{P}_n$ and $\mathcal{N}_n$ are arranged around chunk C, and query-related words appearing at the beginning or end of the chunk are highlighted in red. The statistical significance of the observed differences in $\Delta_{\text{prev}}^{(n)}$ and $\Delta_{\text{next}}^{(n)}$ obtained from the cosine similarity between chunk C and chunk groups $\mathcal{P}_n$ and $\mathcal{N}_n$ is evaluated using hypothesis testing.

In experiments for RQ2, the results of those for RQ1 are classified into incorrect chunks that do not contain answers and correct chunks that contain answers, and the same testing procedure is applied.

4.4 Wilcoxon Signed-Rank Test

In this paper, we use Wilcoxon's signed-rank test [16], a nonparametric test that is effective for verifying the differences between the medians of two corresponding conditions. Here, it is used to examine whether the differences Δ in cosine similarity between chunks C containing related words at the beginning or end of a sentence and the medians of the n preceding and succeeding chunks are significantly biased in the positive direction. The Wilcoxon signed-rank test calculates statistics based on the sign and rank of the difference. Therefore, it does not assume a normal distribution, making it robust to small sample sizes and outliers.

In the implementation, we use SciPy 1.15's scipy.stats.wilcoxon (`mode="auto"`)[15]. If either of the following conditions is met, `mode="approx"` is used to return the p-value based on a normal approximation. If neither condition is met, `mode="exact"` is used to return the exact p-value.

- For the number n of the valid pairs, $n > 50$ holds, or
- Tied ranks are included in the paired differences between two corresponding observations.

In the Case of Exact. For RQ2, the exact mode is used for correct chunks because the number of valid pairs (n) is small. First, the exact mode computes the difference between two corresponding observations, $d_i = x_i - y_i$. The sign of each is recorded, the values $|d_i|$ are then sorted in ascending order and assigned ranks R_i. The rank R_i is defined as the position of $|d_i|$ when all absolute differences $|d_1|, |d_2|, \ldots, |d_n|$ are sorted in ascending order, with average ranks assigned in the case of ties. Subsequently, the sum of the signed ranks for positive differences, denoted as T^+, is calculated.

In this paper, we assume that the difference is positive in a one-sided test, thus we use the sum of ranks corresponding to positive differences T^+ as the test statistic. This assumption came from the observation obtained from a preliminary experiment that examined the order of external knowledge. The experiment was conducted with a dataset consisting of those sections such as *Overview*, *Cause*, and *Treatment*, for which the cause of a disease were questioned. Then, we observed a systematic increase in the similarity scores when the Cause section was put at the beginning. This observation led us to the idea that the similarity increases when the query-related words appear at the beginning of a chunk.

The exact p-value is obtained by calculating T^+ for all 2^n possible sign combinations and determining the proportion of combinations in which $T^+ \geq T^+_{\text{obs}}$.

$$p_{\textbf{exact}} = \frac{\#\left\{T^+ \geq T^+_{\text{obs}}\right\}}{2^n}$$

Here, the numerator represents the number of sign combinations in which T^+ is greater than or equal to the observed value, while the denominator, 2^n represents the total number of sign combinations. This method enables an exact p-value to be calculated independently of the shape of the distribution or the sample size.

In the Case of Approx. For RQ1 and the correct chunks of RQ2, the approx mode is used. The procedure first obtains the rank sum T^+ as in the case of `mode="exact"`. The mean μ_{T^+} and variance $\sigma^2_{T^+}$ under the null hypothesis are given by the following equations.

$$\mu_{T^+} = \frac{n(n+1)}{4}$$

$$\sigma^2_{T^+} = \frac{n(n+1)(2n+1)}{24} - \frac{1}{48}\sum_j t_j(t_j+1)(2t_j+1),$$

where t_j is the number of elements in the group of rank j. The standardized score Z is calculated as follows.

$$Z = \frac{T^+ - \mu_{T^+}}{\sigma_{T^+}}$$

The p-value for a one-sided test assuming a positive difference is calculated using the cumulative distribution function Φ of the standard normal distribution as follows.

$$p_{\text{approx}} = 1 - \Phi(Z)$$

4.5 Effect Size

In the experiments, in addition to statistical significance, effect sizes are also reported as in [17]. The effect size r in the Wilcoxon signed-rank test can be expressed as

$$r = \frac{z}{\sqrt{n}}.$$

As shown in [18], the effect size r is evaluated by calculating

$$z = \Phi^{-1}(1 - p_{\text{approx}})$$

using the inverse function of the standard normal distribution from the obtained p-value. In the Wilcoxon signed-rank test, the effect size is defined as small/medium/large according to Cohen's criteria as $r = 0.1/0.3/0.5$ [19], and the effect sizes are reported in the experimental results section along with the test results.

5 Results

This section reports the experimental results for the research questions in the previous section.

5.1 RQ1

The results of the experiments for RQ1 are shown in Fig. 3. The left axis and bar graph represent the p-values, while the right axis and line graph represent the effect sizes. In Figs. 3(a), (b), and (c), a log-scale is used on the left axis because the p-values are very small. The black line in the figure represents the significance level of 0.05, and values exceeding this level are considered significant. Figure 3(d) uses a linear scale.

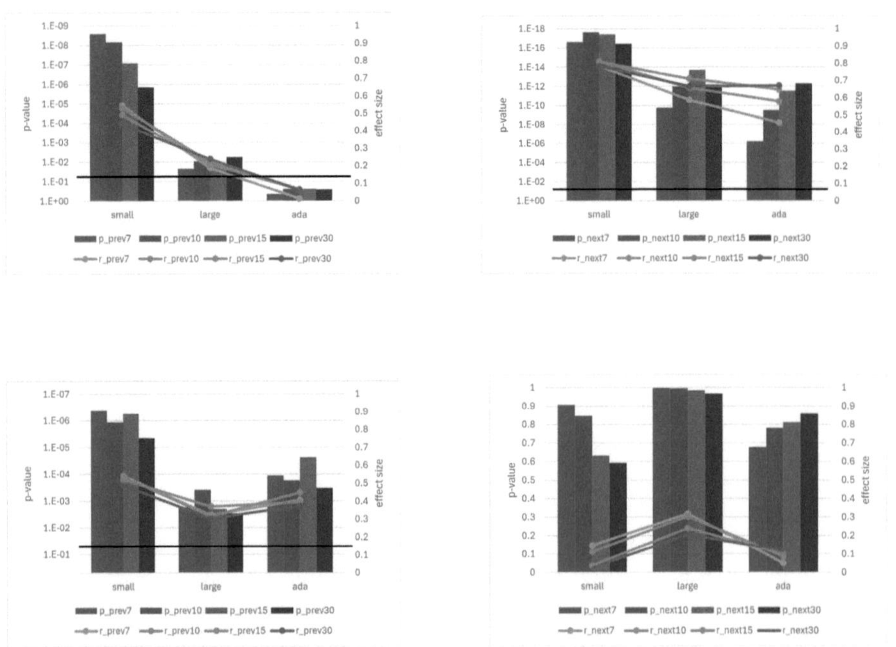

(c) Comparison between chunk with related words at the end and P_n

(d) Comparison between chunk with related words at the end and N_n

Fig. 3. Experimental results of RQ1 – Effect of the position of query-related words within a chunk on cosine similarity.

Figure 3(a) shows cases where related words move from the beginning of the sentence to the middle. The small and large models were significant; however, the ada model was not. When comparing the effect sizes of the two significant models, the small model showed a large value, while the large model showed a value of approximately 0.2, indicating a decreasing trend.

Figure 3(b) compares cases where related words disappear from the beginning of the sentence. All models were significant and showed high effect sizes; however, the large and the ada models at prev 30 showed a significant decrease in effect size.

Figure 3(c) shows the process of related words disappearing from the end of chunk sentences, with all models and prev n being significant. Regarding effect sizes, the small model showed a high effect size, while the large model and ada model showed moderate effect sizes of 0.3 to 0.4. This indicates an overall reduction in effect size compared to Fig. 3 (b) (under similar conditions at the beginning of the sentence).

In Fig. 3(d), we analyzed the differences in cosine similarity between chunks containing query-related words at the end of the chunk and the next n chunks. However, no model showed a significant effect across all values of n.

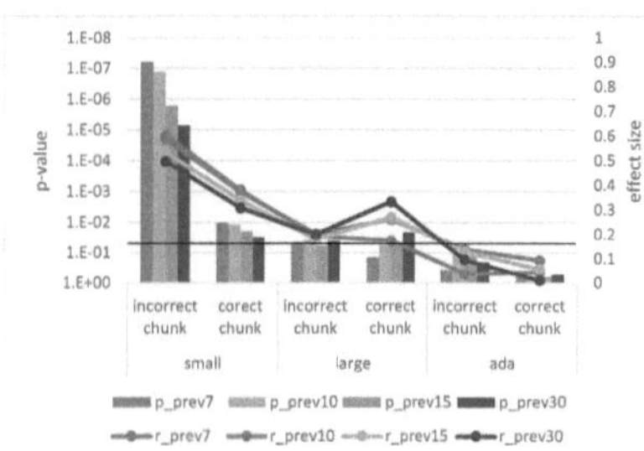

(a) Comparison between chunk with related words at the beginning and P_n

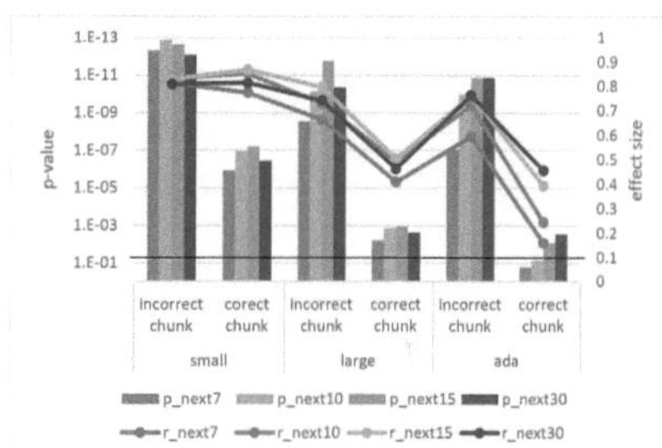

(b) Comparison between chunk with related words at the beginning and N_n

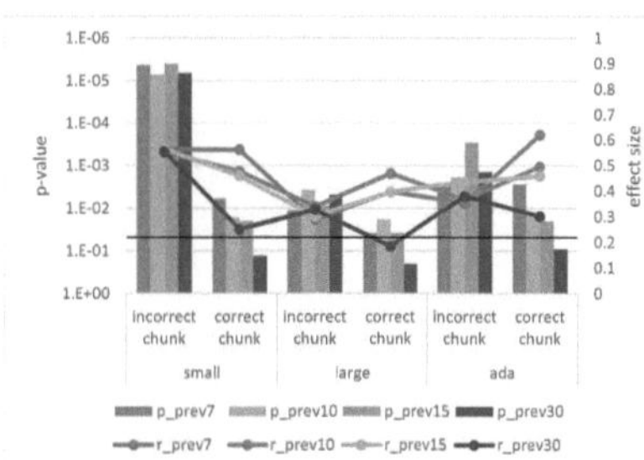

(c) Comparison between chunk with related words at the end and P_n

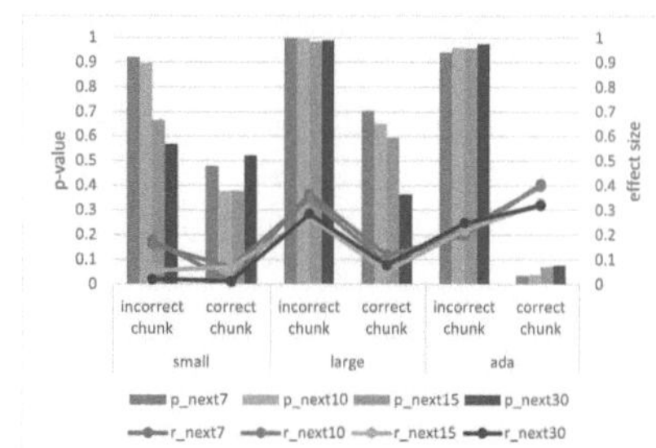

(d) Comparison between chunk with related words at the end and N_n

Fig. 4. Experimental results of RQ2 – Effect of answer inclusion within chunks on cosine similarity.

5.2 RQ2

The experimental results of RQ2 were obtained by classifying the experimental results of RQ1 into chunks that contain answers to the queries and chunks that did not. The results are shown in Fig. 4, where incorrect chunks are those not to contain answers, and correct chunks are those to contain answers. Figure 4(a), (b), and (c) use a log-scale, while Fig. 4(d) uses a linear scale.

In Fig. 4(a), the small model was significant regardless of whether the answer was included. The effect size was large for incorrect chunks; however, it decreased to moderate for correct ones. The large model was not significant for incorrect chunk prev 15, and for correct chunks prev 10 and 15. The effect size was the opposite of the small model, with a tendency for correct chunks to be higher at prev 10, 15, and 30, which were moderate or higher.

In Fig. 4(b), all models except for some results of the ada model were significant for correct chunks. In addition, the effect size tended to decrease when the large model and the ada model were not significant for correct chunks.

When the related words were at the end of the chunk, first, in Fig. 4(c), only prev 30 of each model's correct chunk was not significant, while all others were significant. Furthermore, in terms of effect size, for incorrect chunks, the small model was large, the ada model was moderate or higher, and the large model was moderate and stable for all prev n. However, for correct chunks, there was a tendency for prev 30 to decrease significantly.

In Fig. 4(d), the ada model shows significance and moderate to large effect sizes for correct chunks where $n = 7$ and 10. On the other hand, even the large model, which is completely insignificant, shows moderate effect sizes for incorrect chunks.

6 Discussion

Here, we summarize the discussion.

6.1 RQ1

For some embedding models, the position of query-related words within a chunk affects the similarity scores. This effect was observed in both small and large models, especially in the small models. The reason for this can be derived from a comparison of Figs. 3(a) and (d), as well as Figs. 3(b) and (c).

First, we discuss Figs. 3(a) and (d). In both cases, the chunk groups being compared contain query-related words that specify the reference chunk C, therefore the conditions are equivalent. Figure 3(a) shows the case where the query-related words appear at the beginning of the chunk. In this case, cosine similarity increases significantly in both small and large models, with a particularly large effect size in the small model. Figure 3(d) represents the case where query-related words appear at the end of the chunk, however, no statistical significance was observed. This indicates that the increase in similarity is strongly observed only when related words are located at the beginning of the chunk.

Next, consider a comparison of Figs. 3(b) and (c). In both cases, the chunk groups being compared do not contain query-related words that specify the reference chunk C. Figure 3(b) corresponds to the case where query-related words appear at the beginning of a chunk, while Fig. 3(c) corresponds to the case where they appear at the end. Statistically significant results were obtained in both cases. However, the overall effect size in (b) is larger than in (c). This suggests that having query-related words at the beginning of a chunk has a greater impact on improving similarity scores than having them at the end.

In summary, we can conclude that query-related words tend to increase similarity when they are located at the beginning of a chunk, while their impact on similarity is smaller when they are located at the end. Therefore, RQ1 is partially supported.

6.2 RQ2

For some embedding models, the presence or absence of answers to queries within chunks affected the similarity scores. This effect was observed in both small and large models; however, it was more pronounced in the small model.

As shown in Figs. 4(a) and 4(b), the small model exhibits statistically significant results with at least a medium effect size when query-related words appear at the beginning of a chunk, regardless of whether the chunk contains an answer. Notably, Fig. 4(a) indicates that, when compared with the preceding chunk group $\mathcal{P}_n$, the similarity becomes excessively high when query-related words are located at the beginning of a chunk that does not contain an answer.

Similarly, Figs. 4(a) and (b) show that statistical significance was observed even when query-related words appeared at the beginning of chunks in the large models. However, in Fig. 4(a), the effect size was small for both correct and incorrect chunks, and in Fig. 4(b), the effect size for correct chunks decreased significantly. This is probably because the large model is more expressive than the small model, enabling it to capture the overall semantic context rather than relying solely on the positional effect of query-related words.

On the other hand, in the ada model, the effect size varied considerably depending on the value of n in the correct chunk shown in Fig. 4(a). Furthermore, statistical significance was occasionally observed in the correct chunk shown in Fig. 4. The ada model exhibited tendencies that were different from those of the other two models, which may reflect performance differences due to generational variations among the models.

These results partially support RQ2, as the position effect was stronger in incorrect chunks than in correct ones. However, the extent of this effect varied depending on the model's performance.

7 Conclusion

This study analyzed the similarity between queries and chunks in RAG architecture and examined the influence of the placement of the query-related words within chunks on the similarity. Although differences existed between models, both the latest small and large models showed a tendency for similarity to increase when related words appeared at the beginning of a chunk. This was particularly pronounced in the small model. If query-related words unrelated to the answer appear near the beginning of a chunk, the similarity of that chunk may be unjustifiably inflated. As a result, noise may be introduced into the top-k chunks passed to the LLM, thereby reducing retrieval accuracy and ultimately having a negative impact on response quality. Therefore, the findings of this study suggest that position-aware chunk design is indispensable for improving retrieval accuracy in RAG systems.

Future work includes introducing weighting schemes based on the position of related words and improving RAG accuracy by optimizing the overlap strategy. Furthermore, since this study used only OpenAI models, verification of the impact on other models is also necessary. These efforts are expected to further advance the utilization of RAG across various fields, such as document search and chatbot functionality.

Acknowledgements. Part of this research was supported by Grant-in-Aid for Scientific Research C21K11826.

References

1. Aleksandra, P., et al.: Retrieval-augmented generation for knowledge-intensive NLP tasks. In: Thirty-Fourth Annual Conference on Neural Information Processing Systems, pp. 9459–9474 (2020)
2. Ryan, L.: Training language models to follow instructions with human feedback. In: The Thirty Sixth Annual Conference on Neural Information Processing Systems (2022)
3. Gary, M.: The next decade in ai: four steps towards robust artificial intelligence (2020). https://arxiv.org/abs/2002.06177
4. Alex, M., Akari, A., Victor, Z., Rajarshi, D., Daniel, K., Hannaneh, H.: When not to trust language models: investigating effectiveness of parametric and non-parametric memories. In: Proceedings of the 61st Annual Meeting of the Association for Computational Linguistics (Volume 1: Long Papers) (2023)
5. Akari, A., Zeqiu, W., Yizhong, W., Avirup, S., Hannaneh, H.: Self-RAG: learning to retrieve, generate, and critique through self-reflection. In: The Twelfth International Conference on Learning Representations (2024)
6. Shi-Qi, Y., Jia-Chen, G., Yun, Z., Zhen-Hua, L.: Corrective Retrieval Augmented Generation (2024). https://arxiv.org/abs/2401.15884
7. Nelson, F.L., et al.: Lost in the Middle: How Language Models Use Long Contexts Transactions of the Association for Computational Linguistics, pp. 157–173 (2024)
8. Alec, R., et al.: Learning transferable visual models from natural language supervision. In: Proceedings of the 38th International Conference on Machine Learning, pp. 8748-8763, (2021)
9. Bhavika, D., et al.: Learning spatially-aware language and audio embeddings. In: 38th Conference on Neural Information Processing Systems, pp. 33505–33537 (2024)

10. Vladimir, K., et al.: Dense passage retrieval for open-domain question answering,. In: Proceedings of the 2020 Conference on Empirical Methods in Natural Language Processing, pp. 6769–6781 (2020)
11. Scott, B., Stefanus, K., Srikanth, T., Zach, B., Mohamed, A.: Seven failure points when engineering a retrieval augmented generation system. In: 3rd International Conference on AI Engineering– Software Engineering for AI, pp. 194-199 (2024)
12. Yunfan, G., et al.: Retrieval-Augmented Generation for Large Language Models: A Survey. https://arxiv.org/pdf/2312.10997 (2024)
13. OpenAI: https://openai.com/ja-JP/. Accessed 19 May 2025
14. Ministry of Health, Labour and Welfare. https://www.mhlw.go.jp/stf/seisakunitsuite/bunya/0000084783.html (in Japanese). Accessed 2 Nov 2024
15. Scipy. https://docs.scipy.org/doc/scipy/reference/generated/scipy.stats.wilcoxon.html. Accessed 19 May 2025
16. Jonathan, R., Yoav, B.: Another Argument in Favour of Wilcoxon's Signed Rank Test. https://arxiv.org/abs/1311.5354 (2013)
17. Ronald, L.W., Nicole, A.L.: The ASA's Statement on p-Values: Context, Process, and Purpose, The American Statistician (2016)
18. Maciej, T., Ewa, T.-Ł.: The Need to Report Effect Size Estimates Revisited. An Overview of Some Recommended Measures of Effect Size, rends in Sport Sciences, vol. 1 (21), pp. 19–25, (2014)
19. Nadine, M.N., Alexandle, P., Jony, A.P., Jr., Alex, A.F.: Is p-value < 0.05 enough? a study on the statistical evaluation of classifies. Knowl. Eng. Rev. **35**, e4 (2020)

A Support Tool for Verification of Simulation Relations Between State Machines with Maude

Takanori Ishibashi[1(✉)], Masaki Nakamura[2], and Kazuhiro Ogata[1]

[1] Japan Advanced Institute of Science and Technology (JAIST), Nomi, Japan
{takanori.ishibashi,ogata}@jaist.ac.jp
[2] Toyama Prefectural University, Imizu, Japan
masaki-n@pu-toyama.ac.jp

Abstract. Model checking is a powerful verification technique, but it often suffers from the state space explosion problem. Combining model checking with simulation relations is one possible way to mitigate this problem. However, the integrated formal verification technique requires a plenty amount of manual effort, which is both time-consuming and prone to human error. This paper presents a support tool that automates the major steps of this verification process. The tool is implemented in Maude and leverages its meta-programming facilities to systematically verify the simulation relation for each state transition. It automates a complex sequence of verification commands and handles case splitting for states with associative-commutative properties. We demonstrate the tool's practical effectiveness through a case study where we formally verify that the Alternating Bit Protocol is simulated by a more abstract protocol. The tool enhances the efficiency and reliability of the verification process by reducing manual intervention.

Keywords: Simulation · Meta-programming · Maude · Model checking

1 Introduction

Model checking [5] is a powerful verification technique widely used to ensure the correctness and reliability of hardware and software systems. The primary challenge in model checking is the state space explosion problem, which makes the verification of large systems computationally intractable. Various techniques have been proposed to mitigate this problem, including abstraction [1,2,4,6,8,17] and partial order reduction [2,7]. Nevertheless, the challenge persists. Therefore, developing more scalable verification methods remains a critical research area.

To mitigate the state space explosion problem, Ishibashi and Ogata proposed a technique based on combining model checking with simulation relations [15]. This technique verifies an invariant property of a state machine M via a simulation relation to a more abstract state machine M_A. The approach relies on the

© The Author(s), under exclusive license to Springer Nature Singapore Pte Ltd. 2026
Y. Chen et al. (Eds.): SFPVV 2025, LNCS 16356, pp. 112–129, 2026.
https://doi.org/10.1007/978-981-95-6032-5_8

theorem that if M is simulated by M_A and a state predicate p_A is an invariant property with respect to (wrt) M_A, then the corresponding state predicate p is also an invariant property wrt M. By conducting model checking to verify that p_A is an invariant property wrt M_A, we can formally verify that p is an invariant property wrt M without directly conducting model checking to verify that p is an invariant property wrt M. In the work [15], Maude [9], a rewriting logic-based specification/programming language/system, is used to write formal specifications and conduct model checking and formal verification of simulation relations between state machines.

A principal challenge of the initial approach in [15], however, is that the formal verification of simulation relations is not fully automated and requires a plenty amount of manual intervention. This dependency on manual effort made the process not only time-consuming but also susceptible to human error. To mitigate this problem, this paper describes a support tool designed to automate the major steps of this verification process, thereby enhancing its efficiency and reliability. The tool has been implemented in Maude by using its reflective programming (or meta-programming) facilities. The support tool is available at the webpage[1].

The rest of the paper is organized as follows. Section 2 mentions some preliminaries. Section 3 describes the combining model checking with simulation relations technique. Section 4 outlines, through a simple example, the steps of the technique that are supported by the tool. Section 5 is the core part of the present paper, describing the support tool. Section 6 mentions some existing related work. Finally, Sect. 7 concludes the paper and outlines future directions.

2 Preliminaries

2.1 State Machines

Definition 1 (State Machine). *A State machine M is $\langle S_M, I_M, T_M \rangle$ such that*

- *S_M is a set of states.*
- *$I_M \subseteq S_M$ is the set of initial states.*
- *$T_M \subseteq S_M \times S_M$ is a binary relation over states. $(\upsilon, \upsilon') \in T_M$ may be written as $\upsilon \rightsquigarrow_M \upsilon'$, called a state transition, where υ' is called a successor state of υ.*

For simplicity of notation, the subscript $_M$ is omitted if it is clear from the context that a symbol refers to the state machine M.

Definition 2 (Reachable States). *The set R_M of reachable states wrt M is defined as the smallest set satisfying the following conditions:*

(i) $I_M \subseteq R_M$
(ii) If $\upsilon \in R_M$ and $\upsilon \rightsquigarrow_M \upsilon'$, then $\upsilon' \in R_M$

[1] https://github.com/11Takanori/simulation-checker.

Definition 3 (Invariant Property). *Given a state machine M, a state predicate p is an invariant property wrt M if $p(v)$ is true for all $v \in R_M$, i.e.* $(\forall v \in R_M) \cdot p(v)$.

That a state machine satisfies an invariant property is synonymous with that a state predicate is invariant wrt a state machine. A state predicate p can be interpreted as a set P_M of states such that $(\forall v \in P_M) \cdot p(v)$ and $(\forall v \notin P_M) \cdot \neg p(v)$.

2.2 Simulations

The paper [20] defines the simulation relation of one state machine to another state machine. A type of state machine called Observable Transition Systems (OTS) is used for definitions; however, in this paper we use the state machines defined in the previous subsection, but not OTS.

Definition 4 (Simulation Relation). *Given state machines M and M_A, $r : R_M\, R_{M_A} \to Bool$ is called a simulation relation from M to M_A if it satisfies the following conditions:*

(i) For each $v \in I_M$, there exists $v_A \in I_{M_A}$ such that $r(v, v_A)$.
(ii) For each $v, v' \in R_M$ and $v_A \in R_{M_A}$ such that $r(v, v_A)$ and $v \leadsto_M v'$, there exists $v'_A \in R_{M_A}$ such that $r(v', v'_A)$ and $v_A \leadsto^*_{M_A} v'_A$.

Note that if $v_A \in R_{M_A}$ and $v_A \leadsto^*_{M_A} v'_A$, then $v'_A \in R_{M_A}$.

$\leadsto^*_M$ is a reflexive transitive closure of $\leadsto_M$. When k time applications of transitions move v to v', we write $v \leadsto^k_M v'$.

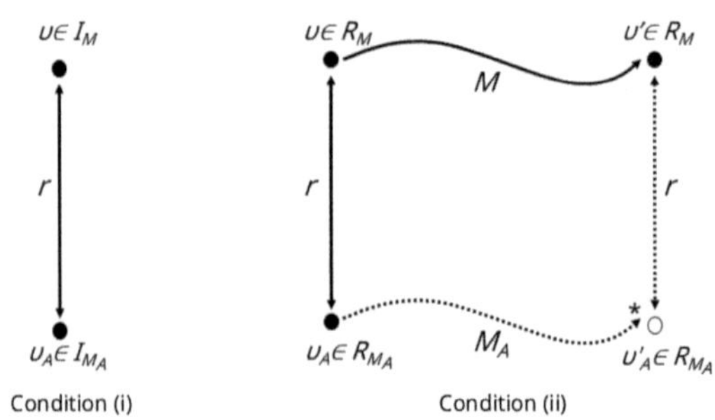

Fig. 1. A simulation relation r from M to M_A.

Figure 1 shows the diagrams corresponding to the two conditions in Definition 4. When there exists a simulation relation r from M to M_A, we may say that M is simulated by M_A, or M_A simulates M. Definition 4 does not say explicitly that for each $v \in R_M$, there exists $v_A \in R_{M_A}$ such that $r(v, v_A)$, and then we need to have the following proposition:

Proposition 1. *Given state machines M and M_A such that there exists a simulation relation from M to M_A and for an arbitrary such simulation relation r and each $v \in R_M$, there exists $v_A \in R_{M_A}$ such that $r(v, v_A)$.*

Proof. By induction on $v \in R_M$. If $v \in I_M$, then there exists $v_A \in R_{M_A}$ such that $r(v, v_A)$ from Definition 4 (i). If $v \rightsquigarrow_M v'$, then there exists $v_A \in R_{M_A}$ such that $r(v, v_A)$ from the induction hypothesis. Then, from Definition 4 (ii), there exists $v'_A \in R_{M_A}$ such that $r(v', v'_A)$ and $v_A \rightsquigarrow^*_{M_A} v'_A$.

If M is simulated by M_A, a state predicate p_A is an invariant property wrt M_A and p_A is preserved by the simulation relation, then the counterpart state predicate p is an invariant property wrt M.

Theorem 1. *Given state machines M and M_A such that there exists a simulation relation from M to M_A and for an arbitrary such simulation relation r and arbitrary state predicates p, p_A such that $p_A(v_A) \Rightarrow p(v)$ for arbitrary states v, v_A with $r(v, v_A)$, if p_A is an invariant property wrt M_A, then p is an invariant property wrt M.*

Proof. For an arbitrary $v \in R_M$, there exists $v_A \in R_{M_A}$ with $r(v, v_A)$ from Proposition 1. Therefore, $p(v)$ holds from the assumption.

2.3 Maude

Maude [9] is a specification and programming language based on rewriting logic. Rewriting logic is reflective; it can faithfully interpret its own theories and therefore enables the construction of sophisticated meta-programming and meta-language applications. States can be represented in various forms. In model checking using `search` command of Maude, we describe a state as a braced associative-commutative collection of name-value pairs, where each name may include parameters. Within the Maude community's terminology, associative-commutative collections are referred to as "soups", and name-value pairs are referred to as "observable components". Therefore, a state is expressed as a braced soup of observable components. The juxtaposition operator serves as the constructor for soups. Let oc_0, oc_1, oc_2 be observable components; then $oc_0\, oc_1\, oc_2$ constructs the soup containing these three observable components. Consequently, a state is expressed as $\{oc_0\, oc_1\, oc_2\}$.

The state transition relation T is defined using rewrite rules. A standard rewrite rule begins with the keyword `rl`, followed by a label enclosed in square brackets, a colon, two patterns separated by `=>`, and concludes with a period. In contrast, a conditional rewrite rule, initiated with `crl`, includes a condition following the `if` keyword and ends with a period. An example of a conditional rewrite rule is `crl [`lb`] :` t `=>` t' `if` ... `/\` c_i `/\` ..., where lb is the rule's label, and c_i forms part of the condition, often represented as an equation tc_i `=` tc_i'. The negation of this equation can be expressed as `(`tc_i `!=` tc_i'`) = true`, with the `= true` part being optional. If the condition ... `/\` c_i `/\` ... is satisfied under a certain substitution σ, then $\sigma(t)$ can be replaced with $\sigma(t')$. The substitution

σ is a function from variables to terms that preserves sorts. The substitution σ can be naturally extended as a function from terms to terms as follows:

$$\sigma\big(f(t_1,\ldots,t_n)\big) = f\big(\sigma(t_1),\ldots,\sigma(t_n)\big)$$

for any function symbol f of arity n and terms $t_1,\ldots,t_n$.

We use the `search` command of Maude for model checking. The `search` command looks for states that are reachable from an initial state through state transitions, aiming to find states that meet certain condition. The `search` command is represented as follows:

`search [`n`] in` M`:` s `=>*` s' `such that` c `.`

Here, M denotes the name of a Maude module. n denotes the upper limit of the number of states (called solutions) that meet the condition. s denotes the initial state, s' denotes the target state, and $=>*$ denotes the exploration through zero or more steps. c is an optional property that has to be satisfied by the target state. In addition to the `search` command, for verification of simulation relations between state machines, the `reduce` command and the `srewrite` command are used. The `reduce` command causes the specified term to be reduced using the equations. `reduce` may be abbreviated to `red`. The `reduce` command is represented as follows:

`red in` M`:` s `.`

M denotes the name of a Maude module, and s denotes the state to be reduced. The `srewrite` command causes the specified term to be rewritten according to the given rewrite rule in the given module. Many results may be obtained. `srewrite` may be abbreviated to `srew`. The `srewrite` command is represented as follows:

`srew in` M`:` s `using` lb `.`

M denotes the name of a Maude module, s denotes the state to which the rewrite rule is applied, and lb denotes the label of the rewrite rule.

Maude provides lists as one of its predefined container data types. The lists are parameterized, allowing for the construction of lists of elements of any data type. The basic representation of lists uses two free constructors: the constant `nil` for the empty list and the juxtaposition operator for list construction. For example, when an element `E` of the same data type as the elements of list `L` is added to the front of the list, we denote it as `E L`.

Maude makes it possible to use fresh constants that represent arbitrary values (meaning that it is possible to do symbolic execution). For example, a fresh constant x of sort `Nat` represents an arbitrary natural number.

3 Combining Model Checking with Simulation Relations

Combining model checking with simulation relations methodology uses model checking to demonstrate that a state machine M is simulated by a more abstract state machine M_A. It further shows that, if M is simulated by M_A and a state predicate p_A is an invariant property wrt M_A, then the corresponding state predicate p is an invariant property wrt M. To prove that p is an invariant property wrt M using the methodology for the state machines M and M_A, and their respective state predicates p and p_A, we follow three steps:

1. Conduct model checking to verify that p_A is an invariant property wrt M_A.
2. Conjecture a simulation relation candidate r from M to M_A, and prove that p can be deduced from p_A assuming the simulation relation candidate r using case splitting and reduction.
3. Demonstrate that M is simulated by M_A using model checking, case splitting, and reduction.

By following the steps, we can formally verify that p is an invariant property wrt M even though it is impossible to directly model check that p is an invariant property wrt M. This is useful when M has a large reachable state space that leads to state space explosion. M_A must have a reachable state space that does not lead to state space explosion. If we successfully carry out steps 1 through 3, then we can conclude that p is an invariant property wrt M from Theorem 1. In the case studies of this paper, M_A is manually constructed and is not automatically generated from M.

The support tool presented in the present paper is designed to demonstrate that Definition 4 (ii). In this section, we describe the technique for showing that Definition 4 (ii) holds. This technique requires case splitting for each state transition of M. Ordinary finite-state model checking usually uses specific concrete values. However, since we aim to demonstrate that the simulation relation is preserved across all state transitions of M with a large reachable state space, where state space explosion occurs, we use fresh constants in addition to concrete values. We define the simulation relation candidate r with an equation in Maude. r takes two states of M and M_A respectively as arguments and returns a Boolean value. It returns true if r holds between the two states, and false otherwise.

We verify that for each state transition of M, for arbitrary states υ, υ' of M, and an arbitrary state υ_A of M_A such that $r(\upsilon, \upsilon_A)$ and $\upsilon \rightsquigarrow_M \upsilon'$, there exists a state υ'_A of M_A such that $r(\upsilon', \upsilon'_A)$ and $\upsilon_A \rightsquigarrow^*_{M_A} \upsilon'_A$. In Maude, state transitions are defined by rewrite rules. As described in the Sect. 2, rewrite rules are defined in two ways: as a rewrite rule (`rl`) and a conditional rewrite rule (`crl`).

- `rl [`lb`] :` t `=>` t'
- `crl [`lb`] :` t `=>` t' `if` $\ldots$ `/\` c_i `/\` $\ldots$

If the *t'* in `rl` or `crl` contains an `if_then_else_fi` expression, a conditional branch occurs. Depending on the condition, different state transitions may occur. We need to do case splitting for (conditional) rewrite rules of M. In the case studies of this paper, we use case splitting based on the conditions of the conditional rewrite rules and the conditions specified in the `if_then_else_fi` expression, ensuring that all possible state transitions of M can be taken into account. In addition to these cases, other types of case splitting may also be required. For example, when using associative commutative pattern matching, multiple substitutions may be obtained, requiring further case splitting based on these substitutions. An arbitrary state before a state transition, caused by a single application of a rewrite rule, corresponds to $\sigma(t)$, and an arbitrary state after the state transition, caused by the same application of the same rewrite rule, corresponds to $\sigma(t')$, where $\sigma(t), \sigma(t') \in S_M$ and $\sigma(t) \rightsquigarrow_M \sigma(t')$. For each case splitting described above, we verify the arbitrary states in which the state transition can occur, including states that are unreachable. This covers a range that broader than or equal to the reachable states and is narrower than or equal to all states. Specifically, we verify for each $v \in D_M$, where D_M satisfies $R_M \subseteq D_M \subseteq S_M$. Similarly, M_A is verified in the same range as M. Specifically, we verify $v_A \in D_{M_A}$, where D_{M_A} satisfies $R_{M_A} \subseteq D_{M_A} \subseteq S_{M_A}$. For each case splitting described above, the following three steps are performed.

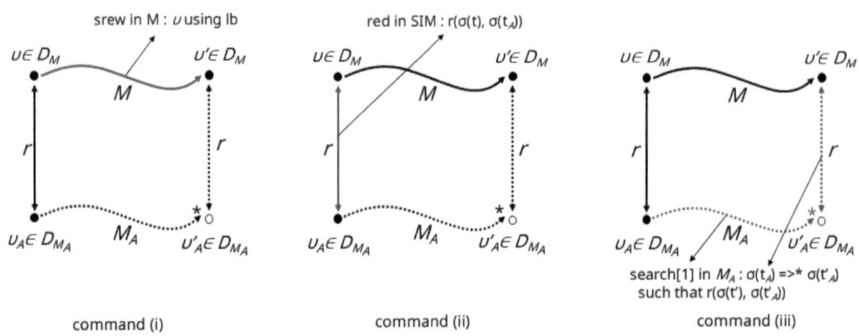

Fig. 2. Verification of simulation relation for each state transition.

First, we find the states resulting from the state transition caused by the application of the rewrite rule using the `srewrite` command of Maude. Specifically, we use the following command:

`srew in` M `:` $\sigma(t)$ `using` lb `.`

where M is the name of the module defining the state machine M, and lb is the label of the rewrite rule. This `srewrite` command finds $\sigma(t')$ that is reachable from $\sigma(t)$ in M by applying the rewrite rule lb. $\sigma(t)$ is the term that represents the most general state for each case in the case splitting. We construct $\sigma(t)$ using fresh constants. For example, if t has associativity or commutativity, multiple substitutions can be obtained. It can be observed that when multiple substitutions are obtained, further case splitting is required. The point at which the `srewrite` command is applied is shown as command (i) in Fig. 2. This command helps to find $\sigma(t')$ required to demonstrate Definition 4 (ii).

Next, we verify that $v_A \in D_{M_A}$ corresponding to $v \in D_M$ has r using the `reduce` command of Maude. Specifically, human users are supposed to construct a state v_A of M_A for each v of M and use the following command:

```
red in SIM : r(σ(t),σ(t_A)) .
```

where SIM is the name of the module defining the simulation relation candidate r with an equation. There are separate modules defining the states of M and M_A, both of which are imported by the module SIM. This reduce command returns a Boolean value. If the command returns true, there is r between $\sigma(t)$ and $\sigma(t_A)$. As with $\sigma(t)$, we use fresh constants to represent $\sigma(t_A)$. We construct a candidate $\sigma(t_A)$ that is expected to hold the r with $\sigma(t)$, and use the command to verify that r holds between $\sigma(t)$ and $\sigma(t_A)$. The point at which the reduce command is applied is shown as command (ii) in Fig. 2.

Finally, we verify that zero or more state transitions make it possible to move υ_A to υ'_A such that the search command is used to confirm that $r(\upsilon', \upsilon'_A)$ holds. Specifically, we use the following command:

```
search[1] in M_A : σ(t_A) =>* σ(t'_A) such that r(σ(t'),σ(t'_A)) .
```

where M_A is the name of the module defining the state machine M_A. The module M_A imports the module SIM. Therefore, r can be used in the module M_A. If this command returns a solution, it indicates that there exists $\upsilon'_A \in D_{M_A}$ such that $r(\upsilon', \upsilon'_A)$ and $\upsilon_A \rightsquigarrow^*_{M_A} \upsilon'_A$. The point at which the search command is applied is shown as command (iii) in Fig. 2.

In our previous work [15], we have proven that performing these three commands for each state transition caused by the rewrite rule of M implies that Definition 4 (ii) is satisfied.

4 An Example Alternating Bit Protocol is Simulated by Simple Communication Protocol

To outline the approach, we use two communication protocols as an example: the Alternating Bit Protocol (ABP) [3] and the Simple Communication Protocol (SCP) [20]. We demonstrate that ABP is simulated by SCP. We begin with a description of ABP and SCP.

ABP is a communication protocol designed to provide reliable communication between a sender and a receiver, even though the two underlying channels may duplicate or drop messages. The protocol consists of a sender process, a receiver process, and two unreliable first-in, first-out channels. The sender maintains a Boolean variable (bit1) and a natural number variable (index), and the receiver maintains a Boolean variable (bit2) and a natural number list (list) that stores the sequence of data elements already delivered. One channel, called queue1, carries messages containing the sender's Boolean value (bit1) and index number (index) to the receiver. The other channel, called queue2, carries acknowledgment messages containing the receiver's Boolean value (bit2) to the sender. The basic flow of the protocol consists of four main steps. First, the sender sends a message containing its current bit (bit1). When the receiver receives the message, it checks the message's bit. If the bit matches its expected bit (bit2), it adds the message's index (index) to the list of delivered data (list) and toggles its bit2 to prepare for the next message. Otherwise, it discards the message as a duplicate. Next, the receiver sends an acknowledgment message containing its current bit (`bit2`) back to the sender. Finally, when the sender receives the acknowledgment message with the correct bit, it knows the message was delivered successfully. The sender then toggles its own bit (`bit1`) and prepares to send the next message. This entire flow, built around the alternating bit, ensures reliable communication even if the underlying channels duplicate or drop messages and their acknowledgment messages. A representative snapshot of ABP is shown in Fig. 3.

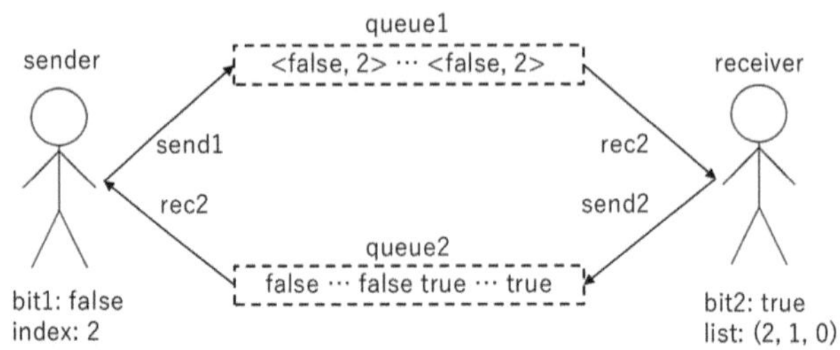

Fig. 3. A snapshot of ABP.

Initially, both `queue1` and `queue2` are empty, both `bit1` and `bit2` are false, `index` is 0, and `list` is nil. T_{ABP} is specified in rewrite rules as follows:

```
crl [send1] :
 {(queue1: PQ) (bit1: B) (index: I) OCs} =>
 {(queue1: (PQ pcell(B, I))) (bit1: B) (index: I) OCs}
 if I <= maxIndex /\ length(PQ) <= maxQueueLength .
rl [rec1] :
 {(queue2: (BC BQ)) (bit1: B) (index: I) OCs} =>
 {(queue2: BQ) (bit1: (if bit(BC) = B then B else not B fi))
 (index: (if bit(BC) = B then I else s(I) fi)) OCs} .
crl [send2] :
 {(queue2: BQ) (bit2: B) OCs} => {(queue2: (BQ bcell(B))) (bit2: B) OCs}
 if length(BQ) <= maxQueueLength .
rl [rec2] :
 {(queue1: (PC PQ)) (bit2: B) (list: L) OCs} =>
 {(queue1: PQ) (bit2: (if bit(PC) = B then not B else B fi))
  (list: (if bit(PC) = B then (index(PC) L) else L fi)) OCs} .
rl [drop1] :
 {(queue1: (PC PQ)) OCs} => {(queue1: PQ) OCs} .
crl [dup1] :
 {(queue1: (PC PQ)) OCs} => {(queue1: (PC PC PQ)) OCs}
 if length(PQ) <= maxQueueLength .
rl [drop2] :
 {(queue2: (BC BQ)) OCs} => {(queue2: BQ) OCs} .
crl [dup2] :
 {(queue2: (BC BQ)) OCs} => {(queue2: (BC BC BQ)) OCs}
 if length(BQ) <= maxQueueLength .
```

OCs denotes a variable of observable components soups. I denotes a variable of index. L denotes a variable of list. PQ denotes a variable of queue1. BQ denotes a variable of queue2. PC denotes a variable of an element in queue1. BC denotes a variable of an element in queue2. B, B1, and B2 denote variables of bit1 or bit2. Both maxIndex and maxQueueLength are natural numbers. They are used to limit the reachable state space during model checking. The rewrite rules drop1 and drop2 indicate that the message at the front of the queue has been removed, while the rewrite rules dup1 and dup2 indicate that the message at the front of the queue is duplicated.

The invariant property candidate of ABP is defined in Maude as follows:

```
eq ABP-inv(ABP) =
 (getBit1(ABP) = getBit2(ABP) implies
   mk(getIndex(ABP)) = (getIndex(ABP) getList(ABP))) and
 (getBit1(ABP) != getBit2(ABP) implies mk(getIndex(ABP)) = getList(ABP))
```

ABP-inv ensures that the protocol's state remains consistent and correct. The parameter ABP is defined as a value of the data type ABPState, which represents the state of the Alternating Bit Protocol. If getBit1(ABP) (the sender's bit) is equal to getBit2(ABP) (the receiver's bit), then mk(getIndex(ABP)) must be equal to (getIndex(ABP) getList(ABP)). If getBit1(ABP) is not equal to getBit2(ABP), then mk(getIndex(ABP)) must be equal to getList(ABP). The functions prefixed with get, including getBit1, getBit2, getIndex, and getList, serve as accessors to extract the bit1, bit2, index, and list components, respectively, from the state. mk takes a natural number k and makes the list *(k k - 1 ... 0)*.

Next, we describe SCP. The only difference between SCP and ABP is in their message handling mechanisms: SCP uses two unreliable cells (which can be seen as unreliable queues of length one), while ABP uses two unreliable queues. These cells are unreliable in the sense that the data they contain may be lost before it can be consumed.

T_{SCP} is specified in rewrite rules as follows:

```
crl [send1] :
 {(cell1: PC) (bit1: B) (index: I) OCs} =>
 {(cell1: pcell(B, I)) (bit1: B) (index: I) OCs} if I <= maxIndex .
crl [rec1] :
 {(cell2: BC) (bit1: B) (index: I) OCs} =>
 {(cell2: empty) (bit1: (if bit(BC) = B then B else not B fi))
  (index: (if bit(BC) = B then I else s(I) fi)) OCs} if BC != empty .
rl [send2] :
 {(cell2: BC) (bit2: B) OCs} => {(cell2: bcell(B)) (bit2: B) OCs} .
crl [rec2] :
 {(cell1: PC) (bit2: B) (list: L) OCs} =>
 {(cell1: empty) (bit2: (if bit(PC) = B then not B else B fi))
  (list: (if bit(PC) = B then (index(PC) L) else L fi)) OCs}
 if PC != empty .
crl [drop1] :
 {(cell1: PC) OCs} => {(cell1: empty) OCs} if PC != empty .
```

```
crl [drop2] :
 {(cell2: BC) OCs} => {(cell2: empty) OCs} if BC != empty .
```

Since SCP uses cells as its message handling mechanism, message duplication does not occur.

An invariant property candidate that ensures that the state of the protocol remains consistent and correct for SCP can be defined similarly to that for ABP.

```
eq SCP-inv(SCP) =
 (getBit1(SCP) = getBit2(SCP) implies
  mk(getIndex(SCP)) = (getIndex(SCP) getList(SCP))) and
 (getBit1(SCP) != getBit2(SCP) implies mk(getIndex(SCP)) = getList(SCP))
```

We conjecture a simulation relation candidate from ABP to SCP. This simulation relation candidate requires that if `SCP-inv` is an invariant property wrt SCP and ABP is simulated by SCP, then `ABP-inv` is an invariant property wrt ABP. The simulation relation candidate from ABP to SCP defined as follows:

```
eq r(ABP, SCP) =
 (getBit1(ABP) = getBit1(SCP)) and (getBit2(ABP) = getBit2(SCP)) and
 (getIndex(ABP) = getIndex(SCP)) and (getList(ABP) = getList(SCP))
```

This demonstrates that `bit1`, `bit2`, `index`, and `list` are identical in ABP and SCP. To verify that Definition 4 (ii) is satisfied, we perform a case splitting for each state transition that we define as a rewrite rule. We confirm the state transitions of the state machine ABP for each rewrite rule. Among the eight rewrite rules, we begin by examining the state transitions induced by the rewrite rule `send1` within the state machine ABP. To accomplish this, we use Maude and execute the following `srew` commands:

```
srew in ABP :
 {(queue1: pqueue) (queue2: bqueue) (bit1: bool1)
  (index: index) (bit2: bool2) (list: list)} using send1 .
```

`pqueue`, `bqueue`, `bool1`, `index`, `bool2`, and `list` are fresh constants. `index` is a value less than or equal to `maxIndex`. The remaining constants represent arbitrary values. The result returned by Maude for the `srew` command is as follows:

```
srew in ABP : {(queue1: pqueue) (queue2: bqueue) (bit1: bool1) (index:
    index) (bit2: bool2) (list: list)} using send1 .
srewrite in ABP : {queue1: pqueue queue2: bqueue bit1: bool1 index: index
     bit2: bool2 list: list} using send1 .
Solution 1
rewrites: 6 in 0ms cpu (0ms real) (~ rewrites/second)
result ABPConfig: {queue1: (pqueue pcell(bool1, index)) queue2: bqueue
    bit1: bool1 index: index bit2: bool2 list: list}
No more solutions.
rewrites: 6 in 0ms cpu (0ms real) (~ rewrites/second)
```

This means that the state `{(queue1: pqueue) (queue2: bqueue) (bit1: bool1) (index: index) (bit2: bool2) (list: list)}` moves to the state `{queue1: (pqueue pcell(bool1, index)) queue2: bqueue bit1: bool1 index: index bit2: bool2 list: list}`.

Then, we verify that the state of the state machine SCP, which corresponds to the state `{(queue1: pqueue) (queue2: bqueue) (bit1: bool1) (index: index) (bit2: bool2) (list: list)}` of the state machine ABP, makes the simulation relation candidate keep holding. We can check this by using the following `reduce` command:

```
red in SIM :
 r(abp(pqueue, bqueue, bool1, index, bool2, list),
   scp(pcell, bcell, bool1, index, bool2, list)) .
```

Maude returns true for this `reduce` command. This means that the state of the state machine SCP, which corresponds to the state `{(queue1: pqueue) (queue2: bqueue) (bit1: bool1) (index: index) (bit2: bool2) (list: list)}` of the state machine ABP, makes the simulation relation candidate keep holding.

Then, we look for v'_A to which zero or more state transitions can move v_A such that $r(v', v'_A)$ holds by using the following `search` command:

```
search[1] in SCP :
 {(cell1: pcell) (cell2: bcell) (bit1: bool1)
  (index: index) (bit2: bool2) (list: list)} =>*
 {(cell1: PC) (cell2: BC) (bit1: B1)
  (index: I) (bit2: B2) (list: L) OCs}
such that
 r(abp((pqueue pcell(bool1, index)), bqueue, bool1, index, bool2, list),
   scp(PC, BC, B1, I, B2, L)) .
```

This `search` command is used to find a state transition from v_A to v'_A within the state machine SCP, while `r` keeps holding for the state machine ABP and the state machine SCP. `abp((pqueue pcell(bool1, index)), bqueue, bool1, index, bool2, list)` is the state found by the `srewrite` command. Maude finds a solution for this `search` command. That is to say, Maude finds a state described above. The results of these commands reveal that, for all state transitions caused by the rewrite rule `send1` in ABP, there exist states within those of SCP that make the simulation relation candidate keep holding. By applying this procedure to all remaining rewrite rules, we have confirmed that Definition 4 (ii) is satisfied.

5 Support Tool Design and Implementation

5.1 System Context and High-Level Design

An overview of the support tool for verifying that Definition 4 (ii) is satisfied, as described in the previous section, is depicted in Fig. 4. The tool accepts as input the module name in which the function representing the simulation relation

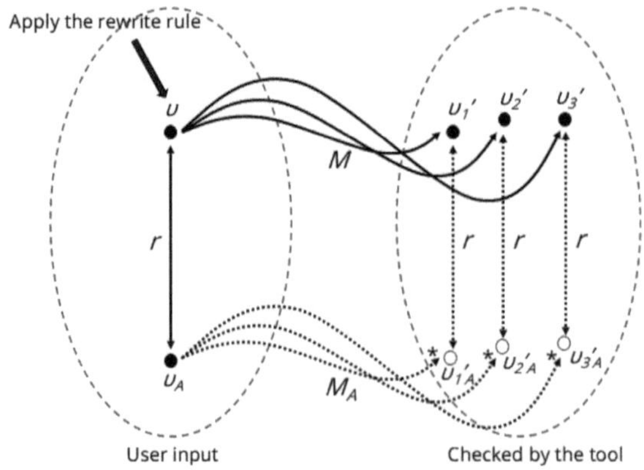

Fig. 4. An overview of a tool supporting the approach.

candidate is defined, the name of that function, the module names of the concrete and abstract state machines, their states before state transitions, and the rewrite rule, and then finds the states for which the simulation relation candidate holds. The technique to verify that Definition 4 (ii) is satisfied is conducted with the support tool as follows:

```
Maude> load specs/communication_protocol.maude
Maude> in simulation_checker
...
Maude> red in SIMULATION-CHECKER-IO : simulate<< "SIM" | "r" > < "ABP" |
    "{(queue1: pqueue) (queue2: bqueue) (bit1: bool1) (index: index) (
    bit2: bool2) (list: list)}" > < "SCP" | "{(cell1: pcell) (cell2:
    bcell) (bit1: bool1) (index: index) (bit2: bool2) (list: list)}" > "
    send1" > .
reduce in SIMULATION-CHECKER-IO : simulate<< "SIM" | "r" > < "ABP" |
   "{(queue1: pqueue) (queue2: bqueue) (bit1: bool1) (index: index) (
       bit2: bool2) (list: list)}" > < "SCP" |
   "{(cell1: pcell) (cell2: bcell) (bit1: bool1) (index: index) (bit2:
       bool2) (list: list)}" > "send1" > .
rewrites: 188 in 16ms cpu (21ms real) (11750 rewrites/second)
result String: "Success"
Maude>
```

where some outputs emitted by Maude are omitted, where ... is written. First, load the modules that specify ABP and SCP; then load the support tool into Maude. The `simulate` function verifies that the simulation relation candidate holds for each state transition. Its arguments are:

- `"SIM"` - the module name in which the simulation relation candidate `r` is defined
- `"r"` - the function name of the simulation relation candidate
- `"ABP"` - the module name in which the ABP state machine is defined.

- `"(queue1: pqueue) (queue2: bqueue) (bit1: bool1) (index: index) (bit2: bool2) (list: list)"` - the state of ABP before the state transition
- `"SCP"` - the module name in which the SCP state machine is defined
- `"(cell1: pcell) (cell2: bcell) (bit1: bool1) (index: index) (bit2: bool2) (list: list)"` - the state of SCP before the state transition
- `"send1"` - the name of the rewrite rule to be applied

The tool's standard output of "Success" indicates that, for the above state transition resulting from the application of the rewrite rule `send1`, `r` keeps holding for the state machine ABP and the state machine SCP. If no state for which the simulation relation candidate holds exists, the tool reports the point at which the verification failed. By executing this procedure for all remaining state transitions and obtaining "Success" in each case, we can conclude that Definition 4 (ii) is satisfied.

The `simulate` function consolidates the three commands described in the previous section into a single invocation. Furthermore, when the state υ before a state transition of the concrete state machine (ABP) possesses the properties of associativity and commutativity, the support tool automatically performs case splitting for each such state transition and verifies each resulting case.

5.2 Implementation Details

We describe the implementation of the support tool, focusing on its key functionalities. First, the tool applies the rewrite rule to the state υ of the concrete state machine, generating successor states by the resulting state transition. Then, the tool verifies that the simulation relation candidate `r` holds between υ and υ_A. For each state produced in the first step, it checks whether there exists a state reachable from υ_A by zero or more state transitions such that `r` holds.

The `srewrite`, `reduce`, and `search` commands described in the previous section are implemented as built-in commands in Maude. Maude supports meta-programming, which enables programs to treat other programs as data. As a result, these commands can themselves be manipulated as data within Maude. By simply importing the predefined `META-LEVEL` module, we can write Maude meta-programs that invoke the built-in functions it provides, such as `metaSrewrite` and `metaSearch`.

The following code constructs all states resulting from state transitions induced by applying a rewrite rule to a given state. It use on Maude's built-in function `metaSrewrite`, which is important for this operation.

```
eq stateTransitionUsingRewriteRule(M, QSL, ST)
  = stateTransitionUsingRewriteRule*(M, QSL, ST, 0) .
ceq stateTransitionUsingRewriteRule*(M, QSL, ST, N)
  = if RP? :: ResultPair then
      RP? stateTransitionUsingRewriteRule*(M, QSL, ST, s(N))
    else
```

```
      nil
    fi
if RP? := rewriteUsingRewriteRule(M, QSL, ST, N) .
eq rewriteUsingRewriteRule(M, QSL, ST, N)
  = metaSrewrite(
      M, getTerm(metaParse(M, QSL, anyType)), ST, breadthFirst, N
    ) .
```

M denotes a variable of the meta-representation of a module. QSL denotes a variable of a list of quoted identifier, which is obtained by prefixing a Maude identifier with a single quote, and is used to represent the state v of the concrete state machine. ST denotes a variable of the meta-representation of a strategy expression; in this paper the relevant strategy expressions are rewrite rules, and N denotes a variable of a natural numbers and is used to indicate the index of a result produced by `metaSrewrite`. The term `s(N)` represents the next natural number after N. The `metaSrewrite` function rewrites a term within the given module according to a specified strategy and, if the rewrite succeeds, returns the result as a value of sort `ResultPair`. In the code shown above, the term is expressed as `getTerm(metaParse(M, QSL, anyType))`. If no result exists for the specified index, it returns the `failure` constant of sort `ResultPair?`. The necessary states are constructed by recursively invoking `stateTransitionUsingRewriteRule*` until `metaSrewrite` returns `failure`. If details of Maude's built-in functions, such as `getTerm` and `metaParse`, are required, we recommend to refer to the document [9].

Next, we describe the code shown above that looks for a state v'_A reachable from v_A by zero or more state transitions such that r keeps holding for the concrete state machine and the abstract state machine.

```
ceq searchStateWithSimulationRelation(QSR, M, QSL, MA, QSAL)
 = metaSearch(
     MA,
     getTerm(metaParse(MA, QSAL, anyType)),
     getTerm(metaParse(MA, V, anyType)),
     getTerm(
       metaParse(
         MA,
         tokenize(
           makeSimulationRelation(
             QSR,
             M,
             tokenize(toState(createState(M, QSL))),
             MA,
             tokenize(toState(string(V))))),
         anyType))
       = 'true.Bool,
     '*, unbounded, 0
   )
 if V := createConfigVar(getType(metaParse(MA, QSAL, anyType))) .
```

QSR denotes a variable of a quoted identifier, which is used to represent the simulation relation candidate r. M and MA denote variables of the meta-representation of modules, where M represents the concrete state machine and MA represents the corresponding abstract state machine. QSL and QSAL denote variables of a list of quoted identifier, where QSL represents the state v' of the concrete state machine and QSAL represents the state v_A of the abstract state machine. The primary function of `metaSearch` is to find terms that match a specific pattern and satisfy a given condition within a specified module and starting from a given initial term. If the search succeeds, it returns the result as a value of sort `ResultTriple`; otherwise, it returns the `failure` constant of sort `ResultTriple?`. Here, since matching a specific pattern is unnecessary, `getTerm(metaParse(MA, V, anyType))` represents a term that matches any state. Furthermore, `getTerm(metaParse(MA, tokenize(makeSimulationRelation(QSR, M, tokenize(toState(createState(M, QSL))), MA, tokenize(toState(string(V))))), anyType)) = 'true.Bool` specifies the condition that the simulation relation candidate holds. `'*` means the exploration through zero or more steps. `unbounded` means that no maximum depth is set for the search. The final argument 0 to `metaSearch` means the index of the search results. Here, it suffices that there exists at least one state with which the simulation relation candidate holds. We do not describe the full code in order to save the space.

6 Related Work

Simulations are used to demonstrate that I/O automata satisfy trace properties, as introduced by Lynch et al. [16]. It establishes a formal relationship between a detailed, concrete solution and its more abstract counterpart. By proving that the abstract solution correctly simulates the concrete one, one can formally verify that the concrete solution adheres to the properties defined in the abstract solution.

In process calculi like Communicating Sequential Processes (CSP) [14] and the Calculus of Communicating Systems (CCS) [18,19], bisimulation is crucial for proving behavioral equivalence between concurrent processes. A bisimulation demonstrates that two processes can mutually simulate each other, meaning any behavior exhibited by one process can be matched by the other. This concept is fundamental to verifying that different system implementations or levels of abstraction are behaviorally identical.

Maude [9] is based on term rewriting using a set of equations and rewrite rules. Its reflective capability, the ability to manipulate specifications themselves as data, enables powerful meta-programming for tasks such as controlling rule application and developing internal strategies. These core features of Maude, namely its foundation in rewriting logic, reflection, and executable specifications, provide the necessary expressiveness and flexibility for building sophisticated formal verification tools. Therefore, a wide range of tools has been developed based on Maude. For instance, Maude-NPA [13] is a tool for the formal analysis of cryptographic protocols, capable of finding attacks by exploring the state space using equational unification. Real-Time Maude [21] extends the formalism with timed rewrite rules to model and analyze the behavior of real-time and hybrid systems through timed reachability analysis and model checking. CafeInMaude [22] serves as an interpreter for the CafeOBJ [10], linking it to the broader verification ecosystem of Maude. NuITP [12] is an inductive theorem prover designed to automate proofs for equational specifications using techniques like narrowing. $|\text{QCEC}\rangle$ [11] focuses on quantum computing, offering a method for checking the equivalence of quantum circuits specified in Dirac notation.

7 Conclusion

This paper describes a support tool for the formal verification of simulation relations between state machines. The tool enhances the verification process by reducing manual effort and minimizing the risk of human error. The practical effectiveness of the tool is demonstrated through a case study. Furthermore, we have presented the high-level design of the tool and its usage. Regarding the implementation, the tool is built in Maude, and we have described the key aspects of how its reflective programming (meta-programming) facilities are leveraged.

The construction of a more abstract state machine from a concrete state machine and the identification of simulation relations still require manual intervention. This lack of automation makes the process challenging, particularly for complex systems. Therefore, the automation of these steps is a key area for future research.

References

1. Bae, K., Escobar, S., Meseguer, J.: Abstract logical model checking of infinite-state systems using narrowing. In: van Raamsdonk, F. (ed.) 24th International Conference on Rewriting Techniques and Applications (RTA 2013). Leibniz International Proceedings in Informatics (LIPIcs), vol. 21, pp. 81–96. Schloss Dagstuhl – Leibniz-Zentrum für Informatik, Dagstuhl, Germany (2013). https://doi.org/10.4230/LIPIcs.RTA.2013.81, https://drops.dagstuhl.de/entities/document/10.4230/LIPIcs.RTA.2013.81
2. Baier, C., Katoen, J.: Principles of model checking. MIT Press (2008)
3. Bartlett, K.A., Scantlebury, R.A., Wilkinson, P.T.: A note on reliable full-duplex transmission over half-duplex links. Commun. ACM **12**(5), 260–261 (1969). https://doi.org/10.1145/362946.362970
4. Clarke, E., Grumberg, O., Jha, S., Lu, Y., Veith, H.: Counterexample-guided abstraction refinement for symbolic model checking. J. ACM **50**(5), 752–794 (2003). https://doi.org/10.1145/876638.876643
5. Clarke, E.M.: The birth of model checking. In: Grumberg, O., Veith, H. (eds.) 25 Years of Model Checking. LNCS, vol. 5000, pp. 1–26. Springer, Heidelberg (2008). https://doi.org/10.1007/978-3-540-69850-0_1
6. Clarke, E.M., Grumberg, O., Long, D.E.: Model checking and abstraction. ACM Trans. Program. Lang. Syst. **16**(5), 1512–1542 (1994). https://doi.org/10.1145/186025.186051

7. Clarke, E.M., Grumberg, O., Minea, M., Peled, D.A.: State space reduction using partial order techniques. Int. J. Softw. Tools Technol. Transf. **2**(3), 279–287 (1999). https://doi.org/10.1007/S100090050035
8. Clarke, E.M., Henzinger, T.A., Veith, H., Bloem, R. (eds.): Handbook of Model Checking. Springer (2018). https://doi.org/10.1007/978-3-319-10575-8
9. Clavel, M., et al.: (eds.): All About Maude - A High-Performance Logical Framework, How to Specify, Program and Verify Systems in Rewriting Logic, Lecture Notes in Computer Science, vol. 4350. Springer (2007). https://doi.org/10.1007/978-3-540-71999-1
10. Diaconescu, R., Futatsugi, K.: CafeOBJ report: the language, proof techniques, and methodologies for object-oriented algebraic specification, vol. 6. World Scientific (1998)
11. Do, C.M., Ogata, K.: Equivalence checking of quantum circuits based on DIRAC notation in Maude. In: Ogata, K., Martí-Oliet, N. (eds.) Rewriting Logic and Its Applications, pp. 84–103. Springer Nature Switzerland, Cham (2024)
12. Durán, F., Escobar, S., Meseguer, J., Sapiña, J.: Nuitp: An inductive theorem prover for equational program verification. In: Proceedings of the 26th International Symposium on Principles and Practice of Declarative Programming. PPDP '24, Association for Computing Machinery, New York, NY, USA (2024). https://doi.org/10.1145/3678232.3678236
13. Escobar, S., Meadows, C., Meseguer, J.: Maude-NPA: cryptographic protocol analysis modulo equational properties. In: Aldini, A., Barthe, G., Gorrieri, R. (eds.) FOSAD 2007-2009. LNCS, vol. 5705, pp. 1–50. Springer, Heidelberg (2009). https://doi.org/10.1007/978-3-642-03829-7_1
14. Hoare, C.A.R.: Communicating sequential processes. Prentice-Hall Inc, USA (1985)
15. Ishibashi, T., Ogata, K.: Combining model checking with simulation-based techniques for protocol verification (2025), manuscript submitted for publication
16. Lynch, N.A.: Distributed Algorithms. Morgan Kaufmann Publishers Inc., San Francisco, CA, USA (1996)
17. Meseguer, J., Palomino, M., MartÃÂŋ-Oliet, N.: Equational abstractions. Theoretical Comput. Sci. **403**(2), 239–264 (2008). https://doi.org/10.1016/j.tcs.2008.04.040, https://www.sciencedirect.com/science/article/pii/S0304397508003605
18. Milner, R. (ed.): A Calculus of Communicating Systems. LNCS, vol. 92. Springer, Heidelberg (1980). https://doi.org/10.1007/3-540-10235-3
19. Milner, R.: Communication and concurrency. PHI Series in computer science, Prentice Hall (1989)
20. Ogata, K., Futatsugi, K.: Simulation-based verification for invariant properties in the OTS/CafeOBJ method. Electron. Notes Theor. Comput. Sci. **201**, 127–154 (2008)
21. Ölveczky, P.C., Meseguer, J.: The real-time Maude tool. In: Ramakrishnan, C.R., Rehof, J. (eds.) Tools and Algorithms for the Construction and Analysis of Systems, pp. 332–336. Springer, Berlin Heidelberg, Berlin, Heidelberg (2008)
22. Riesco, A., Ogata, K., Futatsugi, K.: A Maude environment for CafeOBJ. Formal Aspects Comput. **29**(2), 309–334 (2016). https://doi.org/10.1007/s00165-016-0398-7

Design and Implementation of a Software Tool to Support Agile-SOFL

Ran Chen[1,2] and Shaoying Liu[1(✉)]

[1] East China Normal University, Shanghai, China
syliu@sei.ecnu.edu.cn
[2] Hiroshima University, Hiroshima, Japan

Abstract. Agile development, characterized by rapid delivery and continuous iteration, has become the mainstream paradigm in modern software development. However, ensuring the reliability of systems on a large scale remains a significant challenge within this framework. The Agile-SOFL methodology addresses this gap by integrating the flexibility of Agile with the rigor of formal methods, providing a theoretical foundation for structured and verifiable software development. The rise of Large Language Models (LLMs) presents an opportunity to explore the profound potential of combining classic software engineering theory with modern AI technology. To this end, we introduce a novel software tool that leverages a key component of Agile-SOFL, namely the Functional Scenario Form (FSF), as a semi-formal bridge between user requirements and LLM-based code generation. The approach employs LLMs to automate the code generation phase of the Agile-SOFL process, significantly boosting development efficiency. At the same time, it utilizes the structured nature of FSF specifications to constrain and guide the generative process of LLMs, thereby ensuring the accuracy and reliability of the resulting code. We present the design and implementation of this tool and demonstrate its practical utility through a case study.

Keywords: Functional Scenario Form (FSF) · LLM-based code generation · software tool

1 Introduction

During the past two decades, the field of software development has undergone a profound paradigm shift. Driven by market demands, Agile Development has successfully replaced the traditional waterfall model to become the mainstream paradigm in modern software development. Agile development is characterized by its focus on rapidly building working software and continuously improving the system through feedback and iteration [1]. This methodology enables development teams to respond to changes more flexibly and to deliver functional software earlier, thus maintaining a competitive advantage in the market. However, the success of Agile lies in enhancing, efficiency, and flexibility. When faced

© The Author(s), under exclusive license to Springer Nature Singapore Pte Ltd. 2026
Y. Chen et al. (Eds.): SFPVV 2025, LNCS 16356, pp. 130–140, 2026.
https://doi.org/10.1007/978-981-95-6032-5_9

with large-scale systems, complex business logic, or critical systems with stringent reliability requirements, the limitations of standard Agile practices become apparent. Therefore, how to systematically improve software reliability while maintaining agility has become a critical and unresolved issue in the field of software engineering.

To address this challenge, Agile-SOFL was proposed by Liu [6]. Rather than replacing Agile, its objective is to infuse the Agile process with the rigor of formal methods. It creates a crucial bridge between the flexibility of Agile and the precision of formal engineering. Agile-SOFL offers a systematic theoretical framework centered on the principle of "Specification-Driven Development." This philosophy provides a foundation for the construction of software that is both maintainable and of high quality.

In recent years, AI technologies, particularly Large Language Models (LLMs), have catalyzed a transformative shift in software development. LLMs can rapidly generate code directly from natural language descriptions, significantly increasing the feasibility and speed of automated software construction. This capability aligns perfectly with the Agile goal of "rapid delivery of working software". However, the quality of generated code is highly dependent upon the quality of the input prompts. Without a mechanism to ensure the precision of these inputs, the power of LLMs can hardly be reliably translated into reliable engineering practice.

We recognize that the structured specification philosophy of Agile-SOFL can solve the input dilemma faced by Large Language Models. Specifically, its core component,the Functional Scenario Form (FSF), provides an effective method for capturing and defining precise and machine-friendly requirements. It achieves this by decomposing complex needs into a clear and distinct set of Test Condition and Defining Condition scenarios. The precision of FSF facilitates the LLM to ensure the reliability of generated code, while the LLM, in turn, makes the traditionally time-consuming code implementation phase of Agile-SOFL highly efficient.

To support efficient applications of Agile-SOFL, this paper introduces and implements a novel software tool that deeply integrates the rigorous theory of Agile-SOFL with the automation capabilities of LLMs, with FSF at its core. We describe how the tool is designed and implemented. We also discuss interesting issues related to the construction of the tool.

The remainder of this paper is organized as follows. Section 2 reviews related work on formal methods and LLM-based code generation. Section 3 details the overall architecture and design of our FSF-based tool. Section 4 demonstrates the effectiveness of the tool through a case study. Finally, Sect. 5 concludes the paper and outlines future research directions.

2 Related Work

This section reviews the two primary domains of research related to our work: the evolution of formal and semi-formal methods in software engineering and the recent advancements in LLM-based code generation. We aim to situate our FSF-based approach at the intersection of these two fields.

2.1 Formal and Semi-Formal Methods in Agile Development

The pursuit of software reliability has led to the development of various formal methods, such as VDM [4] and Z [9]. These approaches provide mathematically rigorous notation and proof systems for specifying and verifying software systems. However, their inherent complexity and lack of concrete guidance on writing style have limited their application across a wide range of scenarios, making them challenging to integrate into fast Agile workflows.

To bridge this gap, semi-formal methods have been proposed to balance rigor with practicality. Approaches like the Unified Modeling Language (UML) with Object Constraint Language (OCL) allow for more precise specifications than informal descriptions, yet remain more accessible than fully formal notation. It is within this context that Agile-SOFL was developed. Agile-SOFL is particularly relevant to our work as it explicitly aims to integrate formal engineering principles into an Agile process. Its core component, the Functional Scenario Form (FSF), represents a step towards creating specifications that achieve a balance between human readability and machine parsability, by decomposing system behavior into conditional scenarios.

Recent breakthroughs in Large Language Models (LLMs), particularly their growing capabilities in code generation, have introduced a transformative shift in software development automation. Specifically, LLMs have improved the efficiency of automatically translating high-level, structured specifications into executable code. This technology breaks the manual bottleneck in the traditional "specification-to-code" phase, and more importantly, presents a novel opportunity to revisit the potential of classic methodologies like Agile-SOFL.

2.2 LLM-Based Code Generation and Prompt Engineering

Large Language Models (LLMs), such as GPT-5 [7], GitHub Copilot [3], and AlphaCode [5], have accelerated a transformation in the field of automated code generation. These models demonstrate a remarkable capability to generate complex code segments and even entire functions directly from natural language prompts. However, in practical applications, the specifications that users provide are often incomplete or ambiguous, which reduces the reliability of the generated code. These descriptions may be too brief to provide sufficient context, or they may be excessively detailed. This excessive detail can introduce noise, which misleads the model and leads to deviations from the user's original intent. Furthermore, even when the functional logic is correct, the generated code may not align with user expectations in terms of structure or style, leading to unsatisfactory outcomes.In this context, a critical sub-field that has emerged is Prompt Engineering [8]. It studies how the formulation of the input prompt affects the quality of the LLM's output. Studies have shown that providing more context, examples (few-shot prompting) [2], or breaking down a problem into smaller steps can significantly improve code generation accuracy [10]. Some approaches have explored using intermediate representations, such as code skeletons or test cases, to guide the generation process.

3 Software Tool to Support FSF-Driven Code Generation

In this section, we discuss the issues related to the construction of a software tool to support FSF-driven code generation.

3.1 Tool Architecture

We have designed and implemented a novel software tool, positioned at the intersection of the two research domains previously discussed. The general architecture of our tool, shown in Fig. 1, consists of three core modules. These modules are engineered to guide developers through a "Specify-Generate-Review" workflow. They transform precise user intent into validated code and integrate the rigor of semi-formal specifications with the automation power of LLMs.

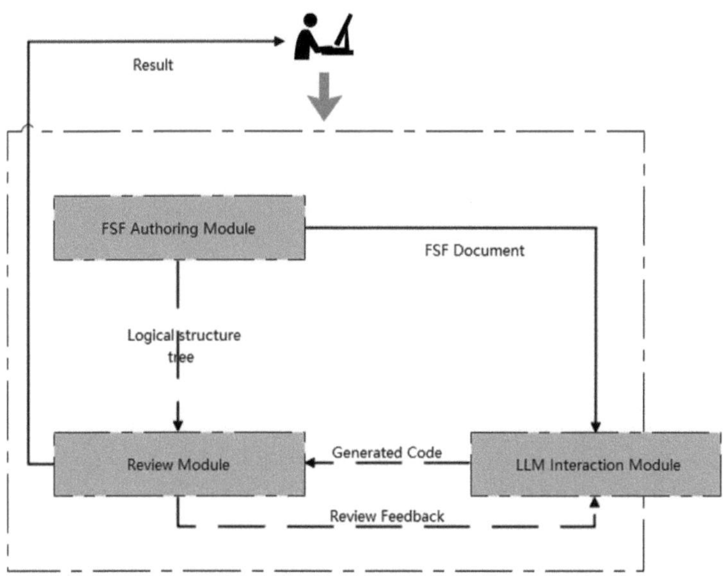

Fig. 1. Overall architecture of our framework. It consists of three core modules engineered to guide developers through a seamless "Specify-Generate-Review" workflow.

1. Specify - The FSF Authoring Module: This module serves as the entry point for user interaction with the framework. It allows developers to invoke FSF (Functional Scenario Form) templates at any point during the coding process to precisely define the functional requirements of a function or module.

Upon completion of a template, the module automatically formats the input into a standard FSF specification, preparing it for the subsequent code generation phase. Figure 2 shows the FSF template.

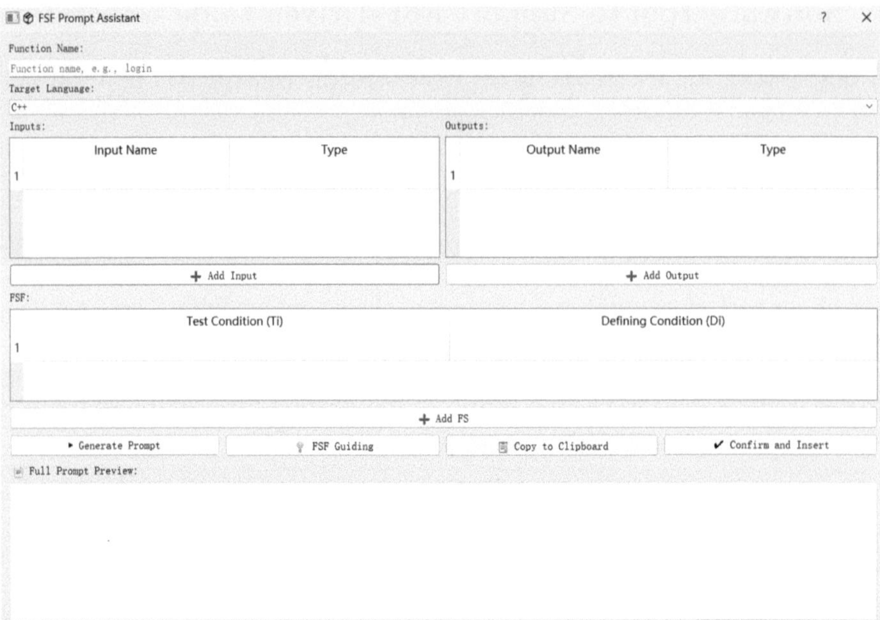

Fig. 2. FSF template interface. The figure illustrates the layout and components of the template used for defining functional requirements.

2. Generate - The LLM Interaction Module: This module acts as the bridge between the specification and the code. It receives the FSF specification from the authoring module and utilizes it as a well-structured prompt. As shown in Fig. 3, this prompt is first inserted into the program generation process. It is then submitted to an integrated Large Language Model (LLM) for code generation. Subsequently, the resulting code segment is routed to the review module for subsequent analysis.

3. Review - The Verification Module: Extending beyond mere code generation, our methodology uses the original specification to guide a crucial verification stage. This module provides an innovative review interface. As shown in Fig. 4, it presents information in a top-and-down view. The top panel displays the FSF specification, which has been automatically converted into a logical tree, while the bottom panel shows the source code generated by the LLM. This dual-view interface facilitates systematic review. It allows users to easily verify that the code implementation completely covers every functional scenario defined in the specification and to flag any identified inconsistencies for further review or refinement.

```
// Mark the book as borrowed
void BorrowManage::markBookAsBorrowed(const std::string& bookID) {
    if (library.find(bookID) != library.end()) {
        library[bookID] = true;
    }
}
// Check the status of a book
### Instruction for LLM:
### You are a precise software engineer. Based on the following FSF specification, please implement the function `UpdateBorrowStatus` in C++.
→ Input:
- userID: string
- bookID: string
→ Output:
- result: string
→ FSF:
bookID not in library &&
  Book not found
OR
book is already borrowed &&
  Book not available
OR
userID has borrowed >= 5 books &&
  Borrowing limit reached
OR
book is available AND user is rligible &&
  update borrow record and Borrow successful
#
// Add a borrowing record for the user
void BorrowManage::addBorrowRecord(const std::string& userID, const std::string& bookID) {
    userRecords[userID].push_back(bookID);
}
```

Fig. 3. Insertion of the FSF-based prompt into the program generation process.

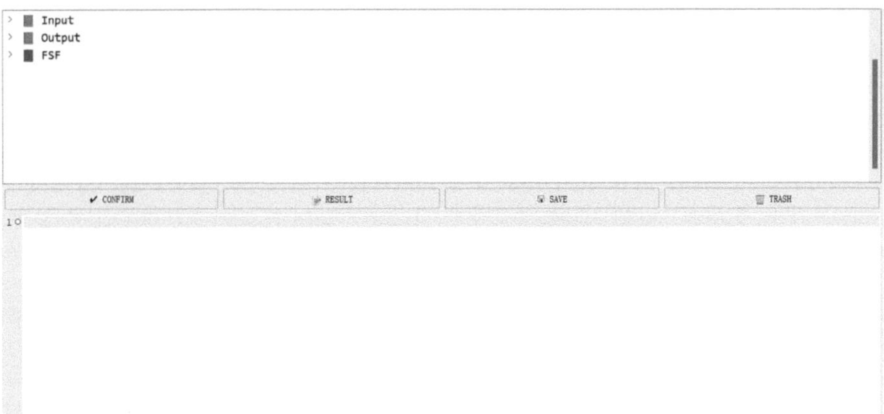

Fig. 4. The review interface displaying FSF specification and generated code.

3.2 Guided Specification Writing Through the FSF Template

Our tool can be directly integrated into the developer's workflow, providing a standardized template to create FSF specifications. Unlike free-form text writing, users are presented with a structured interface that guides them to define the functionality of a software unit (such as a function or method) by completing various fields to complete the specification description. The core structure of this template is composed of multiple "Functional Scenarios" with each scenario containing two main parts: Test Condition: This is used to describe the pre-state or input conditions under which this specific scenario applies. Users are advised to use clear and logical language for their descriptions. Defining Condition: This is used to describe the expected outcome, state change, or return value when the test condition is met. An FSF (Formal Specification Framework) of a process is expressed as a disjunction of multiple functional scenarios (FS1 | | FS2 | |... | | FSn), where each scenario is a conjunction of a test condition (Ti) and a defining condition (Di), separated by the symbol && for readability.

Users can add as many scenarios as needed to cover all expected behaviors, including boundary cases and error conditions. The template also allows us to define the input function name, parameters, and parameter types, while also allowing the target language to be specified. Furthermore, it provides guidance for writing the FSF. After the user has completed the template, they can generate the FSF format as defined in Agile-SOFL with a single click. In its first stage, our framework reduces the cognitive load on developers by providing a structured writing experience based on predefined templates. This enables developers to focus on the logical essence of the requirements rather than the syntactical details of the specification language.

3.3 Systematic Review via Structural Tree Comparison

Our framework does not just use the FSF as a prompt to interact with an LLM to obtain code. It also provides a mechanism for verifying that the LLM-generated code correctly implements the specification by converting the FSF into a tree structure. This mechanism also allows users to annotate the review process, generate a review report, and engage in multiple interactions with the LLM.

The review module is displayed in an interface with two vertically arranged panels. The upper panel shows the FSF parsed into a tree structure, with its child nodes being Input, Output, and FSF. The child nodes under Input and Output are their respective parameters, while under FSF are the various functional scenarios. The tree structure organizes each functional scenario into a "Test Condition -> Defining Condition" format, retaining only the essential conditions and removing symbols. This design ensures that reviewers focus on the core content without being distracted by unnecessary details. When a reviewer clicks on a parameter within Input or Output, the corresponding parameter in the code area below is automatically highlighted. When a functional scenario node in the FSF tree is clicked, the tool automatically highlights the corresponding code block in the code below. The technical implementation of this mapping leverages a key characteristic of LLM behavior: LLMs typically generate code according to the logical order of the prompt. Given that FSF functional scenarios are primarily if-structures, our tool first extracts the if statements from the generated code and maps them to the nodes in the FSF tree. To ensure accuracy, We also perform a comparison of the content. This provides a check on two levels, based on both structure and content, to ensure the accuracy of the highlighting.

Reviewers can systematically browse the FSF tree node by node to ensure that every specified scenario has a corresponding and correctly implemented code block. This transforms the process of code review into a methodical checklist verification task. If a reviewer finds an inconsistency or an issue with a specific line of code, they can directly click on the relevant code line to add an annotation. Annotations can be free-form text or selected from a predefined list of common issues. After the whole review is complete, a review report can be generated with a single click. This report specifically records the locations and content of the issues and can also be used as a new prompt sent to the LLM to conduct iterative interactions, leveraging features like ChatGPT's context memory.

4 Case Study: A Library Management System

4.1 Introduction to the Case Study

To demonstrate the practical application and effectiveness of our FSF-driven framework, this section presents a case study centered on a common software application: a Library Management System. The system comprises several core modules, including user login, book searching, borrowing, returning, and administrative functions for adding new books. While the tool can be applied to any module, we will focus on a function within the borrowing module: the process of updating a book's borrowing status. We chose this function because its logic, while seemingly simple, involves multiple preconditions and state changes that are prone to implementation errors, especially when relying on ambiguous natural language prompts. The objective of this case study is to provide a step-by-step walkthrough of our tool's complete "Specify-Generate-Review" workflow. We will demonstrate how a developer uses the tool.

4.2 Formal Specification and Code Generation

The first step in the workflow involves the developer using our tool to fill out an FSF template. In this case, the developer translates the requirements for the UpdateBorrowStatus function into the structured fields of the template. The detailed information is shown in Fig. 5. This action converts natural language requirements into a structured format.

Once the template is complete, the tool automatically generates the FSF specification. More importantly, it uses this specification to construct a clear prompt ready to be sent to a Large Language Model (LLM), as illustrated in Fig. 6. This generated prompt explicitly defines all necessary components for code generation, including the required parameters (userID, bookID), their data types (string), and the target programming language (C++). It also lays out the four possible execution paths and their corresponding return values.

Compared to traditional natural language requirements, this formal specification significantly reduces ambiguity, enabling the LLM to understand the developer's intent with much higher accuracy. After sending this prompt to the LLM, the tool receives the generated code, which is displayed as shown in Fig. 7. A preliminary inspection shows that the generated code generally conforms to the logic laid out in the FSF specification. However, it is not yet certain whether the code is completely correct or if it contains deviations or potential defects. This necessitates the next step in our workflow: review module. To facilitate this process, the tool automatically parses the FSF into a tree structure, as shown in Fig. 8, providing a visual representation that allows the reviewer to check each

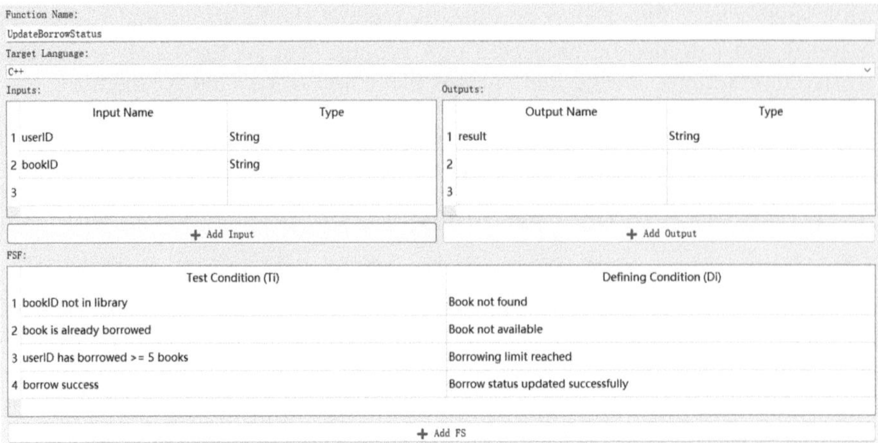

Fig. 5. Filled FSF template for `UpdateBorrowStatus`.

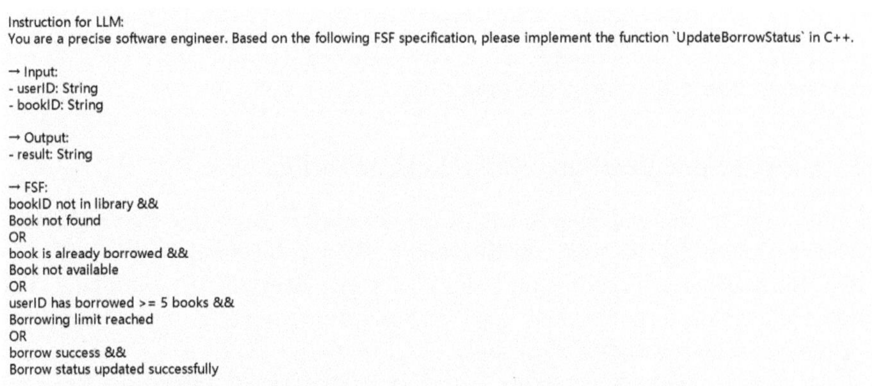

Fig. 6. Generated FSF specification and LLM prompt.

functional scenario against the corresponding code block. By clicking on a functional scenario node in the FSF tree, the reviewer can highlight and navigate to the related section of code.

For example, when reviewing line 5 of the generated code, the reviewer notices a potential improvement. They want to optimize the logic by merging this condition with the previous one and avoiding multiple accesses to library[bookID]. They can directly click on that line and insert an annotation, as shown in Fig. 9. The annotation can be free-form text or selected from a predefined list of common review suggestions (e.g., readability improvements, logic error, or performance optimization). After the completion of all reviews, the tool can generate a review report in a single click. This report documents all identified issues or suggestions, including their locations and comments, and can also serve as an

```
std::string UpdateBorrowStatus(const std::string &userID, const std::string &bookID) {
    if (library.find(bookID) == library.end()) {
        return "Book not found";
    }
    if (library[bookID].isBorrowed) {
        return "Book not available";
    }
    if (userBorrowCount[userID] >= 5) {
        return "Borrowing limit reached";
    }
    library[bookID].isBorrowed = true;
    userBorrowCount[userID]++;
    return "Borrow status updated successfully";
}
```

Fig. 7. LLM-generated C++ code for the function.

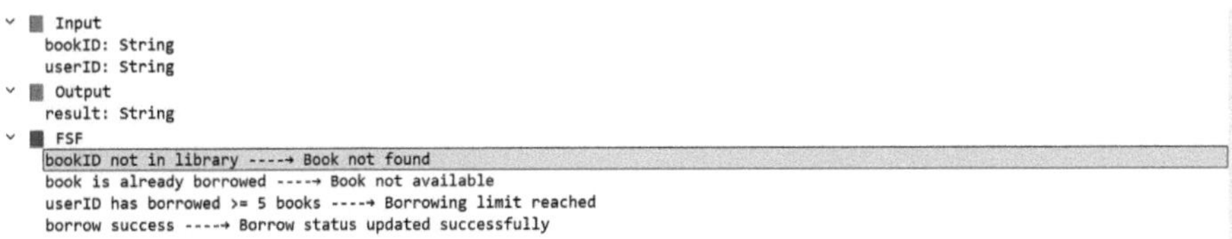

Fig. 8. Visual FSF tree for scenario mapping.

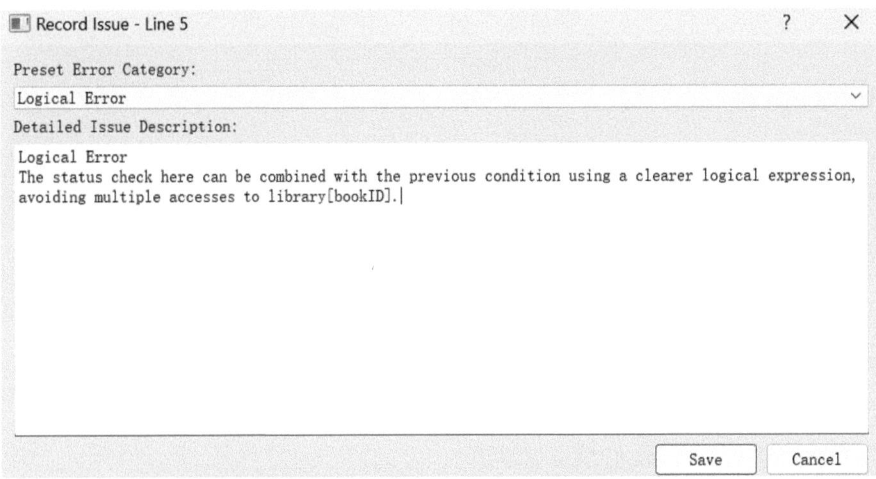

Fig. 9. Code review interface with annotations.

additional prompt for the LLM in subsequent iterations, enabling multi-turn refinement of the generated code.

5 Conclusion and Future Work

In this paper, we introduced and implemented a novel software tool centered on the Functional Scenario Form (FSF) from the Agile-SOFL methodology. The structured and unambiguous nature of FSF specifications provides the precise guidance needed to ensure that LLM generates reliable and verifiable code. In turn, the automation capabilities of LLMs significantly accelerate the code implementation phase in specification-driven development. Our FSF-based tool provides a concrete framework for integrating semi-formal specifications with LLM-based automation. It effectively meets the need for rapid iteration in Agile development and ensures the precision required for high-quality software engineering. Future efforts could be directed towards two key aspects. First, the functionality of the tool can be further extended. This includes support for a wider range of programming languages and strategies to reduce the time required for template input. Second, we plan to conduct more extensive empirical evaluations. While this paper presents an initial validation, future work will involve applying our framework to larger industrial projects.

Acknowledgements. The authors thank Yuxiang Shang and Yanzhao Xia for their support and suggestions on tool construction. This work is supported by a research grant from East China Normal University.

References

1. Beck, K., et al.: Manifesto for agile software development (2001)
2. Brown, T., et al.: Language models are few-shot learners. Adv. Neural Inf. Process. Syst. **33**, 1877–1901 (2020)
3. Chen, M., et al.: Evaluating large language models trained on code. arXiv preprint arXiv:2107.03374 (2021)
4. Jones, C.B.: Systematic Software Development using VDM, vol. 66. Prentice Hall International Englewood Cliffs (1986)
5. Li, Y., et al.: Competition-level code generation with alphacode. Science **378**(6624), 1092–1097 (2022)
6. Liu, S.: Agile-SOFL: agile formal engineering method. Springer (2024)
7. OpenAI: introducing GPT-5 (2025)
8. Sahoo, P., et alA.: A systematic survey of prompt engineering in large language models: Techniques and applications. arXiv preprint arXiv:2402.07927 (2024)
9. Spivey, J.M., Abrial, J.R.: The Z Notation, vol. 29. Prentice Hall Hemel Hempstead (1992)
10. Wei, J., et al.: Chain-of-thought prompting elicits reasoning in large language models. Adv. Neural Inf. Process. Syst. **35**, 24824–24837 (2022)

Model Checking the Two-Phase Commit Protocol for Distributed Database Systems

Yisong Yu[1(✉)], Naipeng Dong[2], Jun Pang[3], and Jin Song Dong[1]

[1] School of Computing, National University of Singapore, Singapore, Singapore
e0792458@u.nus.edu

[2] School of EECS, The University of Queensland, Brisbane, Australia

[3] Department of Computer Science, University of Luxembourg, Luxembourg City, Luxembourg

Abstract. The reliability of distributed database management systems is essential in modern applications with inherently distributed architectures, such as cloud services and e-commerce platforms. The atomicity property of distributed transactions is crucial for data integrity and is typically implemented using the Two-Phase Commit (2PC) protocol. However, the correctness of 2PC in the presence of site failures, timeouts, and recovery scenarios remains complex and challenging to validate through traditional proofs alone. This work presents a formal model and verification of the 2PC protocol, including its recovery and termination subprotocols, using the CSP# language and the PAT model checker. Our approach abstracts certain system behaviors, such as communication reliability and log persistence, to improve verification efficiency while preserving correctness semantics. We explore the impact of bounded site failures and timeout occurrences on the protocol's verifiability, revealing a direct correlation between error frequency and state-space explosion.

Keywords: Model Checking · Distributed Database · 2-Phase Commit

1 Introduction

The rapid digitalisation of the information age has driven computer applications such as web services and e-commerce platforms to adopt distributed architectures for large-scale data processing. This shift has spurred the development of distributed database management systems, which coordinate logically related databases across multiple sites. Compared to centralised systems, distributed databases offer greater reliability through replication, avoiding single points of failure and maintaining service despite site or link outages. To preserve consistency in such environments, user interactions are executed as distributed transactions—atomic units of work spanning multiple sites—whose correctness depends on ensuring atomicity.

Atomicity is achieved through two key primitives, namely *commit* and *abort*, managed by the recovery manager component (that handles both *transaction*

© The Author(s), under exclusive license to Springer Nature Singapore Pte Ltd. 2026
Y. Chen et al. (Eds.): SFPVV 2025, LNCS 16356, pp. 141–159, 2026.
https://doi.org/10.1007/978-981-95-6032-5_10

recovery and *crash recovery*) of a distributed database management system. These operations ensure that transactions can either complete the remaining actions of a transaction by installing its updated pages into the stable storage, or undo the already executed actions of a transaction by restoring the data in its updated pages in the underlying stable storage to their prior values upon recovery from any sort of failure occurred during the execution process of the given transaction. However, the correctness of the actual implementation of these primitives is contingent on distributed reliability protocols that dictate *when* to correctly perform the appropriate commit or abort operation to achieve the overall atomicity, especially in the presence of potential failures.

Our study focuses on the widely adopted atomic commitment protocol (e.g., by Google [4] and Microsoft [2]) - *Two-Phase Commit Protocol* and its companions *Recovery Protocol* and *Termination Protocol*, which collectively coordinate participating sites to reach a consistent decision on whether to *commit* or *abort* a given transaction. 2PC remains widely used in modern distributed systems. Google Spanner [4], a globally distributed SQL database, uses 2PC for transaction coordination. Microsoft uses 2PC in Fast Remote Memory [11], and Azure's Host Integration Server supports 2PC over the internet [2]. Open-source databases such as CockroachDB [3] and FoundationDB [7] also implement variants of 2PC to ensure fault tolerance. Recently, 2PC has been adapted for blockchain e.g., [12] and cross chain applications e.g., [10].

Several efforts have been made to formally verify 2PC. It has been specified using TLA+ to verify safety properties [6], and translated into Lean to verify consistency [5]. However, these models omit abort messages and site failures. The work [9] uses the mCRL2 process algebra to model 2PC, but does not account for timeout and recovery. Other studies such as [13] focus on performance analysis, while [8] used model checking to investigate cheating behaviour of participants rather than site failures.We model both the basic 2PC and its Termination and Recovery protocols using CSP# language supported by the PAT model checker [14], to formally verify their correctness and resilience.

2 Distributed Two-Phase Commit Protocol

We refer to the transaction manager at the transaction originating site as *coordinator*, and the transaction managers at other sites as *participants*.

2.1 Protocol Description

Basic 2PC Protocol. The basic 2PC Protocol (Fig. 1) has two phases:

Preparation (Voting) Phase. The coordinator initiates the commit process by sending a `Prepare` message to all participants. Participants decide to `Vote-Commit` or `Vote-Abort` based on their local state and respond to the coordinator.

Decision Phase. Based on the collected votes, the coordinator decides:Global commit: if all participants vote to commit; Global abort: if any participant votes

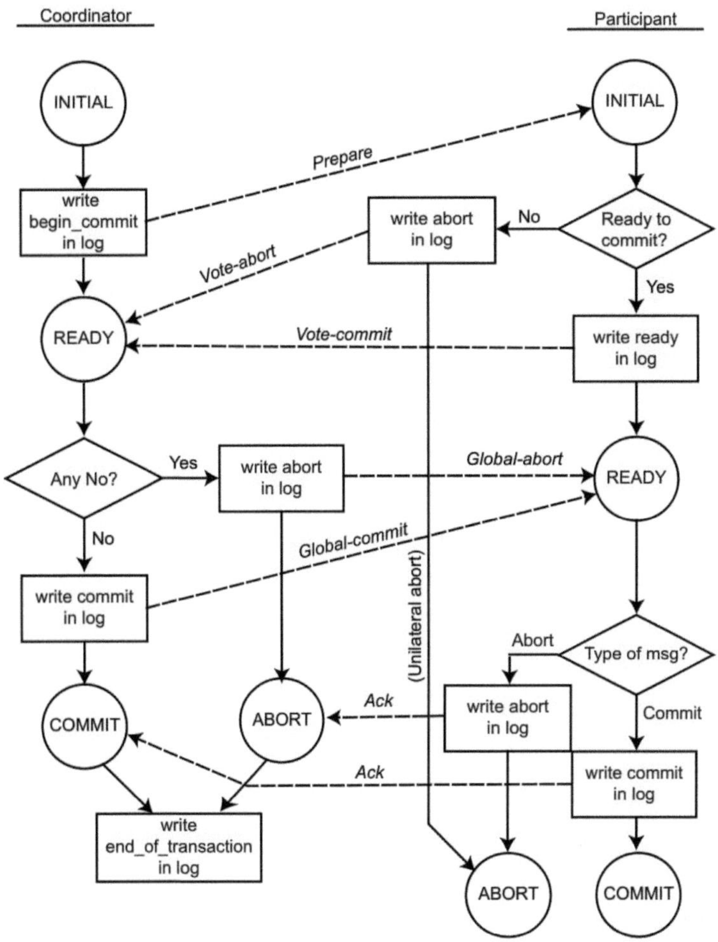

Fig. 1. Basic 2PC [15]. Circles indicate states and dash lines for messages.

to abort. Then, the coordinator communicates the decision to all participants. And participants acknowledge receipt of the decision and update their states.

Two-Phase Termination Protocol. When failures occur, the Termination Protocol handles incomplete transactions to ensure consistency. Failures are detected by the employment of timeout mechanism. The following demonstrates a case-by-case failures occurring at different execution points shown in Fig. 2.

Coordinator Timeouts. There are three states where the coordinator can time out, namely WAIT, COMMIT, and ABORT states. In the WAIT state, the coordinator times out while waiting for votes, and then decides to abort globally.

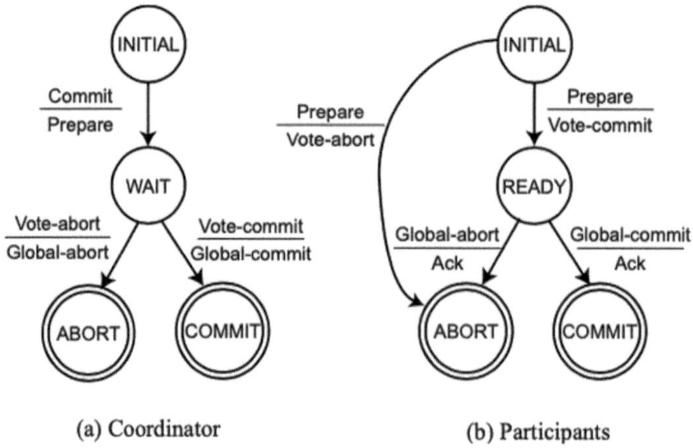

Fig. 2. Termination Based on State Transition [15]. Terminal states are represented by concentric circles. The event that triggers a state transition, by a received message, is at the top; the action taken as a result of a state transition, by a sent message, is at the bottom.

In the COMMIT or ABORT state, the coordinator resends the corresponding global decision to unresponsive participants.

Participant Timeouts. There are two states where a participant can time out namely INITIAL and READY states. In the INITIAL state, a participant times out while waiting for a Prepare message, and then unilaterally aborts. In the READY state, a participant times out while waiting for the coordinator's global decision, and then remains blocked.

Cooperative Termination Protocol. To reduce blocking, participants in the READY state may communicate directly with others. Participants in the INITIAL state unilaterally abort. Participants in ABORT or COMMIT states share their decision to aid others. Participants in the READY state remain uncertain if no conclusive replies are received. While this protocol mitigates blocking, it does not fully resolve it, especially in cases of coordinator failure.

Two-Phase Recovery Protocol. The Recovery Protocol outlines steps for failed sites to rejoin the transaction.

Coordinator Failures: Restart and resend messages depending on last state.

Participant Failures: Resend votes or unilaterally abort based on the logged state. Recovery depends on communication with other sites to synchronize states and ensure consistency.

2.2 Claimed Properties of the Protocol

The 2PC Protocol aims to ensure the following critical properties [15] in the presence of failures, whose formal definitions are presented later in Sect. 4.

Agreement: All participants reach the same global decision.

Abort Preference: If any participant votes abort, the global decision is abort.

Commit Preference: If no failures occur and all participants vote to commit, the global decision is to commit.

Vote Alignment: A global commit implies all participants voted commit.

3 System Modelling

3.1 PAT Model Checker and CSP#

We use PAT model checker for verifying the properties of its capability in handling concurrent processes which is key to the modelling of distributed systems [14]. PAT accepts models in CSP# language, whose syntax is as follows:

Definition 1. (CSP# Syntax)[14])

$$
\begin{aligned}
P,\ Q ::= {} & \mathit{Stop} \mid \mathit{Skip} \mid e \rightarrow P \mid e\{\mathit{prog}\} \rightarrow P \mid c!\mathit{exp} \rightarrow P \mid c?x \rightarrow P \mid P[]Q \mid \\
& \mathit{if}(b)\{P\}\ \mathit{else}\ \{Q\} \mid \mathit{ifa}(b)\{P\}\ \mathit{else}\ \{Q\} \mid P;Q \mid P||Q \mid P|||Q \mid \\
& P\ \mathit{interrupt}\ Q \mid P \backslash A
\end{aligned}
$$

A system is modelled as a process; and a process or subprocess is denoted as P or Q. *Stop* represents inaction, while *Skip* denotes successful termination. An event $e \rightarrow P$ performs e before continuing as P, and $e\{prog\} \rightarrow P$ additionally executes a program fragment *prog* atomically. Channel operations include sending an expression over channel c ($c!exp \rightarrow P$) and receiving over c and referring it as variable x ($c?x \rightarrow P$), namely sending a value of an expression *exp* to channel c or receiving a value from channel c into the variable x. Choices are expressed with external choice ($P[]Q$), conditional ($\mathit{if}(b)\{P\}\ \mathit{else}\ \{Q\}$), and atomic conditional ($\mathit{ifa}(b)\{P\}\ \mathit{else}\ \{Q\}$). Sequential composition is written as $P;Q$, parallel composition with synchronisation as $P||Q$, and interleaved (non-synchronised) parallelism as $P|||Q$. Process $P\ \mathit{interrupt}\ Q$ behaves as specified by P until the first visible event of Q. $P\backslash A$ turns events in A to invisible ones. More details of the modelling language can be found at the PAT User Manual [1].

3.2 Global Constant / Variable Definitions

A list of global constants, channels and variable definitions is shown in Fig. 3, modelling the configurations and messages.

3.3 Coordinator Processes

The Coordinator process (Fig. 4) models a normal execution of the 2PC Protocol starting from the Coordinator_Send_Prepare sub-process that can be interrupted by a random failure event, modelled by the exception event. In such cases, the control is handed over to Coordinator_Error_Handling, which then passes control to Coordinator_Recover. In the worst-case scenario, this recovery process may itself be repeatedly interrupted. To limit the number of allowable site failures, the shared exception event must eventually be disabled, modelled in the parallel Coordinator_Error process that is bounded by the error_count, where the synchronisation of the two parallel processes is modelled by shared alphabet. We detail each sub-processes in the remaining section.

```
#define PARTICIPANT_NUMBER 4;
#define COORDINATOR_BOUNDED_ERROR_COUNT 1; //-1 means unbounded
#define PARTICIPANT_BOUNDED_ERROR_COUNT 1; //-1 means unbounded
#define COORDINATOR_BOUNDED_TIMEOUT_COUNT 2;
enum {C_INITIAL, C_WAIT, C_ABORT, C_COMMIT, P_INITIAL, P_READY, P_ABORT, P_COMMIT,
     C_MSG_PREPARE, C_MSG_GLOBAL_COMMIT, C_MSG_GLOBAL_ABORT, P_MSG_VOTE_COMMIT,
      P_MSG_VOTE_ABORT, P_MSG_ACK, P_MSG_DECISION_REQUEST, P_MSG_DECISION_UNCERTAIN,
     P_MSG_DECISION_COMMIT, P_MSG_DECISION_ABORT, MSG_NULL};
channel network[PARTICIPANT_NUMBER] 5;
channel peer_network[PARTICIPANT_NUMBER * PARTICIPANT_NUMBER] 1;
var coordinator_state = C_INITIAL;
hvar coordinator_sent_messages = [MSG_NULL(PARTICIPANT_NUMBER)];
hvar coordinator_received_messages = [MSG_NULL(PARTICIPANT_NUMBER)];
hvar coordinator_received_messages_are_same = true;
hvar coordinator_timeout = false;
var participants_state = [P_INITIAL(PARTICIPANT_NUMBER)];
hvar participants_received_message = [MSG_NULL(PARTICIPANT_NUMBER)];
hvar participants_sent_message = [MSG_NULL(PARTICIPANT_NUMBER)];
hvar participants_decision_request_responses[PARTICIPANT_NUMBER][PARTICIPANT_NUMBER];
hvar participants_decision_request_result=[P_MSG_DECISION_UNCERTAIN(PARTICIPANT_NUMBER)];
```

Fig. 3. Global Constants and Variables.

```
Coordinator() = Coordinator_Error(COORDINATOR_BOUNDED_ERROR_COUNT) ||
(Coordinator_Send_Prepare(COORDINATOR_BOUNDED_TIMEOUT_COUNT)
interrupt exception -> Coordinator_Error_Handling(COORDINATOR_BOUNDED_TIMEOUT_COUNT));
Coordinator_Error_Handling(timeout_count) =  Coordinator_Recover(timeout_count) interrupt
    exception -> Coordinator_Error_Handling(timeout_count);
Coordinator_Error(error_count) =
[error_count != 0](exception->Coordinator_Error(error_count-1)) [] [error_count == 0]Skip;
```

Fig. 4. The Coordinator Process.

Preparation. The execution of the coordinator (Coordinator_Send_Prepare in Fig. 5) starts with a state transition from C_INITIAL to C_WAIT, followed by concurrently sending a C_MSG_PREPARE message in an interleaved manner

```
Coordinator_Send_Prepare(timeout_count) = c_prepare{coordinator_state = C_WAIT;} ->
(||| i: {0..PARTICIPANT_NUMBER-1} @ ((ifa (coordinator_sent_messages[i] == MSG_NULL) {
atomic{network[i]!C_MSG_PREPARE ->
    c_prepare_sent_to.i{coordinator_sent_messages[i] = C_MSG_PREPARE;} -> Skip}} else {
c_prepare_already_sent_to.i->Skip})\{c_prepare_sent_to.i,c_prepare_already_sent_to.i}));
Coordinator_Collect_Votes(timeout_count);
```

Fig. 5. Coordinator - Preparation.

to each participant `i` through the corresponding channel `network[i]` if it hasn't already done so and recording this message sent in `coordinator_sent_messages[i]`.

We model the coordinator to record sent messages for handling site failures that may occur mid-process, where the `C_MSG_PREPARE` message only reaches some participants but not all. This will trigger recovery which passes the control flow back to the start of this process, causing the same message to be resent and buffered twice for some participants, complicating participant-side handling.

```
Coordinator_Collect_Votes_Auxiliary(timeout_count) =
||| i: {0..PARTICIPANT_NUMBER-1} @ ((
if (coordinator_received_messages[i] == MSG_NULL) {
atomic{network[i]?P_MSG_VOTE_COMMIT ->
 c_vote_commit_collected_from.i{coordinator_received_messages[i] = P_MSG_VOTE_COMMIT;}
    -> Skip []
network[i]?P_MSG_VOTE_ABORT ->
c_vote_abort_collected_from.i{coordinator_received_messages[i] = P_MSG_VOTE_ABORT;}
    -> Skip}
} else {c_vote_already_collected_from.i -> Skip
}) \ {c_vote_commit_collected_from.i, c_vote_abort_collected_from.i,
        c_vote_already_collected_from.i});
Coordinator_Collect_Votes(timeout_count) =
([timeout_count != 0](Coordinator_Collect_Votes_Auxiliary(timeout_count) interrupt
    Coordinator_Terminate(timeout_count - 1)) []
[timeout_count == 0]Coordinator_Collect_Votes_Auxiliary(timeout_count));
Coordinator_Make_Global_Decision(timeout_count);
```

Fig. 6. Coordinator - Vote Collection.

Vote Collection. Once the coordinator sends `C_MSG_PREPARE` to all participants, `Coordinator_Collect_Vote` process (Fig. 6) is invoked to collect the vote from each participant. This process listens on channel `network[i]` to receive `P_MSG_VOTE_COMMIT` or `P_MSG_VOTE_ABORT` if local decision hasn't been received, modelled in `Coordinator_Collect_Votes_Auxiliary`. The received messages are stored in `coordinator_received_message[i]` for decision-making.

The `Coordinator_Collect_Votes` process simulates bounded timeout errors using the `interrupt` construct, when the coordinator is in the `C_WAIT` state. If the initial value passed to the `Coordinator_Collect_Votes` process is greater than 0, it is decremented by 1 each time a timeout occurs. Eventually, it reaches 0, at which point the process can no longer time out and will proceed to decision making. This mechanism effectively bounds the number of allowed timeouts at the coordinator site. The same approach is applied in all subsequent process definitions where coordinator timeouts need to be limited.

Time Modelling. Abstraction is applied on the process level to abstract away the timing details, namely we use the non-timed interrupt construct instead of the timed construct e.g., `interrupt[t]`, as their semantics are considered to be the same in this case. In the matter of result, both of them simulate exactly the same timeout behaviour in this scenario, but the later one using timed `interrupt[t]` would inevitably bloat the state space due to the extra global clock process being concurrently executed with other user-defined processes, resulting in more execution traces being generated with potentially more states that need to be searched for during the verification process. Similarly, the current implementation is considered to be the most efficient with redundant details eliminated as much as possible to simplify the model, and the same idea applies to all subsequent process definitions where timeout errors occur.

```
Coordinator_Make_Global_Decision(timeout_count) =
ifa (!coordinator_timeout) {tau{coordinator_received_messages_are_same = true;
var index = 0; while (index < PARTICIPANT_NUMBER) {
if (coordinator_received_messages[index] == P_MSG_VOTE_ABORT) {
coordinator_received_messages_are_same = false;} index = index + 1;}} ->
ifa (coordinator_received_messages_are_same) {
Coordinator_Send_Global_Commit(timeout_count)
} else {Coordinator_Send_Global_Abort(timeout_count)}};
#alphabet Coordinator_Send_Global_Commit {
i: {0..(PARTICIPANT_NUMBER-1)} @ c_global_commit_already_sent_to.i};
Coordinator_Send_Global_Commit(timeout_count) =
c_global_commit{coordinator_state = C_COMMIT;} -> (||| i: {0..PARTICIPANT_NUMBER-1} @ (
ifa (coordinator_sent_messages[i] == C_MSG_PREPARE) {
atomic{network[i]!C_MSG_GLOBAL_COMMIT ->
c_global_commit_sent_to.i{coordinator_sent_messages[i] = C_MSG_GLOBAL_COMMIT;} -> Skip}
} else {c_global_commit_already_sent_to.i -> Skip }
) \ {c_global_commit_sent_to.i, c_global_commit_already_sent_to.i});
Coordinator_Receive_ACK(timeout_count);
#alphabet Coordinator_Send_Global_Abort {
i: {0..(PARTICIPANT_NUMBER-1)} @ c_global_abort_already_sent_to.i,
i: {0..(PARTICIPANT_NUMBER-1)} @ c_global_abort_no_need_to_send_to.i};
Coordinator_Send_Global_Abort(timeout_count)=c_global_abort{coordinator_state = C_ABORT;}->
(||| i: {0..PARTICIPANT_NUMBER-1} @ (ifa (coordinator_sent_messages[i] == C_MSG_PREPARE &&
coordinator_received_messages[i]!=P_MSG_VOTE_ABORT){atomic{network[i]!C_MSG_GLOBAL_ABORT ->
    c_global_abort_sent_to.i{coordinator_sent_messages[i] = C_MSG_GLOBAL_ABORT;} -> Skip}
} else if (coordinator_sent_messages[i] == C_MSG_GLOBAL_ABORT) {
          c_global_abort_already_sent_to.i -> Skip
} else {c_global_abort_no_need_to_send_to.i -> Skip
}) \ {c_global_abort_sent_to.i, c_global_abort_already_sent_to.i,
        c_global_abort_no_need_to_send_to.i}); Coordinator_Receive_ACK(timeout_count);
```

Fig. 7. Coordinator - Global Decision.

Global Decision. As soon as all the local decision messages are received and recorded by the coordinator, the process `Coordinator_Make_Global_Decision` (Fig. 7) is invoked to discover whether there's any participant voting to abort by looping through all recorded votes. If at least one negative vote if found, rendering the flag `coordinator_received_messages_are_same` to be false, a global abort signal is sent in the process Coordinator_Send_Global_Abort, otherwise Coordinator_Send_Global_Commit is invoked to signal a global commit.

The Coordinator_Send_Global_Commit process starts with a state transition from C_WAIT to C_COMMIT, followed by sending a C_MSG_GLOBAL_COMMIT message concurrently to each participant i through the corresponding channel network[i] and recording this message sent in coordinator_sent_messages[i].

The Coordinator_Send_Global_Abort process starts with a state transition from C_WAIT to C_ABORT, followed by concurrently sending a C_MSG_GLOBAL_ABORT message to each participant i voting to commit through the corresponding channel network[i] and recording this message in coordinator_sent_messages[i].

```
Coordinator_Receive_ACK_Auxiliary() =
||| i: {0..PARTICIPANT_NUMBER-1} @ ((
ifa (coordinator_received_messages[i] == P_MSG_VOTE_ABORT ||
        coordinator_received_messages[i] == P_MSG_VOTE_COMMIT) {
atomic{network[i]?P_MSG_ACK ->
          c_ack_received_from.i{coordinator_received_messages[i] = P_MSG_ACK;} -> Skip}
} else {c_ack_no_need_to_receive_from.i -> Skip
} \ {c_ack_received_from.i, c_ack_no_need_to_receive_from.i}) );
Coordinator_Receive_ACK(timeout_count) =
[timeout_count != 0](Coordinator_Receive_ACK_Auxiliary()
    interrupt Coordinator_Terminate(timeout_count - 1)) []
[timeout_count == 0]Coordinator_Receive_ACK_Auxiliary();
```

Fig. 8. Coordinator - Ack Collection.

Ack Collection. No matter the global decision is to commit or abort, the process moves to the execution of Coordinator_Receive_ACK (Fig. 8). The process collects an acknowledgement from each participant. Similarly, listening to channel network[i] for the P_MSG_ACK message is modelled in an auxiliary process Coordinator_Receive_ACK_Auxiliary, and the received message is recorded in coordinator_received_messages[i] for each participant i. The main process Coordinator_Receive_ACK simulates the bounded timeout errors of the coordinator in C_ABORT or C_COMMIT state, in a similar manner as above.

```
Coordinator_Recover(timeout_count) =
ifa (coordinator_state == C_COMMIT) {Coordinator_Send_Global_Commit(timeout_count)
} else if (coordinator_state == C_ABORT) {Coordinator_Send_Global_Abort(timeout_count)
} else {Coordinator_Send_Prepare(timeout_count) };
```

Fig. 9. Coordinator - Recovery.

Recovery. The `Coordinator_Recover` process is invoked whenever a site failure occurs to help the coordinator to recover its state. The modelling is straightforward following the protocol specification (Fig. 9). Note that since duplicate messages sent to the same participant multiple times will be strictly prohibited by each individual process defined previously, we do not need to guard against these cases again. And considering that the coordinator will always resume in `C_INITIAL` state no matter it fails in `C_INITIAL` or `C_WAIT`, these two scenarios are consolidated into one for simplicity, collectively handled by the `Coordinator_Send_Prepare` process in the else block(Figs. 10,11,12,13 and 14).

```
Coordinator_Terminate(timeout_count) = tau{coordinator_timeout = true;} ->
ifa (coordinator_state == C_COMMIT) { Coordinator_Send_Global_Commit(timeout_count)
} else if (coordinator_state == C_ABORT) { Coordinator_Send_Global_Abort(timeout_count)
} else { c_global_abort{coordinator_state = C_ABORT;} ->
(||| i: {0..PARTICIPANT_NUMBER-1} @ (atomic {if (!call(cempty, network[i])) {
network[i]?message -> case {
message == P_MSG_VOTE_ABORT:tau{coordinator_received_messages[i] = P_MSG_VOTE_ABORT} -> Skip
message == P_MSG_VOTE_COMMIT:tau{coordinator_received_messages[i] = P_MSG_VOTE_COMMIT}->Skip
default: Skip //default covers the case where message == C_MSG_PREPARE}};
network[i]!C_MSG_GLOBAL_ABORT ->
c_global_abort_sent_to.i{coordinator_sent_messages[i] = C_MSG_GLOBAL_ABORT;} ->
network[i]?P_MSG_ACK ->
c_ack_received_from.i{coordinator_received_messages[i] = P_MSG_ACK;} -> Skip } )) };
```

Fig. 10. Coordinator - Termination.

Termination. The `Coordinator_Terminate` process is invoked when a site failure is detected to help the coordinator to gracefully terminate the current active transaction. Similar to how the recovery protocol is implemented, timeout in `C_COMMIT` or `C_ABORT` state is handled in an elegant manner by delegating the control back to `Coordinator_Send_Global_Commit` process and `Coordinator_Send_Global_Abort` process respectively.

However,timeout in the `C_WAIT` state must be handled as a special case instead of simply passing the control back to `Coordinator_Send_Global_Abort`. If there's a message sitting in the buffer of `network[i]` for a participant `i`, message must be one of the following: `P_MSG_VOTE_ABORT` or `P_MSG_VOTE_COMMIT` if that participant `i` has already sent its decision to the coordinator and transitioned from `P_INITIAL` to `P_ABORT` or `P_READY`; `C_MSG_PREPARE` if participant `i` remains in `P_INITIAL` and hasn't processed it yet. In all cases, the coordinator should consume (i.e. by reading) the obsolete message to clear the channel buffer. Recall that `network[i]` supports bidirectional communication, any unprocessed message in the channel can block subsequent communication, stalling the entire system. To prevent this, the coordinator must clear the channel buffer before sending the global abort message (`C_MSG_GLOBAL_ABORT`) to the `network[i]`, and then wait for an acknowledgement(`P_MSG_ACK`). Because each `network[i]` is independent, the above actions are encapsulated in a separate sub-process per participant, interleaved within the `Coordinator_Terminate` process.

```
Participant_Receive_Prepare(i) = ((atomic{network[i]?C_MSG_PREPARE->p_prepare_received_by.i{
   participants_received_message[i] = C_MSG_PREPARE;} -> Skip
} interrupt Participant_Terminate(i)) \ {p_prepare_received_by.i});
(Participant_Send_Vote_Commit(i) [] Participant_Send_Vote_Abort(i));

Participant_Send_Vote_Abort(i)=(ifa(participants_received_message[i]==C_MSG_GLOBAL_ABORT &&
    participants_sent_message[i]==P_MSG_ACK){p_global_abort_prematurely_received_by.i->Skip
} else { atomic{network[i]!P_MSG_VOTE_ABORT -> p_vote_abort_sent_by.i{
participants_sent_message[i] = P_MSG_VOTE_ABORT; participants_state[i] = P_ABORT;
} -> Skip } }) \ {p_global_abort_prematurely_received_by.i};

Participant_Send_Vote_Commit(i)=(ifa(participants_received_message[i]==C_MSG_GLOBAL_ABORT &&
    participants_sent_message[i]==P_MSG_ACK){p_global_abort_prematurely_received_by.i->Skip
} else if (participants_sent_message[i] == MSG_NULL) {
atomic{ network[i]!P_MSG_VOTE_COMMIT -> p_vote_commit_sent_by.i{
participants_sent_message[i] = P_MSG_VOTE_COMMIT; participants_state[i] = P_READY;
} -> Skip }; Participant_Collect_Decision(i)
} else { p_vote_commit_already_sent_by.i -> Participant_Collect_Decision(i)
}) \ {p_global_abort_prematurely_received_by.i, p_vote_commit_already_sent_by.i};

Participant_Collect_Decision(i) = ((ifa(participants_received_message[i] == C_MSG_PREPARE){
atomic{network[i]?C_MSG_GLOBAL_COMMIT -> p_global_commit_received_by.i{
participants_received_message[i] = C_MSG_GLOBAL_COMMIT; } -> Skip  []
network[i]?C_MSG_GLOBAL_ABORT -> p_global_abort_received_by.i{
participants_received_message[i] = C_MSG_GLOBAL_ABORT;}->Skip}; Participant_Send_ACK(i)
} else { p_global_decision_already_received_by.i -> Participant_Send_ACK(i)
}) \ {p_global_commit_received_by.i, p_global_abort_received_by.i,
    p_global_decision_already_received_by.i}) interrupt Participant_Terminate(i);

Participant_Send_ACK(i) = (ifa (participants_received_message[i] == C_MSG_GLOBAL_COMMIT &&
    participants_sent_message[i] != P_MSG_ACK) {
atomic{network[i]!P_MSG_ACK->p_ack_commit_sent_by.i{participants_state[i]=P_COMMIT;}->Skip}
} else if (participants_received_message[i] == C_MSG_GLOBAL_ABORT &&
    participants_sent_message[i] != P_MSG_ACK) {
atomic{ network[i]!P_MSG_ACK->p_ack_abort_sent_by.i{participants_state[i]=P_ABORT;}->Skip}
} else { p_ack_already_sent_by.i -> Skip }) \ {p_ack_already_sent_by.i};
```

Fig. 11. Participant i - Recovery, Termination and Error Handling

3.4 Participant Processes

Site failures invoke `Participant_Recover(i)` to recover. If failure occurs in `P_INITIAL`, the participant unilaterally aborts. If in `P_READY`, it can resume from `Participant_Send_Vote_Commit(i)`. `Participant_Terminate(i)` models a graceful termination. Timeout in `P_INITIAL` results in an abort, and timeout in `P_READY` invokes `Participant_Cooperative_Terminate(i)` for recovery.

A special feature for participants is that cooperative termination may be invoked by a participant `i` when the coordinator is unavailable, modelled in `Participant_Cooperative_Terminate(i,j)`. It spawns a thread for each participant `j` executed as `Participant_Cooperative_Terminate_Thread(i,j)`. Each thread sends a `P_MSG_DECISION_REQUEST` for participant `j` over the channel `peer_network[i * PARTICIPANT_NUMBER + j]`, waits for a response, and records them in `participants_decision_request_responses[i][j]`. Once all threads complete, participant `i` scans the collected responses. If any participant replies with a `P_MSG_DECISION_ABORT` or `P_MSG_DECISION_COMMIT`, `i` transitions from `P_READY` to `P_ABORT` or `P_COMMIT` accordingly. If all responses are

P_MSG_DECISION_UNCERTAIN, i must wait for the coordinator's recovery and the eventual global decision broadcast.

At the end of Participant_Cooperative_Terminate(i), a guarded Skip is used to ensure correct semantics, preventing termination unless i reaches a terminal state, namely P_ABORT or P_COMMIT. Note that global decision receipt is handled separately by Participant_Daemon(i).

The Participant_Error(i,error_count) process models bounded site failures using the exception.i event. Each invocation decrements error_count,

```
Participant_Recover(i) = ifa (participants_state[i] == P_INITIAL) {
p_unilaterally_abort_by.i{participants_state[i] = P_ABORT;} -> Skip
} else if (participants_state[i] == P_READY) {Participant_Send_Vote_Commit(i)} else {Skip};

Participant_Terminate(i) =  ifa (participants_state[i] == P_INITIAL) {
p_unilaterally_abort_by.i{participants_state[i] = P_ABORT;} -> Skip
} else { Participant_Cooperative_Terminate(i) };

Participant_Cooperative_Terminate(i) =
(||| j: {0..PARTICIPANT_NUMBER-1} @ Participant_Cooperative_Terminate_Thread(i, j));
tau{participants_decision_request_result[i] = P_MSG_DECISION_UNCERTAIN;
var j = 0; while (j < PARTICIPANT_NUMBER) {
if (participants_decision_request_responses[i][j] == P_MSG_DECISION_ABORT) {
participants_decision_request_result[i] = P_MSG_DECISION_ABORT;
} else if (participants_decision_request_responses[i][j] == P_MSG_DECISION_COMMIT) {
participants_decision_request_result[i] = P_MSG_DECISION_COMMIT;
} j = j + 1; } } -> case {
participants_decision_request_result[i] == P_MSG_DECISION_ABORT:
        p_cooperatively_abort_by.i{participants_state[i] = P_ABORT} -> Skip
participants_decision_request_result[i] == P_MSG_DECISION_COMMIT:
        p_cooperatively_abort_by.i{participants_state[i] = P_COMMIT} -> Skip
default: [participants_state[i] == P_COMMIT || participants_state[i] == P_ABORT] Skip };

Participant_Cooperative_Terminate_Thread(i, j) =
atomic{ peer_network[i * PARTICIPANT_NUMBER + j]!P_MSG_DECISION_REQUEST ->
( peer_network[i * PARTICIPANT_NUMBER + j]?P_MSG_DECISION_ABORT ->
p_decision_abort_received_from_by.j.i{
participants_decision_request_responses[i][j] = P_MSG_DECISION_ABORT; } -> Skip []
peer_network[i * PARTICIPANT_NUMBER + j]?P_MSG_DECISION_COMMIT ->
p_decision_commit_received_from_by.j.i{
participants_decision_request_responses[i][j] = P_MSG_DECISION_COMMIT; } -> Skip []
peer_network[i * PARTICIPANT_NUMBER + j]?P_MSG_DECISION_UNCERTAIN ->
p_decision_uncertain_received_from_by.j.i{
participants_decision_request_responses[i][j] = P_MSG_DECISION_UNCERTAIN; } -> Skip ) };

#alphabet Participant_Error {exception.i};
Participant_Error(i, error_count) =
[error_count!=0](exception.i->Participant_Error(i, error_count-1)) [] [error_count==0]Skip;

Participant_Error_Handling(i) =
  Participant_Recover(i) interrupt exception.i ->Participant_Error_Handling(i);
```

Fig. 12. Overall Participants Process.

```
Participant(i) = Participant_Error(i, PARTICIPANT_BOUNDED_ERROR_COUNT) ||
Participant_Receive_Prepare(i) interrupt exception.i -> Participant_Error_Handling(i);

Participants() = ||| i: {0..PARTICIPANT_NUMBER-1} @ Participant(i);
```

Fig. 13. Participant Daemon Process.

limiting how many failures can occur. Once error_count reaches 0, no further failures are simulated for participant i. To avoid runtime exception during verification, the process alphabet must be explicitly specified due to its recursive nature with decreasing error_count. Participant_Error_Handling(i) wraps Participant_Recover(i) to allow site failure during recovery. This design enables thorough verification by exposing edge cases.

The Overall Participant Process. With all necessary primitives defined, we can now assemble the complete participant(i) process. This process models two concurrent components: the Participant_Error process that models bounded random site failures, and the normal execution of the 2PC Protocol starting from the Participant_Receive_Prepare(i), including potential interruptions.

A natural question may arise: why are timeout events not similarly bounded for a participant i. The reason lies in the structure of Participant_Terminate(i). Unlike Coordinator_Terminate, which may loop back to earlier stages and thus tolerate multiple timeouts, Participant_Terminate(i) does not return control to Participant_Send_Vote_Abort(i) or Participant_Send_Vote_Commit(i). Therefore, a timeout error can occur at most once, eliminating the need for explicit bounding in the model. The Participants() process models the behaviour of all participants in the system by interleaving the execution of all Participant(i) processes, where i ranges from 0 to PARTICIPANT_NUMBER-1.

3.5 Participants Daemon Processes

As previously mentioned, the Participants_Daemon operates independently in the background, separated from each Participant(i) process. It spawns multiple threads—modelled as Participant_Daemon_Thread(i, j)—equal to the number of participants. Each thread performs two key tasks:

- Handling decision requests: Each thread listens on the channel peer_network[j * PARTICIPANT_NUMBER + i] for a P_MSG_DECISION_REQUEST message from participant j. Upon receipt, it replies with: P_MSG_DECISION_ABORT if in P_INITIAL or P_ABORT state, P_MSG_DECISION_COMMIT if in P_COMMIT state, or P_MSG_DECISION_UNCERTAIN if in P_READY state.
- Processing the global decision from the coordinator: Each thread also listens on network[i] for a C_MSG_GLOBAL_COMMIT message or C_MSG_GLOBAL_ABORT message. Upon receipt, it records the message in participants_received_message[i], sends a P_MSG_ACK acknowledge the decision, records the ACK in participants_sent_message[i], and transitions to P_COMMIT or P_ABORT based on the message received.

Participants_Daemon() interleaves the execution of Participant_Daemon(i) processes (for i = 0 to PARTICIPANT_NUMBER-1), modelling the collective background behaviour of all participants.

```
Participants_Daemon() = ||| i: {0..PARTICIPANT_NUMBER-1} @ Participant_Daemon(i);

Participant_Daemon(i) =
(||| j: {0..PARTICIPANT_NUMBER-1} @ Participant_Daemon_Thread(i, j)) |||
atomic{network[i]?C_MSG_GLOBAL_COMMIT -> p_daemon_global_commit_received_by.i{
participants_received_message[i] = C_MSG_GLOBAL_COMMIT;} -> network[i]!P_MSG_ACK ->
p_daemon_ack_commit_sent_by.i{participants_sent_message[i] = P_MSG_ACK;
participants_state[i] = P_COMMIT;} -> Skip []
network[i]?C_MSG_GLOBAL_ABORT -> p_daemon_global_abort_received_by.i{
    participants_received_message[i] = C_MSG_GLOBAL_ABORT;} -> network[i]!P_MSG_ACK ->
p_daemon_ack_abort_sent_by.i{participants_sent_message[i] = P_MSG_ACK;
participants_state[i] = P_ABORT;} -> Skip };

Participant_Daemon_Thread(i, j) =
peer_network[j * PARTICIPANT_NUMBER + i]?P_MSG_DECISION_REQUEST -> case {
participants_state[i] == P_INITIAL:
peer_network[j*PARTICIPANT_NUMBER + i]!P_MSG_DECISION_ABORT->Participant_Daemon_Thread(i,j)
participants_state[i] == P_READY:
peer_network[j*PARTICIPANT_NUMBER+i]!P_MSG_DECISION_UNCERTAIN->Participant_Daemon_Thread(i,j)
participants_state[i] == P_COMMIT:
peer_network[j*PARTICIPANT_NUMBER + i]!P_MSG_DECISION_COMMIT->Participant_Daemon_Thread(i,j)
participants_state[i] == P_ABORT:
peer_network[j* PARTICIPANT_NUMBER + i]!P_MSG_DECISION_ABORT->Participant_Daemon_Thread(i,j)
default: Participant_Daemon_Thread(i, j)};
```

Fig. 14. The Overall System.

3.6 The Overall System Process

The full system, i,e, the `Distributed_System()` process, is an interleaved execution of `Coordinator()`, `Participants()`, and `Participants_Daemon()`[1].

It abstracts communication link failures, avoiding the complexity of simulating unreliable networks. Log writes are also abstracted as atomic state transitions to reduce interleaving and improve verification efficiency. To keep the state space finite and tractable, site failures and timeouts are bounded. Communication link failures may cause delay or message loss. As this model does not implicitly model time for efficiency, latency before timeout is equivalent to message received, and latency after timeout is the same as message loss, as the message being sent will not be persisted but instead dropped. Message loss is captured by no further message sending or receiving after timeout.

```
Distributed_System() = Coordinator() ||| Participants() ||| Participants_Daemon();
```

Fig. 15. Formulation of Properties (Snippet of Four Participants Example)

4 Investigated Properties and Verification Results

Agreement. This property is formulated by the following three sub-properties

[1] Available at https://github.com/YuuYouYoo/CS5219-CS5232-Project.

1. *Agreement 1:* All participants will eventually reach the same global decision—either all commit or all abort.
2. *Agreement 2:* If the coordinator reaches the COMMIT state, then all participants must eventually reach COMMIT.
3. *Agreement 3:* If the coordinator reaches the ABORT state, then all participants must eventually reach ABORT.

Abort Preference. If at least one participant reaches the ABORT state, then all participants must eventually reach ABORT.

Commit preference. This property includes a "no failures" condition. However, in our model, sites are assumed to always recover from failures; therefore, this constraint is omitted for clarity. The property is formulated as: If all participants vote to commit a transaction, then the coordinator must eventually decide to globally commit it.

Vote alignment. If the coordinator decides to globally commit the protocol, then it must be the case that all participants have voted to commit the transaction.

We define a set of assertions to formulate the important properties claimed in the 2PC Protocol, shown in Fig. 15 (four participants as an example).

Verification Results. We verified these properties of models with two, three and four participants using PAT 3.5.1 with Intel Core i7 11800H / 32GB RAM. The result is shown in Table 1, where"-" indicates that no value can be provided. When PAT times out, the values in the *States*, *Transitions*, and *Memory* columns reflect the status at the termination of verification. These are indicative only and do not represent complete verification results.

For two and three participants, the protocol satisfies all specified properties, demonstrating correctness and robustness. In contrast, verification for four participants either timed out after two hours or resulted in an Out-of-Memory error, reflecting the exponential growth in state space. The number of states and transitions for *Commit Preference* and *Vote Alignment* are identical for two and three participants, owing to the structural similarity of the corresponding formulas. However, the verification algorithms diverge, as PAT applies formula-specific optimisations, which in turn account for the observed differences in memory consumption. For *Vote Alignment*, memory usage is lower than that of the other properties; however, verification with four participants still exhausted memory due to exponential growth, whereas the other properties terminated by timeout before memory exhaustion.

5 Experiments and Evaluations

One particularly important direction for further investigation is analysing how key parameters—such as the number of participants, the number of allowed site failures (for both the coordinator and participants), and the permitted coordinator timeout—affect state-space size and verification time. This analysis provides deeper insights into the state-space explosion problem.

Table 1. Verification Results

Property	#Participant	Result	States	Transitions	Time(s)	Memory(KB)
Agreement 1	2	Valid	145218	409901	3.95	105705
	3	Valid	23629458	98961221	1099	15355173
	4	Time Out	39177688	235443330	-	33458016
Agreement 2	2	Valid	124093	314115	3.11	904484
	3	Valid	18638427	64918577	817	10557383
	4	Time Out	43363694	211240199	-	32599380
Agreement 3	2	Valid	140383	388727	3.67	102038
	3	Valid	23355117	97301121	1066	15022524
	4	Time Out	35760192	213465259	-	30358774
Abort Preference	2	Valid	142495	401165	3.93	105368
	3	Valid	23597859	98722316	1116	15173606
	4	Time Out	38179569	228487994	-	32276466
Commit Preference	2	Valid	124093	314115	3.07	91678
	3	Valid	18638427	64918577	793	10895478
	4	Time Out	43571006	21281683	-	32545493
Vote Alignment	2	Valid	124093	314115	2.68	12330
	3	Valid	18638427	64918577	689	824183
	4	OutOfMemory	-	-	-	-

5.1 Impact of Participant Number on Verification Time

We investigated how increasing the number of participants could affect the verification time, by varying the value of `PARTICIPANT_NUMBER` from 2 to 4.

As shown in Table 1, increasing the participant count from 2 to 3 already leads to a dramatic rise in verification time—from a few seconds to several thousand seconds—while keeping all others unchanged. This trend suggests an exponential growth in complexity, and indeed, with 4 participants, verification becomes infeasible: none of the assertions complete within two hours. The number of visited states approximately doubles, and the total transitions quadruple on average. Notably, verifying the *Vote Alignment* property under the four-participant configuration resulted in an Out-of-Memory Exception, underscoring the severity of state explosion and the limitations of verification scalability.

Table 2. Experimental Results with Varying Error and Timeout Counts

Configuration	Average Visited States	Average Total Transitions	Average Time Used
0/0/0	1190	2739	0.0341742 s
0/0/5	8003	15227	0.2069795 s
0/5/0	60033	178209	1.5335324 s
5/0/0	10850	24128	0.2838439 s
5/5/0	836960	3450350	22.6993082 s
0/5/5	666922	1827464	18.6319547 s
5/0/5	82698	219370	2.1904446 s
5/5/5	6105938	22161937	186.7857362 s
-1/-1/-1	N/A (TIMEOUT)	N/A (TIMEOUT)	N/A (TIMEOUT)

5.2 Relationship Between Error Counts and Verification Time

To understand the impact of bounded failures and timeouts on verification time, we conducted a series of experiments using various configurations. Each configuration is denoted by a triplet $c/p/t$, where c is the value assigned to `COORDINATOR_BOUNDED_ERROR_COUNT`, p to `PARTICIPANT_BOUNDED_ERROR_COUNT`, and t to `COORDINATOR_BOUNDED_TIMEOUT_COUNT`. For each configuration, we ran multiple experiments across all properties and reported the aggregated (average) metrics for better clarity. Each individual verification result is available online.

From the first four entries in Table 2, we observe that the participant failures (p) have the most significant effect on state-space growth among the three error types. The next three entries explore combinations of two error types while disabling the third (i.e., assigning a value of 0). Among these, the combination of coordinator and participant failures (i.e., $c/p/0$) leads to the largest increase in state-space size and verification time.

The configuration 5/5/5 demonstrates a compounded, exponential effect of combining all three error types. In comparison, the unbounded configuration $-1/-1/-1$, which allows failures and timeouts to occur an unlimited number of times, and causes verification to fail due to time and memory exhaustion. PAT does not complete within the default 120-minute timeout, and increasing the timeout to 24 hours has no practical benefit due to severe system thrashing. These are intuitive: Failures may occur at nearly any execution point, whereas timeouts are restricted to specific waiting states, making site failures more impactful overall. However, the exponential growth in the state space is not immediately obvious from the empirical data alone. We therefore provide a mathematical model to illustrate the underlying combinatorial complexity.

Assume the following parameters:

- X: Number of coordinator execution points that may be interrupted by a site failure;

- Y: Number of execution points per participant that may be interrupted by a site failure;
- Z: Number of coordinator execution points that may be interrupted by a timeout, where $Z << X$;
- n: Maximum number of site failures allowed for the coordinator;
- m: Maximum number of site failures allowed for each participant;
- s: Maximum number of timeouts allowed for the coordinator;
- p: Number of participants involved.

Assuming failures and timeouts occur independently and uniformly across valid execution points, we can estimate the number of execution traces as follows:

- The number of possible execution traces for the coordinator is $X^n * Z^s$.
- The number of possible execution traces for each participant is Y^m.
- Assuming participants operate independently (a simplification, since synchronisation occurs in practice), the total number of possible interleaved execution traces for all participants is $(Y^m)^p$.
- Assuming further that the coordinator operates independently of participants, the total number of possible system execution traces becomes:

$$X^n * Z^s * (Y^m)^p.$$

This estimation assumes exactly n, m and s failures/timeouts. If we relax the constraint to allow *up* to those bounds (i.e., allowing fewer than the maximum), the number of possible traces increases substantially due to the explosion in branching behaviours. Each branch may correspond to a distinct execution path, resulting in exponential growth in explored states with respect to n, m, s, and the number of participants p. Techniques like partial-order reduction may mitigate this to some extent by merging equivalent states, but the fundamental combinatorial explosion remains.

This mathematical model provides strong evidence of the inherent complexity of verifying the 2PC protocol under failure conditions, and underscores the importance of bounding error parameters to achieve practical verification.

6 Conclusion and Future Work

We presented a formal model of the 2PC protocol with bounded failures, timeouts, recovery, and termination, and verified key correctness properties using PAT. Our results confirmed protocol robustness for up to three participants but revealed significant state-space explosion. Through detailed analysis, key contributors were identified: the number of sites involved, and the number of error types. These reflect two inherent properties of distributed systems—scalability and uncertainty—which together introduce intertwined layers of non-determinism.

Addressing this limitation remains an important area for future work, particularly in improving the efficiency of verification engines. One promising direction is the application of nested model checking on system abstractions. If a system exhibits hierarchical structure and can be decomposed into independent subproblems, these can be verified in parallel with reduced need for synchronisation. This approach offers a potential pathway to mitigate state-space explosion in complex distributed systems.

References

1. Process analysis toolkit (pat) 3.5 user manual print. https://pat.comp.nus.edu.sg/resources/OnlineHelp/htm/
2. Network integration. https://learn.microsoft.com/en-us/host-integration-server/what-is-his,Accessed on 13 June 2025
3. Parallel commits: an atomic commit protocol for globally distributed transactions . https://www.cockroachlabs.com/blog/parallel-commits/,Accessed on 13 June 2025
4. Spanner: truetime and external consitency . https://cloud.google.com/spanner/docs/true-time-external-consistency,Accessed on 13 June 2025
5. Specifying and simulating two-phase commit in lean4 . https://protocols-made-fun.com/lean/2025/04/25/lean-two-phase.html,Accessed on 13 June 2025
6. Tlaplus examples module twophase . https://github.com/tlaplus/Examples/blob/master/specifications/transaction_commit/TwoPhase.tla,Accessed on 13 June 2025
7. Using FDB clusters as 2pc participants . https://forums.foundationdb.org/t/using-fdb-clusters-as-2pc-participants/1060,Accessed on 13 June 2025
8. Al-Bataineh, O.I., Reynolds, M.: Epistemic model checking of distributed commit protocols with byzantine faults. In: Proceedings of FormaliSE@ICSE 2019, pp. 51–60. IEEE CS (2019)
9. Atif, M.: Analysis and verification of two-phase commit & three-phase commit protocols. In: Proceedings of International Conference on Emerging Technologies, pp. 326–331 (2009)
10. Dang, H., et al.: Towards scaling blockchain systems via sharding. In: Proceedings of the 2019 International Conference on Management of Data, pp. 123–140. ACM Press (2019)
11. Dragojevic, A., Narayanan, D., Castro, M., Hodson, O.: Farm: fast remote memory. In: Proceedings of the 11th USENIX Symposium on Networked Systems Design and Implementation. USENIX Association (2014). https://www.microsoft.com/en-us/research/publication/farm-fast-remote-memory/
12. Hellings, J., Sadoghi, M.: Byshard: sharding in a byzantine environment. Proc. VLDB Endow. **14**(11), 2230–2243 (2021)
13. Kamil, S.N.S., Thomas, N.: Modelling and Analysis of Commit Protocols with PEPA. In: Reinecke, P., Di Marco, A. (eds.) EPEW 2017. LNCS, vol. 10497, pp. 266–281. Springer, Cham (2017). https://doi.org/10.1007/978-3-319-66583-2_17
14. Sun, J., Liu, Y., Dong, J.S., Pang, J.: PAT: Towards Flexible Verification under Fairness. In: Bouajjani, A., Maler, O. (eds.) CAV 2009. LNCS, vol. 5643, pp. 709–714. Springer, Heidelberg (2009). https://doi.org/10.1007/978-3-642-02658-4_59
15. Özsu, M.T., Valduriez, P.: Principles of distributed database systems. Springer Publishing Company, 3rd edn. (2011)

Formal Verification of Measurement-Based Quantum Computation in Maude

Ryuichi Nagoshi and Tsubasa Takagi(✉)

Japan Advanced Institute of Science and Technology, Ishikawa, Japan
{nagoshi,tsubasa}@jaist.ac.jp

Abstract. Measurement-based quantum computation (MBQC) is a key paradigm for quantum computing, offering advantages in blind quantum computation, for example. However, guaranteeing the correctness of MBQC protocols is challenging due to the inherent nondeterminism of quantum mechanics. Formal verification is therefore needed to provide systematic assurance. We propose an automated verification framework for MBQC. Our method formalizes MBQC using the Measurement Calculus (MC) and implements it in Maude, an algebraic specification language. We represent quantum states and operations symbolically using Dirac notation, enabling exhaustive exploration of all computational paths by rewrite-based reduction rather than direct matrix calculation. We use fidelity to automatically verify that the final quantum state is the desired state. In case studies, we successfully verified seven MBQC protocols.

Keywords: Formal verification · Measurement-based Quantum Computation · Maude · Symbolic Reasoning

1 Introduction

Quantum computing is expected to offer computational advantages for problems that are intractable on classical computers, such as integer factorization [11] and approximate combinatorial optimization (for example, with the Quantum Approximate Optimization Algorithm (QAOA) [6]). In cryptography, protocols that exploit quantum-mechanical effects to distribute keys securely, known as Quantum Key Distribution (QKD), have attracted significant attention as highly secure key-distribution methods [7].

Measurement-based quantum computation (MBQC) is a model of quantum computation that originated from the one-way model proposed by Raussendorf and Briegel [8,9]. MBQC is computationally equivalent to the standard circuit model of quantum computation [10], but its computational process is completely different from the circuit model. MBQC calculations progress by repeating measurements: MBQC prepares a multipartite entangled resource state and then repeatedly performs single-qubit local measurements, along with Pauli corrections based on the measurement outcomes.

© The Author(s), under exclusive license to Springer Nature Singapore Pte Ltd. 2026
Y. Chen et al. (Eds.): SFPVV 2025, LNCS 16356, pp. 160–178, 2026.
https://doi.org/10.1007/978-981-95-6032-5_11

MBQC has advantages for physical implementations on specific physical platforms, such as photonic and light-matter systems, as well as for parallelization. It also cleanly separates quantum operations from classical control, a property that is especially useful in cryptography and security. For example, blind quantum computation [1] utilizes this separation to enable a client to delegate a quantum computation to a remote quantum server while keeping the data and the algorithm secret.

In such delegated computing environments, it is crucial to eliminate design-level defects. This is necessary to guarantee both the correctness of the computational result and the privacy of the computation itself for the client. However, because the nondeterminism and entanglement essential to quantum computation impose inherent coverage limits on testing- and simulation-centered approaches, exhaustive assurance is difficult. Therefore, formal verification, which mathematically proves properties of a specification and thereby provides systematic assurance of safety and reliability, is indispensable.

Formal verification of quantum computation has been studied across multiple layers of abstraction, from high-level approaches that address the correctness of quantum programs to low-level methods that establish the equivalence of quantum circuits [2]. High-level approaches target the verification of quantum programs. Examples include Quantum Hoare Logic (QHL) and dedicated verification frameworks such as QBRICKS [2, §7.2] and SQIR [2, §7.3]. In contrast, low-level techniques focus on guaranteeing functional equivalence of circuits during compilation and optimization. For instance, VOQC [2, §5.4] uses the Coq proof assistant to prove the correctness of circuit transformations, and the ZX-calculus [2, §5.1] provides a graph-based algebraic calculus for reasoning about circuit equivalence. Furthermore, within the ZX-calculus, there are diagrammatic rewriting frameworks that establish the determinism of MBQC patterns [5]. In this context, determinism ensures the final output is determined independent of random measurement outcomes.

Compared with prior research, our aim and scope differ. QHL, QBRICKS, and SQIR focus on proving high-level specifications, whereas verifying low-level specifications is not their primary objective. VOQC provides a framework for establishing circuit equivalence, and property checking falls outside its scope. The ZX-calculus is well-suited to the theoretical justification of equivalence and determinism, but it is not designed to automatically and exhaustively check properties of the final quantum state along each measurement branch.

By contrast, we formalize MBQC computations according to the Measurement Calculus (MC) [3] and propose a tool that automatically verifies properties by exhaustively exploring all measurement branches. Our method employs algebraic specification. We formalize MBQC following the MC and encode its behavior using as `eq` (equations) and `ceq` (conditional equations) in Maude [13], a specification language that supports membership equational logic and rewriting logic. Matrices are represented as symbolic terms in Dirac notation, and execution proceeds as rewrite-based reduction rather than by direct matrix calculation.

We perform automatic verification using fidelity. We use fidelity to quantify the closeness between the desired state and the state produced by a pattern. Because simple equality of state vectors does not capture physical equivalence, we use fidelity to verify whether the produced state is physically equivalent to the specification. In our case studies, we automatically verified seven patterns mentioned in [3], including quantum teleportation and GHZ-state preparation, and confirmed that in every case the generated state satisfied the desired properties.

2 Preliminaries

In this section, we briefly review basic linear-algebraic notation for quantum mechanics and the main concepts of MBQC.

2.1 Fundamentals of Quantum Computation

In classical computation, the basic unit is the bit, 0 or 1, whereas in quantum computation, the basic unit is the quantum bit (*qubit*). A qubit has, as a basis, the two column vectors corresponding to the classical bit values, which in Dirac notation are written as

$$|0\rangle = \begin{pmatrix} 1 \\ 0 \end{pmatrix}, \quad |1\rangle = \begin{pmatrix} 0 \\ 1 \end{pmatrix}.$$

An arbitrary (pure) state of a single qubit can be written as

$$|\psi\rangle = \alpha|0\rangle + \beta|1\rangle, \quad \alpha, \beta \in \mathbb{C}, \quad |\alpha|^2 + |\beta|^2 = 1,$$

where $\mathbb{C}$ stands for the set of all complex numbers. We denote the inner products of $|i\rangle$ and $|j\rangle$ by $\langle i|j\rangle$, and denote the matrix multiplication of $|i\rangle$ and $\langle j|$ by $|i\rangle\langle j|$.

The evolution of a closed quantum system is described by a unitary operator U satisfying $U^\dagger U = UU^\dagger = I$. When applied to a state $|\psi\rangle$, it yields $|\psi'\rangle = U|\psi\rangle$. A quantum gate is a fundamental operation on qubits and is represented by a unitary operator. In this work, we use the following one- and two-qubit gates:

$$I = \begin{pmatrix} 1 & 0 \\ 0 & 1 \end{pmatrix}, X = \begin{pmatrix} 0 & 1 \\ 1 & 0 \end{pmatrix},$$

$$Y = \begin{pmatrix} 0 & -i \\ i & 0 \end{pmatrix}, Z = \begin{pmatrix} 1 & 0 \\ 0 & -1 \end{pmatrix}, H = \frac{1}{\sqrt{2}} \begin{pmatrix} 1 & 1 \\ 1 & -1 \end{pmatrix},$$

$$\mathrm{CX} = \begin{pmatrix} 1 & 0 & 0 & 0 \\ 0 & 1 & 0 & 0 \\ 0 & 0 & 0 & 1 \\ 0 & 0 & 1 & 0 \end{pmatrix}, \quad \mathrm{CZ} = \begin{pmatrix} 1 & 0 & 0 & 0 \\ 0 & 1 & 0 & 0 \\ 0 & 0 & 1 & 0 \\ 0 & 0 & 0 & -1 \end{pmatrix}.$$

For example, the Pauli-X gate performs a bit flip. Its action on the computational basis is:

$$X|0\rangle = |1\rangle, \quad X|1\rangle = |0\rangle.$$

Quantum measurements are described by a set of operators $\{M_m\}$ satisfying $\sum_m M_m^\dagger M_m = I$, where the index m labels the measurement outcome. If the system is in a state $|\psi\rangle$ before measurement, the probability of obtaining outcome m is given by

$$p(m) = \langle\psi|M_m^\dagger M_m|\psi\rangle,$$

and the post-measurement state, provided $p(m) > 0$, is

$$|\psi_m\rangle = \frac{M_m|\psi\rangle}{\sqrt{p(m)}}.$$

For a measurement in the computational basis, $M_0 = |0\rangle\langle 0|$ and $M_1 = |1\rangle\langle 1|$, which yields $p(0) = |\alpha|^2$ with $|\psi_0\rangle = |0\rangle$, and $p(1) = |\beta|^2$ with $|\psi_1\rangle = |1\rangle$.

An n-qubit system is described by the 2^n-dimensional tensor product space $\mathcal{H}^{\otimes n}$, the n-fold tensor product of the single-qubit Hilbert space $\mathcal{H}$ with computational basis $\{|0\rangle, |1\rangle\}$. The basis for $\mathcal{H}^{\otimes n}$ is $\{|m\rangle \mid m \in \{0,1\}^n\}$, where for a bit string $m = m_1 \cdots m_n$, we write $|m\rangle$ as shorthand for $|m_1\rangle \otimes \cdots \otimes |m_n\rangle$.

A state that cannot be expressed as the tensor product of single-qubit states is called an entangled state. An example is the EPR (Einstein–Podolsky–Rosen) state

$$|\mathrm{EPR}\rangle = \tfrac{1}{\sqrt{2}}(|00\rangle + |11\rangle).$$

2.2 Fundamentals of MBQC

The circuit model of quantum computation is widely used today. In this model, quantum gates are applied to qubits in sequence, and the qubits are measured at the end of the whole computation to obtain measurement outcomes. These outcomes represent the output of the computation, such as a factorization result, the solution to a search problem, and so on.

By contrast, MBQC first prepares a graph state, a highly entangled multi-qubit resource state. The subsequent computation proceeds solely by performing local measurements on individual qubits, together with classical computation on the measurement outcomes and conditional single-qubit Pauli corrections.

Graph states used in MBQC are prepared by the following steps:

1. Prepare all qubits in
$$|+\rangle = \frac{1}{\sqrt{2}}(|0\rangle + |1\rangle).$$
2. Apply controlled-Z (CZ) gates between the prepared qubits to generate entangled states.

We refer to the states obtained by this procedure collectively as graph states.

In MBQC, local measurements play the role of gates in the circuit model. The projective measurement on a qubit i is defined by

$$M_i^{\pm\alpha} = |\pm_\alpha\rangle\langle\pm_\alpha|, \quad |\pm_\alpha\rangle = \frac{1}{\sqrt{2}}(|0\rangle \pm e^{i\alpha}|1\rangle), \quad \alpha \in [0, 2\pi].$$

By choosing an angle α, we realize a single-qubit rotation. Because measurement outcomes are randomly obtained, we adjust subsequent measurement angles and, when necessary, apply Pauli-X and/or Pauli-Z corrections based on the measurement outcomes. These adjustments ensure that, after applying the prescribed corrections, every branch yields the same final output state, thereby making the result independent of the measurement outcomes. The complete MBQC procedure is as follows:

1. Prepare an N-qubit graph state.
2. Measure qubit i in the basis $\{|+_\alpha\rangle, |-_\alpha\rangle\}$.
3. Update the measurement angle for the next qubit and determine the required Pauli corrections X or Z determined by the outcome, and then apply the required corrections.
4. Repeat the steps 2 and 3 for all qubits to be measured.
5. The remaining unmeasured qubits (or the outcomes of the measurement) are the desired output state.

2.3 Measurement Calculus Formalism

MBQC can be decomposed into four primitive operations: (1) qubit initialization, (2) entanglement generation, (3) angle-dependent measurement, and (4) correction based on measurement outcomes. The Measurement Calculus (MC) [3] formulates these operations with five basic commands and organizes MBQC procedures into *patterns*. In this paper, we introduce only the definitions needed for our implementation.

Commands. In the MC, MBQC operations are expressed by the following five commands:

- N_i: initialize qubit i in the state

$$|+\rangle = \frac{1}{\sqrt{2}}(|0\rangle + |1\rangle).$$

- E_{ij}: applying the controlled-Z (CZ) gate between qubits i and j.
- M_i^α: measuring a qubit i in the basis $\{|+_\alpha\rangle, |-_\alpha\rangle\}$, where

$$|\pm_\alpha\rangle = \frac{1}{\sqrt{2}}\big(|0\rangle \pm e^{i\alpha}|1\rangle\big).$$

- X_i^s, Z_i^t: apply the X- or Z-gate on the qubit i based on classical bits $s, t \in \{0, 1\}$.

The measurement angle itself is also updated depending on preceding measurement outcomes. In the MC, this dependence is denoted by the following abbreviation:

$${}^t\big[M_i^\alpha\big]^s := M_i^{(-1)^s \alpha + t\pi},$$

where s and t are classical bits obtained from previous measurement outcomes, $(-1)^s$ indicates the sign flip of the angle, and $t\pi$ denotes the phase flip. In this paper, when $s = t = 0$, that is, when there is no dependence on previous measurement outcomes, we omit them (for example, ${}^0\big[M_i^\alpha\big]^0 = \big[M_i^\alpha\big]^0 = M_i^\alpha$).

Patterns. A *pattern* is a tuple (V, I, O) together with a finite sequence of commands $A_n, \ldots, A_1$ executed from right to left, where:

- V is a set of all qubits used.
- $I \subseteq V$ is a set of input qubits.
- $O \subseteq V$ is a set of output qubits.
- $A_n, \ldots, A_1$ are commands.

A valid pattern must satisfy:

1. Commands must not depend on measurement outcomes that have not yet been obtained.
2. No commands are applied to a qubit after it has been measured.
3. No commands are applied to an unprepared qubit.
4. Measured qubits are not in the output set O.

Example 1: Quantum Teleportation. Quantum teleportation transmits an unknown quantum state from one qubit to another using entanglement (with classical communication). Let $V = \{1, 2, 3\}$, $I = \{1\}$, and $O = \{3\}$. The command sequence is

$$X_3^{s_2} \, Z_3^{s_1} \, M_2^0 \, M_1^0 \, E_{23} \, E_{12},$$

executed from right to left. These commands execute as follows:

1. E_{12} entangles qubits 1 and 2, and then E_{23} entangles qubits 2 and 3.
2. M_1^0 and M_2^0 measure qubits 1 and 2 at the angle $\alpha = 0$, yielding classical bits $s_1, s_2 \in \{0, 1\}$.
3. $Z_3^{s_1}$ and $X_3^{s_2}$ apply Pauli corrections on the qubit 3: Z if $s_1 = 1$; X if $s_2 = 1$.

After these steps, the state $|\psi\rangle$ initially on qubit 1 is transmitted to that on qubit 3.

Example 2: GHZ State A GHZ (Greenberger–Horne–Zeilinger) state is a special entangled state of three or more qubits. In particular, the three-qubit GHZ state is

$$|\text{GHZ}\rangle = \frac{1}{\sqrt{2}}(|000\rangle + |111\rangle).$$

We now present a pattern for generating this state. Let $V = \{1, 2, 3, 4, 5\}$, $I = \emptyset$, and $O = \{1, 3, 5\}$. The command sequence is

$$X_5^{s_2+s_4} \, X_3^{s_2} \, M_4^0 \, M_2^0 \, E_{45} \, E_{34} \, E_{23} \, E_{12}.$$

where $+$ denotes the exclusive OR on bits. These commands execute as follows:

1. E_{12}, E_{23}, E_{34}, E_{45} entangle qubits 1 through 5 with the controlled-Z gates.
2. M_2^0 and M_4^0 measure qubits 2 and 4 respectively at angle $\alpha = 0$, obtaining classical bits $s_2, s_4 \in \{0, 1\}$.
3. $X_5^{s_2+s_4}$, $X_3^{s_2}$ apply corrections: X on the qubit 3 if $s_2 = 1$; X on the qubit 5 if $s_2 + s_4 = 1$.

This procedure generates the GHZ state on qubits 1, 3, and 5.

3 Symbolic Reasoning

In this section, we define *terms* as the basic symbolic elements for representing quantum computational operations, and we introduce a set of rewrite rules for their reduction. These definitions, including basic matrix representations in Dirac notation, mainly follow [4,12]. However, [4, 12] address only the quantum circuit model. We add some rules to cover MBQC and implement the entire framework in Maude.

3.1 Terms

The basic elements of the symbolic system for quantum computation in this paper are implemented using the following sorts:

- `PNat`: the Peano natural numbers.
- `Cpx`: complex numbers.
- `Bit`: qubit measurement outcomes (`zeroB`, `oneB`, `nullB`).
- `Ket`: the elements of the computational basis $\{|0\rangle, |1\rangle\}$).
- `Bra`: the adjoints of `Ket` elements ($\langle 0|$, $\langle 1|$).
- `Vect`: complex column vectors.
- `CoVect`: complex row vectors.
- `Mat`: complex square matrices.
- `Command`: operations that constitutes a pattern.

Terms are formed using the operators for scalar multiplication (`.`), addition (`+`), matrix multiplication (`*`), and tensor product (`(x)`).

In Dirac notation, the Pauli-X gate can be written as

$$X = \begin{pmatrix} 0 & 1 \\ 1 & 0 \end{pmatrix} = |0\rangle\langle 1| + |1\rangle\langle 0|.$$

In Maude, this is expressed as

```
|0><1| + |1><0|.
```

Thus, the quantum gates introduced in Sect. 2 are formulated in Maude as linear combinations of `|0>`, `|1>`, `<0|`, `<1|`, and complex scalars of sort `Cpx`.

3.2 Rewrite Rules

To enable automatic reduction of terms, we introduce a set of rewrite rules for quantum operations and matrix algebra. Table 1 lists the main rules, which are implemented as rewriting rules in Maude.

Example: Term Reduction As a concrete example, we show the steps by which the term

```
CXx((H(x)I)x(|0>x|0>))
```

is reduced to

```
1./sqrt(2).(|0>(x)|0>)+1./sqrt(2).(|1>(x)|1>).
```

First, we demonstrate the single-qubit state reduction by the H gate, and then the two-qubit state reduction by the controlled-X gate.

```
Hx|0>
→ 1./sqrt(2).((X + Z)x|0>)
→ 1./sqrt(2).((|0><1|+|1><0|)+(|0><0|+(-1).(|1><1|))(x)|0>
→ 1./sqrt(2).(((|0>x<1|)x|0>)+((|1>x<0|)x|0>))
+(|0>x(<0|)x|0>)+(-1).((|1>x<1|)x|0>)
→ 1./sqrt(2).(|1>+|0>)
```

```
(H(x)I)x(|0>(x)|0>)
→ (Hx|0>)+(Ix|0>)
→ 1./sqrt(2).(|1>+|0>)(x)|0>
→ 1./sqrt(2).((|1>(x)|0>) + (|0>(x)|0>)
```

```
CXx((H(x)I)x(|0>(x)|0>))
→ CXx(1./sqrt(2).((|1>(x)|0>)+(|0>(x)|0>)))
→ ((P0+(P1xX))x(1./sqrt(2).((|1>(x)|0>)+(|0>(x)|0>)))
→ (((P0+(P1xX))x(1./sqrt(2).(|1>(x)|0>)))
+((P0+(P1xX))x(1./sqrt(2).(|0>(x)|0>)))
→ 1./sqrt(2).((|1>(x)|1>)+(|0>(x)|0>))
```

In Maude, reduction applies the rules recursively until no further rule is applicable. The Maude's built-in module for rational numbers is extended by adding the rewrite rules in Table 1 to the module for complex numbers and quantum computation. For brevity, we omit the full details in this paper.

4 Proposed Method

In this section, based on the Measurement Calculus (MC), we formally define the MBQC commands. We then introduce *patterns*, consisting of a pattern computation space V, a pattern inputs I, and a command list. After that, we show how to specify some quantum protocols using these patterns. The formal specification for the MC captures the entire workflow, from qubit preparation and entanglement, through measurement and classical control, to output extraction, providing the foundation for automatic verification.

Our tool, implemented by Maude, is publicly available at https://github.com/ryuichi-nagoshi/MBQC_Maude.

Table 1. Set of rules used in symbolic reasoning

```
A + 0 = A, A . 0 = 0 . A = 0
I . A = A, A . I = A
(A + B) + C = A + (B + C)
(A . B) . C = A . (B . C)
A . (B + C) = A . B + A . C
(A + B) . C = A . C + B . C
c . (A + B) = c . A + c . B
c1 . (c2 . A) = (c1 . c2) . A
c . (A . B) = (c . A) . B = A . (c . B)
c . (A (x) B) = (c . A) (x) B = A (x) (c . B)
A (x) (B + C) = A (x) B + A (x) C
(A + B) (x) C = A (x) C + B (x) C
(A (x) B) . (C (x) D) = (A . C) (x) (B . D)
|0><0| = |0> x <0|, |1><1| = |1> x <1|
|0><1| = |0> x <1|, |1><0| = |1> x <0|
(K x <1|) x |0> = 0, (K x <0|) x |1> = 0
(K x <0|) x |0> = K, (K x <1|) x |1> = K
P0 = |0><0|
P1 = |1><1|
X = |0><1| + |1><0|
Z = |0><0| + (-1) . |1><1|
Y = (-i) . |0><1| + i . |1><0|
H = 1./sqrt(2) . (X + Z)
CX = P0 (x) I + P1 (x) X
CZ = P0 (x) I + P1 (x) Z
```

4.1 Overall Architecture

This subsection presents the overall execution flow of our implementation. The user provides a pattern computation space V, pattern inputs I (the input qubits and their quantum states), and a command list CL. The `MBQC-LANG` command `pattern` uses V and I to generate the initialization commands N and to construct the initial state vector, then input V and CL to `runPattern`. The `runPattern` procedure reads the elements of CL from right to left and invokes `measure.maude` to execute them. During the execution, for each measurement branch, the system records the list of outcomes `LB` and applies the remaining commands to the current state vector. After all commands have been executed, `traceOut` extracts the unmeasured qubits and selects the components corresponding to the output qubits, returning the list of results, one for each branch. We then input this list to the verifier `check`, which compares it with the target specification and produces a verification result. Figure 1 shows a schematic overview of our implementation.

4.2 Generic List Specification

In this subsection, we describe a generic list structure, provided as a parameterized module in Maude, for storing measurement outcomes, qubit indices, and related data. This enables a uniform treatment of list operations, irrespective of what `X` is.

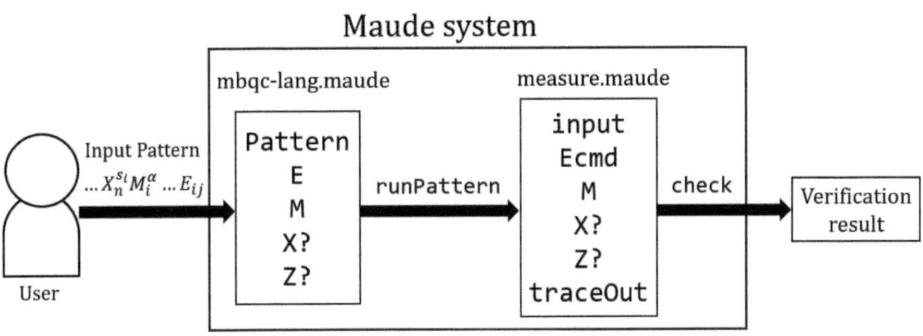

Fig. 1. Architecture of the Maude-based MBQC verifier.

```
1. fth TRIV is
2. sort Elt .
3. endfth
4. fmod LIST-GENERIC{X :: TRIV} is
5. sort List{X} .
6. subsort X$Elt < List{X} .
7. op nil : -> List{X} [ctor] .
8. op _ _ : List{X} List{X} -> List{X} [assoc ctor id: nil] .
9. endfm
```

The sort `Elt` in the module `TRIV` (line 1) is a data (parameter) sort; by replacing `Elt` with another sort, we obtain a list over that sort. The notation `List{X}` (line 5) denotes the list sort whose data sort is `X$Elt` (line 5). The empty list is represented as `nil` (line 7), and concatenation is represented as the infix operator `_ _` (line 8), where `_` denotes a placeholder. By declaring `[assoc id:nil]` (line 8), the operator is associative and `nil` behaves as the identity. All list sorts used below are instantiations of this parameterized module.

4.3 Definition of Sorts

We first present the principal sorts that appear in the command definitions below, together with the operators used to build them.

- `PairPV`: a sort for a pair of an input qubit index and a complex column vector.
  `op <_@_> : PNat Vect -> PairPV.`
  Example of a term: `< 0 @ |1> >.`
- `PairPP`: a sort for a pair of qubit indices to generate entanglement.
  `op <_&_> : PNat PNat -> PairPP.`
  Example of a term: `< 0 & 1 >.`
- `PairBV`: a sort for a pair consisting of a list of classical outcome bits and a complex column vector.
  `op <_,_> : ListTRIV2BIT Vect -> PairBV.`
  Example of a term: `< nullB oneB zeroB, |0> (x) |0> (x) |0> >.`
- `Outcome`: a sort for a triple consisting of (1) a list of classical outcome bits, (2) a list of indices of qubits that remain unmeasured, and (3) a normalized complex column vector.
  `op [_,_,_] : ListTRIV2BIT ListTRIV2PNAT Vect -> Outcome.`
  Example of a term: `[ nullB zeroB oneB , 0 , |0> + |1> ].`

In the following, we concisely list the instantiated list sorts obtained by replacing the parameter `X` in `LIST-GENERIC{X}` with each of the primitive sorts:

- `List{TRIV2BIT}`: list of `Bit` (measurement outcomes).
- `List{TRIV2PNAT}`: list of `PNat`.
- `List{TRIV2VECT}`: list of `Vect` (sequences of complex column vectors).
- `List{TRIV2PAIRPV}`: list of `PairPV`.
- `List{TRIV2PAIRBV}`: list of `PairBV`.
- `List{TRIV2OUTCOME}`: list of `Outcome`.
- `List{TRIV2COMMAND}`: list of `Command`.

4.4 Pattern Execution Commands: `pattern`, `runPattern`, `input`

In this subsection, we define the user-facing operators `pattern` and `runPattern`, as well as `input`, which constructs an initial state. The rewrite rules of `runPattern` for each command are presented in the corresponding subsections below.

10. `op pattern : PNat ListTRIV2PAIRPV ListTRIV2COMMAND -> ListTRIV2OUTCOME .`
11. `op runPattern : PNat ListTRIV2COMMAND Vect -> ListTRIV2OUTCOME .`
12. `op runPattern : PNat ListTRIV2COMMAND ListTRIV2PAIRBV -> ListTRIV2OUTCOME .`
13. `eq pattern(N, LPPV, CL) = runPattern(N, CL, input(N, LPPV)) .`

```
14. -- input
15. op input : PNat ListTRIV2PAIRPV -> Vect .
16. eq input(N, LPPV) = cmV(gatherInputs(N, LPPV)) .
```

The operator `pattern` (line 10) takes three arguments: (1) `N : PNat`, which denotes the size of the pattern computation space $N + 1$ with $N \geq 0$; (2) a list `LPPV` of pairs of input-qubit indices and complex column vectors; (3) a command list `CL`. The operator `pattern` uses `input` to build an initial state vector, then passes the vector together with `CL` to `runPattern` (line 13). The procedure `runPattern` (line 13, line 14) interprets the command list, executing from right to left. Until the first measurement occurs, the quantum state is treated as a value of sort `Vect`; after the first measurement, it is treated as a list of branches of sort `List{TRIV2PAIRBV}`. Detailed rules for `runPattern` are given in the following sections for the individual commands.

The operator `input` receives `N` and `LPPV`. First, it calls `gatherInputs` to construct a list of the length $N + 1$ whose elements are single-qubit states. All unspecified positions are filled with $|+\rangle$, and specified positions are populated with the single-qubit state vectors provided in `LPPV`. Next, `cmV` folds this list from left to right with the tensor product to obtain a single complex column vector, which becomes the initial state. During the execution, duplicate indices or out-of-range indices are treated as errors. In such cases, `input` returns `errV` (an error term of sort `Vect`) and then halts.

Intuitively, `pattern` constructs the initial state for execution. Given the number of qubits `N` and the input specification `LPPV`, it prepares the initial state by `input`. It then passes the command list `CL` to `runPattern` to start execution. Execution proceeds from right to left: if `CL` $= C_3C_2C_1$, then C_1 is applied first, followed by C_2, and finally C_3.

4.5 Entanglement Generation Command: E,Ecmd

In this subsection, we define the entanglement generation command `E` and the corresponding `runPattern` rule used when applying `E`.

```
17. op E : PNat PNat -> Command .
18. eq runPattern(N, CL E(N1,N2), V) = runPattern(N, CL , Ecmd(N,
    < N1 & N2 >, V)) .
19. -- entanglement command
20. op Ecmd : PNat PairPP Vect -> Vect .
21. eq Ecmd(N, < N1 & N2 >, V) = CZ(N1, N2, N) x V .
```

The operator `E` (line 17) specifies the two qubits `N1` and `N2` on which to apply a controlled-Z gate. When `runPattern` detects `E(N1,N2)` at the end of the command list, it passes the pair `< N1 & N2 >` and the current state vector `V` to `Ecmd`. The operator `Ecmd` (line 21) then applies a controlled-Z gate to the designated qubits and updates the state accordingly.

4.6 Measurement Command: M

In this subsection, we define the measurement command M and its rewrite rules, together with the runPattern rule that is used when M is applied.

```
22. op (_,_)[M(_,_)](_,_) : Bit ListTRIV2PNAT PNat AngReal Bit
    ListTRIV2PNAT -> Command .
23. -- evalDependency
24. op evalDep : Bit ListTRIV2PNAT ListTRIV2BIT -> Bit .
25. eq evalDep(B, nil, LB) = B .
26. eq evalDep(B, N LN, LB) = evalDep(B + retrieve(N, LB), LN, LB)
    .
27. -- Mdep
28. op Mdep : PNat PNat Bit ListTRIV2PNAT Bit ListTRIV2PNAT
    ListTRIV2PAIRBV AngReal -> ListTRIV2PAIRBV .
29. eq Mdep(N1, N2, B1, LN1, B2, LN2, nil, ANG-X) = nil .
30. eq Mdep(N1, N2, B1, LN1, B2, LN2, < LB, V > LPBV, ANG-X) =
    M(N1, N2, evalDep(B1, LN1, LB), evalDep(B2, LN2, LB), < LB, V
    >, ANG-X) Mdep(N1, N2, B1, LN1, B2, LN2, LPBV, ANG-X) .
31. -- runPattern
32. eq runPattern(N, CL (B2, LN2)[M(N1, ANG-X)](B1, LN1), V) =
    runPattern(N, CL, M(N1, N, B1, B2, < reset(N), V > , ANG-X)) .
33. eq runPattern(N, CL (B2, LN2)[M(N1, ANG-X)](B1, LN1), < LB, V
    > LPBV) = runPattern(N, CL, Mdep(N1, N, B1, LN1, B2, LN2, <
    LB, V > LPBV , ANG-X)) .
34. -- measurement
35. op M : PNat PNat Bit Bit ListTRIV2PAIRBV AngReal ->
    ListTRIV2PAIRBV .
36. eq M(N1, N2, B1, B2, nil, ANG-X) = nil .
37. ceq M(N1, N2, B1, B2, < LB , V > LPBV, ANG-X) = < insert(N1,
    zeroB, LB), P0(N1,N2) x (preMeas(N1, N2, ANG-X, B1) x V) > <
    insert(N1, oneB, LB), P1(N1,N2) x (preMeas(N1, N2, ANG-X, B1)
    x V) > M(N1, N2, B1, B2, LPBV, ANG-X) if retrieve(N1, LB) ==
    nullB = true /\B2 == zeroB .
38. ceq M(N1, N2, B1, B2, < LB , V > LPBV, ANG-X) = < insert(N1,
    zeroB, LB), P1(N1,N2) x (preMeas(N1, N2, ANG-X, B1) x V) > <
    insert(N1, oneB, LB), P0(N1,N2) x (preMeas(N1, N2, ANG-X, B1)
    x V) > M(N1, N2, B1, B2, LPBV, ANG-X) if retrieve(N1, LB) ==
    nullB = true /\ B2 == oneB .
39. ceq M(N1, N2, B1, B2, < LB , V > LPBV, ANG-X) = errCmd if
    retrieve(N1, LB) =/= nullB or B1 == nullB or B2 == nullB .
```

The operator on line 22 encodes a measurement whose angle and basis may depend on previous measurement outcomes, and it specifies these dependencies in the form

```
(B2, LN2)[M(N1, ANG-X)](B1, LN1).
```

Here, (B1, LN1) corresponds to the outcome s that flips the sign of the measurement angle (that is, ${}^{t}[M_i^{\alpha}]^{s}$), and (B2, LN2) corresponds to the outcome t that flips the measurement basis (that is, $\alpha \mapsto \alpha + \pi$). For example, the expression ${}^{0}[M_3^{0}]^{1+s_2}$ can be written as

```
(zeroB, nil)[M(2, 0pi)](oneB, 1).
```

The dependence signals are evaluated by evalDep. Given LB, the list of prior measurement outcomes, the call evalDep(B, LN, LB) XOR-reduces the outcomes at the qubit indices listed in LN, starting from the fixed bit B. Thus we obtain

$$s = \texttt{evalDep(B1, LN1, LB)},$$
$$t = \texttt{evalDep(B2, LN2, LB)}.$$

The behavior of runPattern when it encounters M depends on whether this is the first measurement. If it is the first measurement (that is, no branches have been created yet), the current state vector V is wrapped as <reset(N), V> to form a pair of an outcome list and a state, and this single branch is inputed to M (line 35). If a branch list <LB, V> LPBV already exists, then for each branch <LB, V> we evaluate s and t by Mdep and input the results to M (line 35). Concretely, for each branch <LB, V> we execute

```
M(N1, N2, B1, B2, < LB , V > LPBV, ANG-X).
```

If the measurement target N1 has already been measured (that is, retrieve(N1, LB) =/= nullB), or if any dependence signal refers to an as-yet-unmeasured outcome (nullB), the command is treated as invalid and errCmd is returned, where errCmd is an error term of sort Command indicating an invalid dependency.

4.7 Pauli Corrections: X?, Z?

In this subsection, we define the correction commands X? and Z? and their rewrite rules, together with the runPattern rules used when they are applied.

```
40. -- X?
41. op X? : PNat ListTRIV2PNAT -> Command .
42. eq runpattern(N, CL X?(N1, N2 LN), < LB, V > LPBV) =
    runpattern(N, CL X?(N1, LN), X?(N1, N2, N, < LB, V > LPBV)) .
43. eq runpattern(N, CL X?(N1, nil), < LB, V > LPBV) =
    runpattern(N, CL, < LB, V > LPBV) .
44. op X? : PNat PNat PNat ListTRIV2PAIRBV -> ListTRIV2PAIRBV .
45. ceq X?(N1, N2, N3, < LB, V > LPBV) = < LB, X(N1, N3) x V >
    X?(N1, N2, N3, LPBV) if retrieve(N1,LB) == nullB = true /
    \retrieve(N2,LB) == oneB = true .
46. ceq X?(N1, N2, N3, < LB, V > LPBV) = < LB, V > X?(N1, N2, N3,
    LPBV) if retrieve(N1,LB) == nullB = true /\retrieve(N2,LB) ==
    zeroB = true .
```

```
47. -- Z?
48. op Z? : PNat ListTRIV2PNAT -> Command .
49. eq runpattern(N, CL Z?(N1, N2 LN), < LB, V > LPBV) =
    runpattern(N, CL Z?(N1, LN), Z?(N1, N2, N, < LB, V > LPBV)) .
50. eq runpattern(N, CL Z?(N1, nil), < LB, V > LPBV) =
    runpattern(N, CL, < LB, V > LPBV) .
51. op Z? : PNat PNat PNat ListTRIV2PAIRBV -> ListTRIV2PAIRBV .
52. ceq Z?(N1, N2, N3, < LB, V > LPBV) = < LB, Z(N1, N3) x V >
    Z?(N1, N2, N3, LPBV) if retrieve(N1,LB) == nullB = true /\
    retrieve(N2,LB) == oneB = true .
53. ceq Z?(N1, N2, N3, < LB, V > LPBV) = < LB, V > Z?(N1, N2, N3,
    LPBV) if retrieve(N1,LB) == nullB = true /\retrieve(N2,LB) ==
    zeroB = true .
```

The commands `X?` (line 41) and `Z?` (line 48) are defined with two arguments: a target-qubit index `N1` and a list `LN` of measurement outcomes to be referenced. When `runPattern` encounters one of these commands, it consumes the elements of `LN` from left to right and, at each step, invokes `X?` (line 44) with the size `N` of the pattern computation space and the current branch list `LPBV`. When `LN` becomes empty, the command is removed.

Applying `X?` (line 44) affects a branch only when the referenced outcome is `oneB`: in that case `X(N1, N3)` is applied to the state `V`; when the outcome is `zeroB`, the state `V` is left unchanged. The command `Z?` behaves analogously, applying `Z(N1, N3)` only when the condition is satisfied. In both cases, the procedure scans all elements of `LPBV`, applies the corresponding updates, and then halts.

4.8 Output Extraction: `traceOut`

We define `traceOut`, which runs after all commands have been executed. For each element `<LB, V>` in the list `LPBV`, it extracts (1) the list of measurement outcomes, (2) the list of indices of qubits that remain unmeasured, and (3) the complex column vector, and then returns an `Outcome` triple.

```
54. op traceOut : List{TRIV2PAIRBV} -> List{TRIV2OUTCOME} .
55. eq traceOut(nil) = nil .
56. eq traceOut(< LB, V >  LPBV) = [LB , ri(LB),
    norm(traceV(V, ri(LB)))] traceOut(LPBV) .
57. eq runpattern(N, nil, LPBV) = traceOut(LPBV) .
```

When the command list `CL` is exhausted, `runPattern` (line 58) calls `traceOut`. After extraction, it returns a list of `Outcome` values. In `traceOut`, we scan `LPBV` from the head and, for each element `<LB, V>`, generate the triple

- the measurement outcomes `LB`.
- the list of indices of unmeasured qubits `ri(LB)`.
- the state vector restricted to the unmeasured-qubit subsystem.

Here, `ri` (short for "remember indices") is an auxiliary operator that, given `LB`, extracts the indices of qubits that have not been measured. The operator `traceV` is an auxiliary operator that extracts the quantum state supported on the unmeasured qubits identified by `ri`. The operator `norm` normalizes a state vector. Following our verification policy in this paper, we apply `norm` only to the final output.

In the MC, post-measurement quantum states are handled in an unnormalized form, and the squared norm of a state represents the probability of reaching that branch. This convention simplifies the overall computation, reducing the number of rewriting steps in Maude. Our implementation follows this convention and performs all computations in `runPattern` without normalization until all commands have been executed. For verification, however, we apply normalization in `traceOut` in order to decide whether the pattern realizes the desired unitary U.

5 Case Study

In this section, we automatically verify whether the proposed execution system realizes the desired properties for each pattern. Verification is performed using the notion of fidelity between (1) the final state vectors of each branch after all commands are executed and (2) the desired state.

Concretely, after enumerating all branches of a pattern, we normalize each output state vector to obtain the corresponding branch state $|\phi\rangle$, and then evaluate the fidelity between $|\phi\rangle$ and the desired state $|\psi\rangle$,

$$F(|\psi\rangle, |\phi\rangle) = |\langle\psi|\phi\rangle|^2.$$

For the patterns under consideration, some branches may differ by a global phase (the complex scalar $e^{i\theta}$ of $e^{i\theta}|\psi\rangle$) depending on measurement outcomes. We therefore use fidelity as the decision criterion, since it is invariant regardless of the global phase of $|\psi\rangle$. If $F(|\psi\rangle, |\phi\rangle) = 1$, then we successfully verify that all the results obtained by every possible measurement are desired states.

5.1 Verification Results

We have successfully verified the following seven patterns mentioned in [3] using our tool, which is publicly available at https://github.com/ryuichi-nagoshi/MBQC_Maude.

1. **Hadamard**: simulating the Hadamard gate in the quantum circuit model of the MBQC protocol.
2. **Quantum Teleportation**: transmit a sender's unknown state to the receiver's qubit.
3. **X-rotation**: simulating the $R_x(\theta)$ gate in the quantum circuit model of the MBQC protocol.

4. **Z-rotation**: simulating the $R_z(\theta)$ gate in the quantum circuit model of the MBQC protocol.
5. **CNOT**: simulating the CNOT gate in the quantum circuit model of the MBQC protocol.
6. **General rotation**: simulating the composite rotation $R_z(\gamma)R_x(\beta)R_z(\alpha)$ in the quantum circuit model of the MBQC protocol.
7. **GHZ preparation**: generate the GHZ state

$$|\mathrm{GHZ}\rangle = \frac{1}{\sqrt{2}}(|000\rangle + |111\rangle)\,.$$

The experiments were conducted on a machine with a 3.3 GHz, 8-core CPU and 16 GB of memory. First, we executed the command list with `runPattern`, then extracted the final outputs of all branches with `traceOut`. We next normalized output states $|\phi\rangle$ of each branch and evaluated its fidelity with respect to the desired state $|\psi\rangle$ using `check`. For each case, we confirmed $F(|\psi\rangle, |\phi\rangle) = 1$.

The experimental results are summarized in Table 2. In Table 2, "Qubits" means the size of the pattern computation space, "Branches" means the number of branches generated by measurement when executing each pattern, that is, the number of final states produced, "Rewrite Steps" means the number of rewrite steps to complete the formal verification, and "Time" means the time taken to complete the formal verification.

Table 2. Experimental Result

Pattern	Qubits	Branches	Rewrite Steps	Time
Hadamard	2	2	671	1 ms
Quantum Teleportation	3	4	3,426	4 ms
X-rotation	3	4	4,461	4 ms
Z-rotation	3	4	5,114	4 ms
CNOT	4	4	3,072	4 ms
General rotation	5	16	30,225	36 ms
GHZ	5	4	14,535	20 ms

6 Conclusion and Future Work

In this paper, we formalized MBQC using Maude. Concretely, we used basic matrix representations in Dirac notation and implemented patterns based on the Measurement Calculus (MC) [3]. This enabled pattern execution, branch enumeration, output extraction with normalization, and automatic verification of patterns.

As case studies, we formally verified the seven patterns mentioned in [3]: for every branch induced by the outcomes of the measurements, we confirmed that the normalized output states are equivalent to the desired states. These results demonstrate the feasibility of exhaustively exploring MBQC branches and automatically verifying their outputs.

Future work includes verifying more practical blind quantum computation protocols, in particular the BFK protocol [1], which is formulated in the MBQC model, to further demonstrate the utility of our framework.

The BFK protocol enables a client to delegate a quantum computation to a server while keeping the computation private by exploiting the structure of MBQC. In MBQC, quantum operations are separated from classical control, and this separation aligns with the protocol's division of labor: the server performs the quantum part, whereas the client carries out the classical processing. With only the ability to prepare and transmit single-qubit states, the client can delegate the entire task, including the input, the computation, and the output, without revealing any information about them to the server.

Verifying the correctness of delegation protocols such as the BFK protocol is significant. A client that outsources a computation often lacks an efficient way to check whether the server's answer is valid, a difficulty that is particularly problematic when the underlying problem is hard to verify classically. In addition, these protocols branch into many possible sequences of measurement outcomes, and the correct final state must be obtained in every branch. For these reasons, a rigorous formal proof of protocol correctness is indispensable.

Acknowledgments and Disclosure of Funding. The authors wish to thank anonymous reviewers who commented on drafts of this article. This work was supported by JSPS KAKENHI Grant Number 24K23858 and 24KK0185, and also by the Okawa foundation for information and telecommunications research grant.

Disclosure of Interests. The authors have no competing interests to declare that are relevant to the content of this article.

References

1. Broadbent, A., Fitzsimons, J., Kashefi, E.: Universal blind quantum computation. In: 2009 50th Annual IEEE Symposium on Foundations of Computer Science, pp. 517–526. IEEE (2009). https://doi.org/10.1109/focs.2009.36
2. Chareton, C., Bardin, S., Lee, D., Valiron, B., Vilmart, R., Xu, Z.: Formal methods for quantum programs: a survey (2022). https://arxiv.org/abs/2109.06493
3. Danos, V., Kashefi, E., Panangaden, P.: The measurement calculus. J. ACM **54**(2), 8–es (2007). https://doi.org/10.1145/1219092.1219096
4. Do, C.M., Takagi, T., Ogata, K.: Automated quantum protocol verification based on concurrent dynamic quantum logic. ACM Trans. Softw. Eng. Methodol. **34**(6) (2025). https://doi.org/10.1145/3708475
5. Duncan, R.: A graphical approach to measurement-based quantum computing (2012), https://arxiv.org/abs/1203.6242

6. Farhi, E., Goldstone, J., Gutmann, S.: A quantum approximate optimization algorithm (2014). https://arxiv.org/abs/1411.4028
7. H., B.C.: Quantum cryptography: public key distribution and coin tossing. In: International Conference on Computer System and Signal Processing, pp. 175–179. IEEE (1984). https://cir.nii.ac.jp/crid/1573950399056246784
8. Raussendorf, R., Briegel, H.: Computational model underlying the one-way quantum computer (2002). https://arxiv.org/abs/quant-ph/0108067
9. Raussendorf, R., Briegel, H.J.: A one-way quantum computer. Phys. Rev. Lett. **86**, 5188–5191 (2001). https://doi.org/10.1103/PhysRevLett.86.5188
10. Raussendorf, R., Browne, D.E., Briegel, H.J.: Measurement-based quantum computation on cluster states. Phys. Rev. A **68**(2) (2003). https://doi.org/10.1103/physreva.68.022312
11. Shor, P.: Algorithms for quantum computation: discrete logarithms and factoring. In: Proceedings 35th Annual Symposium on Foundations of Computer Science, pp. 124–134 (1994). https://doi.org/10.1109/SFCS.1994.365700
12. Takagi, T., Do, C.M., Ogata, K.: Automated quantum program verification in dynamic quantum logic. In: Gierasimczuk, N., Velázquez-Quesada, F.R. (eds.) Dynamic Logic. New Trends and Applications. pp. 68–84. Springer, Cham (2024). https://doi.org/10.1007/978-3-031-51777-8_5
13. The Maude Team: The Maude System. https://maude.cs.illinois.edu/w/index.php/The_Maude_System

Author Index

C
Chen, Ran 130

D
Do, Canh Minh 17
Dohi, Tadashi 1
Dong, Jin Song 34, 141
Dong, Naipeng 141
Duy, Truong Vinh Truong 78

G
Guo, Xiujing 59

I
Igaki, Haruto 48
Ishibashi, Takanori 112

L
Liu, Shaoying 34, 130

N
Nagoshi, Ryuichi 160
Nakajima, Shin 98
Nakamura, Masaki 112
Noguchi, Shun 98

O
Ogata, Kazuhiro 17, 112
Ogata, Shipei 98
Okamura, Hiroyuki 1
Okano, Kozo 98
Okubo, Toshiya 78

P
Pang, Jun 141

S
Shang, Yuxiang 34

T
Takagi, Tsubasa 160
Takeuchi, Hironori 78
Tsuchiya, Tatsuhiro 48, 59

U
Ubayashi, Naoyasu 78

W
Washizaki, Hironori 78

Y
Yoshioka, Nobukazu 78
Yu, Yisong 141

Z
Zheng, Junjun 1

© The Editor(s) (if applicable) and The Author(s), under exclusive license
to Springer Nature Singapore Pte Ltd. 2026

Y. Chen et al. (Eds.): SFPVV 2025, LNCS 16356, p. 179, 2026.
https://doi.org/10.1007/978-981-95-6032-5

MIX
Papier aus verantwortungsvollen Quellen
Paper from responsible sources
FSC® C105338

If you have any concerns about our products,
you can contact us on
ProductSafety@springernature.com

In case Publisher is established outside the EU,
the EU authorized representative is:
Springer Nature Customer Service Center GmbH
Europaplatz 3, 69115 Heidelberg, Germany

Printed by Libri Plureos GmbH
in Hamburg, Germany